OMNIPAGE POWER!

Myra J. Fox and Michael C. Read

OmniPage Power!

Credits: Senior Editor, Mark Garvey; Production Editor, Rodney A. Wilson; Technical Editor, Yael Li-Ron; Cover Design, Chad Planner, *Pop Design Works*; Interior Design and Layout, Val Brandenburg, Amy Francis, *Custom Editorial Productions*; Indexer, Kevin Broccoli, *Broccoli Information Management*.

Publisher: Andy Shafran

Library of Congress Catalog Number: 2001099815

ISBN 1-929685-58-0

5 4 3 2 1

Muska & Lipman Publishing
2645 Erie Avenue, Suite 41
Cincinnati, Ohio 45208

www.muskalipman.com

publisher@muskalipman.com

About the Authors

Myra Fox and Michael Read, originally from New Zealand, have lived in Sydney, Australia for twenty years. Michael has been involved in computers for over thirty years. He first started servicing punch card machines and valve card sorters in the early 70s. He has had a number of roles in technical support, management, consulting, business analysis, and training. Myra started her own computer training company in 1984, using some of the first PCs: twin floppy drive machines with 64 K of memory and the CPM operating system. She set up one of the first multimedia-training centers in Australia using accelerated learning techniques. They have been training, supporting, and selling OmniPage products since 1995. The vast size of Australia and the demand for OmniPage training led them to create several interactive training CDs for OmniPage (visit www.omnipagetraining.biz for more information). To balance the computer side of life, Myra holds diplomas in Marketing, NLP (Neuro Linguistic Programming), life counseling, and coaching, and she studies natural therapies. Michael also renovates and build houses and enjoys scuba diving, water skiing, and sailing.

Acknowledgments

We would like thank our editor, Mark Garvey, of Muska & Lipman for his eye for detail, for capturing the essence of what we were saying, and for his patience. We thank all our friends and family for their enthusiasm, and ScanSoft for supporting this book.

Contents

Introduction

Welcome to OmniPage Power! Document Scanning Made Easy with OmniPage Pro. This is the only book available that covers OCR (Optical Character Recognition) scanning with OmniPage, apart from our other classroom training manuals. Many books and magazines show how scanners work. There are numerous books on how to manage and manipulate pictures. However, none of them covers OmniPage in detail. The primary use for OmniPage is to scan and recognize text and photos for editing, printing, or archiving. *OmniPage Power!* is an instructional training manual with exercises. The exercises are for beginners, intermediate, advanced, and frequent users. It teaches a process for scanning rather than discussing each function separately. Whether you are just beginning to scan documents or have been using OmniPage for some time, this book clearly and simply explains all the ins and outs of scanning a single page text document, as well as complex pages with graphics, photos, logos, signatures, columns, and tables.

A scanner is not like a photocopier. Getting a perfect copy every time you push the scanner button just doesn't happen. The software controls how your scanned documents look, and understanding how and why to set up your options in OmniPage prior to scanning will lead you to become an OmniPage power user, saving you hours of wasted time. This book will get you there.

We have worked with end users of OmniPage and ScanSoft/Caere products for six years. We have supported and conducted training courses on OmniPage for thousands of users—from corporations, governments, universities, and schools to small businesses, home users, and retirees. This book has been written from the contents of our training courses and from listening to and solving end-user issues. We have written step-by-step training manuals for OmniPage since Version 6. We design, develop, and produce interactive multimedia training CD-ROMs for OmniPage, and ScanSoft, Inc. recommends this book. For full details on our training products for OmniPage, please visit http://www.omnipagetraining.biz or http://www.mylearningsystems.com.

What You Will Find in This Book

- ▶ Hands-on examples that teach you the keys to mastering scanning.
- ▶ Easy scanning techniques and options for all types of documents—from business and government documents to resumes, school assignments, and exams—any small and large documents that you don't want to retype.
- ▶ Techniques for scanning spreadsheets and tables while maintaining lines and columns.
- ▶ Time-saving tips for creating templates, to make scanning similar documents fast and easy.
- ▶ Tips for making electronic copies of existing forms—timesheets, order forms, etc.
- ▶ Techniques for successful scanning of logos, signatures, line art, and photographs—with simple techniques for reducing the size of your image files for e-mailing and the Web, plus tips on resolution.
- ▶ Instructions for integrating OmniPage with Word and Excel for easy scanning and document editing of simple, complex, and long documents.
- ▶ An introduction to OmniPage's sister applications to make your scanning jobs work better for you. You'll discover the right tool for the right job—OmniForm for scanning forms with fill-in fields and checkboxes, and PaperPort to manage your files and Windows Explorer.
- ▶ A host of tips and tricks that aren't in the OmniPage user's manual.

Who This Book Is For

This book is for anyone who has a scanner and doesn't want to retype existing text documents. It's for professionals, business people, government departments and divisions, retirees, lecturers, teachers, legal professionals, authors, students, and kids. It's for anyone who wants to make brochures, fliers, magazines, and desktop publications.

This book is also for you if:

- ▶ You have experienced problems scanning with OmniPage or other OCR programs.
- ▶ You have spent more than an hour trying to scan a document.
- ▶ Your scanned documents don't turn out looking like the originals, and you want to know why and how to fix them. You want to know how to get rid of unwanted shading and squiggly characters and how to stop your photos from going to the bottom of the page.
- ▶ You have trouble formatting scanned resumes, contracts, newsletters, catalogs, books, manuals, tenders, lists of numbers, spreadsheets, tables, faxes, newspaper and magazine articles, brochures, and advertising materials.
- ▶ You want to know how to create an electronic signature or capture a logo.

How This Book Is Organized

OmniPage Power! has fourteen chapters and an appendix with exercises. Most of the exercises are for scanning in black and white; however, Chapter 8 has a section on scanning a colored photo. To make it easy for you, we have set up an area on our Web site to download this photo, plus all the other exercises for the chapters. You can download the photo and exercises from: http://www.omnipagetraining.biz or from http://www.muskalipman.com.

▶ Chapter 1: "Document Scanning and OCR." This chapter introduces the basic terms and concepts of scanning and Optical Character Recognition. It shows you how to install or reinstall OmniPage. It also walks you through the OmniPage scanner setup. Plus, it will introduce you to some of the example exercises you will work through in the book.

▶ Chapter 2: "Navigating OmniPage." This chapter provides a detailed walk-through of the OmniPage desktop and its three primary views: Document Manager, Original Image, and Text Editor. We'll also take a look at the menus and toolbars available to you, including the OmniPage toolbox, the interface from which you initiate and control scanning. Chapter 2 also includes coverage of the OCR Wizard, a step-by-step interactive tool that helps you obtain great character recognition results.

▶ Chapter 3: "Basic Document Scanning." There are decisions to be made before scanning begins. This chapter walks you through that decision-making process, from describing your original documents in terms of OmniPage parameters, to establishing goals for your end results. Then, you will learn the process of scanning and OCR step-by-step, by working through examples of scanning a test document, proofing the results, and saving your file. We'll also cover using OmniPage's dictionaries and converting text to speech.

▶ Chapter 4: "Working With Zones." Understanding how OmniPage creates and uses zones is key for achieving great results with your scans. This chapter covers zones from top to bottom—from defining zone types and properties to using the zone toolbar to draw and edit your zones. You'll learn how OCR settings interact with zones, and you'll get plenty of practice in drawing and working with zones in the step-by-step examples.

▶ Chapter 5: "Multi-Column Documents." OmniPage is great for scanning newspaper articles, resumes, legal documents, newsletters, magazines, or any text that's arranged in columns. This chapter provides thorough instructions on scanning and OCR'ing documents whose text is in multiple columns. In step-by-step exercises, you'll learn how zone settings affect scanning results for multi-column documents and how to arrange those settings for optimal results. And you'll learn how to properly recognize the scanned image and save your results.

► Chapter 6: "Direct OCR." One of the handiest features of OmniPage, Direct OCR allows you to scan and recognize text using the OmniPage software from within applications such as Word or Excel, or even from within Windows Explorer. This chapter will walk you through the steps necessary to set up Direct OCR to work seamlessly with your other applications. Examples in the chapter will guide you through using Direct OCR and setting up options for best results.

► Chapter 7: "Tables and Spreadsheets." OmniPage's table feature does a great job of scanning things like price and/or parts lists, telephone bills, schedules, and tables. The results are exportable to Excel and, from there, into a database of your choosing. This chapter will teach you options and settings to optimize your results when working with tables and spreadsheets. You will also learn your way around the Table toolbar, a special set of formatting tools for working with spreadsheets and tables. A series of exercises will help you sharpen your skills.

► Chapter 8: "Logos, Signatures, Line Art, and Color Photos." OmniPage has some impressive capabilities to help you work with graphic images of all sorts. In this chapter, you'll learn how to use OmniPage to capture and manipulate a variety of graphics. You'll cover image editing and cropping, with particular attention to the process of scanning and working with color photographs.

► Chapter 9: "Multiple-Page and Long Documents." Some documents are much longer than others and, as such, require somewhat different handling. In this chapter, we'll cover the differences you'll encounter when working with long documents. We'll also cover ADFs (Automatic Document Feeders), how to scan books and double-sided pages, and using Schedule OCR to set your scanner up to run unattended.

► Chapter 10: "Saving, Publishing, and Sending Documents." You have a lot of options when it comes to saving and sending documents you've scanned and recognized with OmniPage. This chapter covers all the possibilities, including basic and advanced save options, turning documents into HTML files, scanning and creating PDF files, and e-mailing scanned files.

► Chapter 11: "Managing Documents and Images with PaperPort." You have enough details to stay on top of—managing your files and documents should not be one more source of complexity in your life. ScanSoft's PaperPort software helps alleviate file clutter and keeps you organized. In this chapter, we'll cover the basics of file organization in general and discuss file sharing, archiving, searching, and document management via PaperPort.

▶ Chapter 12: "Form Scanning With OmniForm." Just as we use a hammer to knock in a nail and a spade to dig a hole, computer applications are also specific tools meant for specific tasks. Different jobs call for different tools. This chapter introduces OmniForm, an application specifically designed to handle the job of scanning and recognizing forms such as tenders, legal forms, credit applications, surveys, questionnaires, enrollment forms, a variety of in-house forms, bank forms, employment forms, and more. You'll learn about optimizing your form-scanning results with OmniForm's Form Designer and Form Filler. You'll learn how to transfer data from OmniForm to an external database, and you'll learn all about e-mailing a form.

▶ Chapter 13: "OmniPage Advanced Configuration Options." Make the most of OmniPage by learning how to fine-tune the option settings to match the type of documents you are scanning in order to get the results you're after. OmniPage's advanced configuration options allow you full control over a wide variety of parameters, including language and proofing options, scanner options, layout, processing, and saving.

▶ Chapter 14: "Troubleshooting." This chapter is a list of Frequently Asked Questions from OmniPage users. If you're having trouble with a particular function, feature, or process, refer to this chapter for quick answers.

▶ Appendix. Sample documents with the appropriate settings, plus the exercises for this book. You can also download these exercises, plus additional documents to practice with, at http://www.omnipagetraining.biz and at http://www.muskalipman.com.

1

Document Scanning and OCR

In this chapter, you'll discover how to get a document from the scanner into OmniPage. We'll discuss different types of documents you can scan with OmniPage and show you some examples. We'll look at basic OCR (Optical Character Recognition) principles and how OmniPage interprets the document you are scanning. Plus, we'll discuss the importance of starting out with a good-quality document. As a result, you'll understand what is meant by document and OCR scanning, you'll know the important steps involved in installing your scanner to work with OmniPage, and you'll learn the correct procedure for installing OmniPage and how to register your software.

Documents are scanned for a wide variety of purposes, from simple home use to high-speed image and document management systems. The home user may scan photos for use in image-editing programs, or use the scanner for the occasional OCR—the process of turning the scanned image of a paper-based document into editable text—of text for invoices, school assignments, and other projects. Small businesses may use OCR document scanning for administration and for scanning parts and price lists, reports, and many different business documents. Those scanned documents can then be saved as Excel spreadsheets and imported into databases. OCR programs can also be used to create electronic forms.

Larger organizations may use document scanning with sophisticated programs that can read hand printing, bar codes, and checkboxes. You may often see surveys, exam questions, or application forms that have registration marks on the sides. Document scanning also encompasses image archiving of documents. Large organizations, municipal councils, freight companies, and other organizations use scanning to archive masses of documents that need to be kept for future reference.

What Is Document Scanning?

Simply put, a scanner is a device for taking pictures and getting them into your computer. For instance, a scanner can take a picture of a page of text. A software program such as OmniPage then converts this picture into editable text, so you can then use your word processing or spreadsheet program to edit sand rearrange the text. A scanner can also take a picture of a black and white or color photograph. You can then use an image editing program such as Adobe PhotoDeluxe to remove red eye, to crop, and to make other changes.

Document scanning should begin with a clear goal in mind for the end purpose of the scanned image. Most people think document scanning is nothing more than putting a document or page in a scanner and pressing the button to have it miraculously appear in their PC. But there's more to it than that.

NOTE

We are often asked, "How do I scan my document?" Our standard reply is, "What do you want to do with it?" Scanning must begin with the end result in mind. Do you want to fax your document, edit it in Word, save it into a spreadsheet so you can edit it, keep it as a high-resolution image for archiving, e-mail it . . . ?"

Scanning and OCR with OmniPage

OmniPage is a scanning software program that converts scanned documents and PDF files into editable text and images for use in computer software applications such as Microsoft Word or Excel. OmniPage retains other nontext elements of a document during OCR, including:

- ▶ **Graphics:** Photographs, graphics, drawings, signatures, logos, etc.
- ▶ **Text Formatting:** Bold and italic font types, font sizes, font styles, and more.
- ▶ **Page Formatting**: Column structure, paragraph spacing, and placement of graphics, for example.

OmniPage scans resumes, legal documents, schedules, price and parts lists, multiple column documents, contracts, letters, memos, invoices, logos, signatures, newspaper and magazine articles, brochures, manuals, tables of numbers like a phone bill, spreadsheets, advertisements, line-art drawings, maps, both color and black and white photos, recipes, school exam papers, medical literature, and plain text documents with no format layouts. Also, OmniPage will scan a document with a combination of a table of text and numbers, single and multiple columns, a logo, signature, and color photo all on one page while keeping these elements in their original positions—and the photo will not go to the bottom of the page. The following are examples of types of documents you can scan with OmniPage. We will use these examples as exercises. Some of these exercises are in color. Since this book is printed in black and white, the photos, obviously, are not in color; however, you can log on to http://www.omnipagetraining.biz or http://www.muskalipman.com or use your own color document. Plus, we'll be using many more examples throughout this book. As you move through the book, you'll find all the tips, tricks, and techniques necessary to scan all these types of documents.

Sample Documents

These example images are available to download from http://www.omnipagetraining.biz or http://www.muskalipman.com. Some are also in the appendix.

True Page Sample

OmniPage Professional allows you to recognize, edit, and save documents in their original, full page formats when you use True Page recognition. With True Page, you can even edit any images on the page by simply clicking on the image. This opens a complete set of editing tools in our Image Assistant editing package. Image Assistant features are highlighted

Image Editing for Every Business

Image Assistant has automatic, intelligent tools that anyone in your office can use. And, for the professional graphic artist, it has the most complete set of professional features available in image editing software. Whether your business consists of you and your computer or you and a cast of thousands,

Image Assistant is your image editing tool. Image Assistant is a 24 bit color image editor that lets just about anyone, even beginners, produce professional color output: from a color slide to a four color separation.

Assist Mode

You may not be a graphic artist, but you know how your image should look. In Assist Mode, you choose just the right effect for your image by looking at sample thumbnails onscreen. For example, if you're setting contrast, you'll see 15 samples of how your image will look with 15 different contrast settings. You just click on the sample that looks right to you, and your image is transformed. And, multiple levels of Undo and Redo let you experiment to your heart's content.

Imaging for Pros

Image Assistant's true power and versatility are clear to the professional graphic artist. You can edit in bilevel, grayscale, RGB, or CYMK and access complete PANTONE color support. Image Assistant has all the tools and features you expect from a high end image processing product.

Automatic Scanning Controls

Image Assistant completely automates the task of capturing images. For example, it can separate a scanned photo from unwanted text, crop it and rotate it. It determines whether you're working with a line art, grayscale, or color image and opens it in the appropriate environment. You also have complete manual control for all settings if you need it.

Editing Tools

Image Assistant provides all the features you need to edit color, grayscale and black and white images. It can even convert images to a different type; for example, you can convert grayscale images into line art and vice versa. Grayscale images are made of various shades and tones. Consequently, the editing tools in Image Assistant let you paint and edit in shades and tones of grays. You can smudge grays together, paint with any gray from within an image, and even create custom brushes from different patterns and textures in the image. Electronic tools such as the pencil, eraser, paintbrush and airbrush are also available.

10 Aug	01:05 pm	15435482	0:21	0.25
12 Aug	10:02 am	18259253	0:37	0.25
17 Aug	12:15 pm	18415485	0:35	0.25
17 Aug	01:27 pm	18865586	2:35	1.00
17 Aug	02:53 pm	18415485	0:27	0.25
22 Aug	09:14 am	15230053	0:51	0.50
22 Aug	11:31 am	18265761	1:24	0.75
22 Aug	02:56 pm	18415485	0:32	0.25

Figure 1.1

Example of document that has multiple columns, a table, and photo

---

10.

Mortgage; and

(d) **(Notices):** on receipt, provide to the Mortgagee any summons, process, notice, order or other document received by the Mortgagor from any Government Authority relating to or affecting the Mortgaged Property.

5.4 **Repair**

The Mortgagor will maintain the Mortgaged Property, keeping it in good and tenantable repair and condition. Without limiting the generality of the foregoing, the Mortgagor will:

(a) **(Repair):** promptly and in a good and workmanlike manner make any repairs, renovations, additions and constructions to the Mortgaged Property necessary for:

(i) keeping all Buildings comprising the Mortgaged Property in good and tenantable repair and condition;

(ii) complying with the requirements of any Government Authority in relation to the Mortgaged Property; and

(iii) complying with any notice in writing from the Mortgagee to repair any defect in the condition of the Mortgaged Property;

(b) **(No alteration without consent):** not make or permit to be made any alteration or addition to the Mortgaged Property or pull down, remove or demolish any Buildings from time to time comprising the Mortgaged Property without the prior written consent of the Mortgagee;

(c) **(Clean):** keep the Mortgaged Property clean, tidy and clear of rubbish; and

(d) **(Maintenance Contracts):** enter into and keep in force contracts with respectable and qualified contractors for the maintenance and repair of all plant, equipment and electrical, mechanical and fire services to the Mortgaged Property.

5.5 **Use of Mortgaged Property**

The Mortgagor will:

(a) **(Approved use):** itself, and will cause every person from time to time in occupation of the Mortgaged Property to only use the Mortgaged Property for purposes permitted under any Statute, development consent or other like consent, approval or permission affecting the Mortgaged Property;

(b) **(Maintain current use):** not discontinue or vary the current use of the Mortgaged Property without the prior written consent of the Mortgagee;

(c) **(Conduct of business):** conduct and maintain every business carried on by the Mortgagor on the Mortgaged Property from time to time in a proper and efficient manner;

(d) **(No offensive use):** not carry on or permit to be carried on any noxious, noisome, immoral or offensive art, trade, business or occupation upon the Mortgaged Property; and

(e) **(No nuisance):** not cause or contribute to any nuisance to or disturbance of the owners, occupiers or users of any property adjoining the Mortgaged Property.

Figure 1.2

Example of a contract

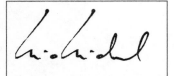

Figure 1.3
Example of a signature

10 Aug	01:05 pm	Mobile		015435482	Peak	0:21	0.25
12 Aug	10:02 am	Mobile		018259253	Peak	0:37	0.25
17 Aug	12:15 pm	Mobile		018415485	Peak	0:35	0.25
17 Aug	01:27 pm	Mobile		018865586	Peak	2:35	1.00
17 Aug	02:53 pm	Mobile		018415485	Peak	0:27	0.25
22 Aug	09:14 am	Mobile		015230053	Peak	0:51	0.50
22 Aug	11:31 am	Mobile		018265761	Peak	1:24	0.75
22 Aug	02:56 pm	Mobile		018415485	Peak	0:32	0.25
26 Aug	09:07 am	Mobile		018617249	Peak	0:44	0.50
26 Aug	01:34 pm	Mobile		018415866	Peak	0:42	0.50
29 Aug	10:11 am	Mobile		018969363	Peak	0:29	0.25
30 Aug	12:30 pm	Mobile		015431007	Peak	2:34	1.00
30 Aug	12:54 pm	Mobile		018044682	Peak	11:03	4.50
30 Aug	04:14 pm	Mobile		018153040	Peak	0:26	0.25
31 Aug	12:21 pm	Mobile		018256063	Peak	0:19	0.25
31 Aug	12:45 pm	Mobile		018256063	Peak	0:32	0.25
31 Aug	02:27 pm	Mobile		018617249	Peak	0:31	0.25
31 Aug	03:02 pm	Mobile		018617249	Peak	1:27	0.75
05 Sep	02:12 pm	Mobile		018969363	Peak	0:48	0.50
05 Sep	02:59 pm	Mobile		018212472	Peak	0:30	0.25
05 Sep	03:17 pm	Mobile		018212472	Peak	4:04	1.75
05 Sep	04:34 pm	Mobile		018617249	Peak	0:43	0.50
Telephone Service							
10 Aug	12:08 pm	Mobile		015435482	Peak	1:00	0.50
23 Aug	10:23 am	Mobile		018617249	Peak	0:20	0.25
31 Aug	04:49 pm	Mobile		018293791	Peak	4:38	2.00
01 Sep	10:22 am	Mobile		018617249	Peak	1:35	0.75
05 Sep	03:06 pm	Mobile		018617249	Peak	0:23	0.25
Telephone Service							
24 Aug	11:46 am	Mobile		018278366	Peak	0:44	0.50

Continued page 5

Figure 1.4
Example of a phone bill

Figure 1.5
Example of a color
photo (shown here in
black and white)

Figure 1.6
Example of a logo

Omnipage Training

Figure 1.7
Example of a
newspaper article

Figure 1.8
Example of a letter

TECHNOLOGY * SIMPLE

4 June 1998

Chief of Division:

OmniPage Training
Fax: 9888 7400

Dear Sir

I attended an OmniPage Pro 8 Training course last week at Parramatta and just wanted to let you know how informative it was. I have been using Omnipage for a few years now, mostly making it do what I wanted, but now I realise I was doing things a very long way around indeed.

To be able to scan tables and spreadsheets (a big part of my job) and have them arrive in Word or Excel correctly is just wonderful, something I had never got totally right before. Knowing how to now handle graphics and text together, and those odd shaped pieces you need from time to time put the finishing touches on very informative day.

I particularly liked before the course started the trainer asked everyone in the room what they used Omnipage for and what they would like to do and made a very long list, but by the end of the day every item on the list was crossed off.

Great trainer, great program. great day.

Many thanks indeed

Signature went here

Filename: Letter

Basic OCR Principles

When a document is scanned, it is converted into an image made up of dots. These dots are called pixels. When using OmniPage, the resolution—or "dots per inch" (DPI)—is set to 300. Every square inch of the image is made up of 300 dots. Each dot is either black or white when scanned in black and white mode. When scanned in grayscale, each dot can be one of 256 shades of gray. When scanned in color, each dot can be one of millions of different colors! The dots make up patterns that form text characters and graphics (see Figure 1.9).

Figure 1.9
Characters are made up
of a pattern of dots

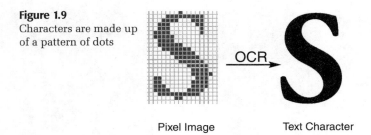

Pixel Image   Text Character

However, to the PC it is just a page of different-colored dots. OmniPage recognizes the text by using "maps" or "templates" of what each character looks like. It compares these character maps to find the matching pattern. When it finds a match, OmniPage places the text character in that location on the page. It does this very quickly—sometimes at a rate of up to 8,000 words per minute. OmniPage also uses intelligent built-in spelling dictionaries and training files. OmniPage uses several "recognition engines" to achieve an amazing level of accuracy. Sometimes, OmniPage may mistake what looks to us like a graphic or a smudge for text, and it will produce stray characters. This is easily fixed.

During OCR, OmniPage uses specific settings to determine how the page is evaluated. The settings also create ordered zones around areas of a page. These zones identify what will be recognized as text or retained as a graphic. The recognized text and graphics are then placed in the new text document based on settings you select in the Text window.

OmniPage identifies words by looking at the average spacing between characters and the font size. When it sees a larger-than-average space, it assumes this must be the end of a word. It then starts looking for the beginning of the next word. OmniPage applies this same principle to line and paragraph spacing. For columns and tables, OmniPage looks for similar word spacing and larger gaps on consecutive lines. It also looks for grid lines of tables and graphics. OmniPage uses this information to determine where and what type of zones to draw. See Figure 1.10.

Character space
–the gap between each character is of the same or similar size.

Characters on a page

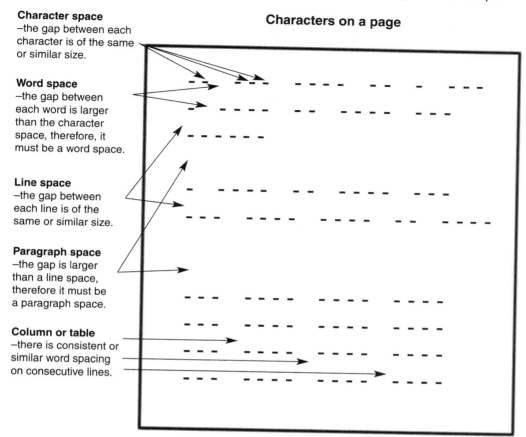

Word space
–the gap between each word is larger than the character space, therefore, it must be a word space.

Line space
–the gap between each line is of the same or similar size.

Paragraph space
–the gap is larger than a line space, therefore it must be a paragraph space.

Column or table
–there is consistent or similar word spacing on consecutive lines.

Figure 1.10
The characteristics of a page—OmniPage uses these characteristics to determine how and where to break words, lines, and paragraphs and where to create columns

If you have headings, titles, or text in a very large, bold font, or if there is more than normal space between characters, OmniPage may recognize groups of letters within words as separate words. For example, the word "SCAN" written in a large font with wide spacing between letters may end up, after the OCR process, as two "words": "SC" and "AN."

Calculating Font Size

We get many calls from users asking why their scanned fonts turn out smaller or larger than they are in their original documents. The explanation below will give you some insight as to why this can happen and how a slight difference in the scanned font can change the size of the recognized font.

The font size reproduction is very good on font sizes between 8 points and about 28 points. For anything less than 8 points, it is better to scan at a higher resolution. This will give OmniPage more pixels to measure the font size and more pixels to help recognize the shape of the character. If the font size is incorrect, you can easily change the font size in OmniPage's Text Editor view or in your word processing program.

OmniPage calculates the size of the font based on the resolution at which the document was scanned—which, remember, is usually 300 dpi—and the height of the character in pixels.

Fonts are measured in "points" (10-point, 12-point, etc.). A point is equal to 1/72nd of an inch. A 10-point character would be 10 divided by 72, or 0.138 inches high. So, OmniPage calculates a 10-point character is 41 pixels high (300 dpi multiplied by 0.138 inch). An 11-point character is 45.9 pixels high (300 dpi multiplied by 0.153 inch).

So, you can see the difference between recognizing a character as 10 points or as 11 points is only four pixels, which is just over thirteen one thousandths of an inch (Figure 1.11).

Figure 1.11
The difference in character size between 10 points and 10.5 points

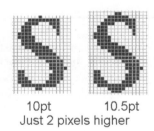

10pt   10.5pt
Just 2 pixels higher

The Importance of Document Quality

There's an old saying: "Garbage in, garbage out." You will get the best scanning results using first-generation documents (original of a document, not a photocopy or fax). For OmniPage to work effectively, the characters must be clear and clean. OmniPage needs to see a clear gap between characters for good recognition. Best results are obtained using laser-quality originals. The characters should not bleed into one another, nor be too light or broken. That said, OmniPage can often give amazing results even on poor quality documents.

If the document contains a script font, where the characters are joined together (Figure 1.12), no OCR program, including OmniPage, will be able to recognize the text, as there is no gap or clear separation between the characters.

Figure 1.12
Script font

A similar problem is when characters in documents are unintentionally joined together. This is called bleeding, meaning that one character "bleeds" into the one beside it. This can happen with third- or fourth-generation (or worse) photocopies. Bleeding can typically be seen in photocopies of newspaper articles, documents with shaded backgrounds, documents with poorly formed or broken characters, or poor-quality faxes. Serif characters are more prone to bleeding than are sans because of the "tails" on the characters.

Figure 1.13 shows an example of a word from a poor-quality document. The word is "dog," but, as you can see, the scanned image is missing some of the dots that make up the characters. Since OmniPage is looking for gaps between characters to define each one, and since there are dots missing in the "d," OmniPage will interpret the "d" as two separate characters: "c" and "l." The OmniPage recognition engines and spell checkers will produce the word "clog." A valid result; however, the sentence "I took my clog for a walk" is very different from "I took my dog for a walk."

Figure 1.13
Clog or dog?

How Your Computer Works with Your Scanner

There are many components of hardware and software between you and your scanner. You interact with the OmniPage desktop screen; the commands you send to OmniPage are then sent to Microsoft Windows. Windows talks to the OmniPage Scanner Wizard, which talks to the scanner's TWAIN driver, which then talks to your scanner. The scanner sends the image all the way back through this chain until you see it on the screen. All these components must be working properly and be able to talk to each other for OmniPage to function correctly.

Scanner manufacturers know you need software to be able to use their scanner, so they provide it with the hardware they sell. But at the price for which they sell the scanners, they can't include the full version of all the different software programs. They don't know if you want tea or coffee, so to speak. So, you get an instant tea and a trial-size coffee. They bundle cut-down or limited versions of software applications with their hardware—and not always the latest versions. This allows you to perform basic OCR of plain text documents and basic image/picture editing.

It pays to shop around and look at what software is included with scanners you are considering purchasing. The OCR program that often comes bundled with scanners is OmniPage Limited Edition. Some Scanners come with OmniPage Version 9, which lets you scan tables, spreadsheets, and color pictures. Some of the higher-range HP scanners come with OmniForm, for scanning forms, or PaperPort. PaperPort is an excellent document manager with OCR capabilities. Now, if you want the full cappuccino with froth and powdered chocolate on top, you need to purchase OmniPage 11 for OCR.

CAUTION

If you buy the latest scanner and it has OmniPage 9 bundled with it, remember that OmniPage 9 came out many years prior to the release of your new scanner. If you are not getting the accuracy you are expecting, it's most likely that you have not completed two important tasks.

1. You have not set up your scanner to talk to OmniPage. Because OmniPage 9 does not have a Scanner Wizard to set up your scanner to talk to OmniPage as does Pro 11, you must select the scanner driver through Scan Manager 5.0. To do this, go to Start > Settings > Control Panel > Scan Manager 5.0. Click Add Scanner. Click Generic and then TWAIN Scanner. Click Next, name this driver TWAIN (and then the name of your scanner, i.e., Canon). All you are doing here is setting up another scanner driver to use. Click Next and select your Scanner Twain Driver from the list. *If it is not in the list, you haven't installed your scanner driver*. Click Finish. You will see the new Generic Twain Driver icon in the Caere Scan Manager Window. Now, OmniPage Pro 9 is set up to talk to your scanner. If you have more than one scanner, this is where you will need to select which scanner to use before launching OmniPage. You can download Scan Manager 5.0 from ScanSoft's Support Web site at http://support.scansoft.com/cu/library/downloads/index.asp.

2. You are not actually using OmniPage to scan the document, but rather using the OCR engine built into the new scanner driver.

Some scanner driver menus—Canoscan and Epson Smart Panel, for example—give you the option to select the OCR program to use. Often, these OCR programs are the limited versions that are embedded in the scanner program. They are not the same as the full OmniPage product. If you are scanning this way and not launching OmniPage correctly as indicated below, accuracy will suffer and the layout of the document may be all over the place.

You do not start OmniPage through your scanner driver menu—i.e., through CanoScan or Epson Smart Panel. For OmniPage 9, you access OmniPage by launching OmniPage from Start > Programs > Caere > OmniPage. For OmniPage 11, click Start > Programs > Scansoft OmniPage Pro 11 > OmniPage Pro 11.

Telling your scanner how to talk to OmniPage and launching it correctly will improve your scanning accuracy.

Table 1.1
A comparison of OCR speeds using the document "test" on computers with varying specifications

PC system specs	OCR characters	Recognition time	Recognition words per minute
Pentium II 233MHz 128Mb memory 100Mb free disk space	3588	19.7sec	1948
Pentium II 660MH 128Mb memory 2Gb free disk space	3588	6.0sec	6707
Pentium III 850MHz 256Mb memory 12Gb free disk space	3588	2.9sec	13,036

Installing and Setting Up Your Scanner Software

Before you install OmniPage, you must install your scanner and the scanner driver according to the scanner manufacturer's specifications. Remember, if you have an older scanner and you upgrade to OmniPage 11, you'll need to check the compatibility.

A scanner driver is software that is required to allow the Windows operating system to communicate with your scanner. Every scanner has its own driver. The scanner drivers are on the CD that came with your scanner.

All scanners have a special driver called a TWAIN driver. Some say it stands for "Technology Without An Interesting Name." It sounds like a fun acronym, given how many of them we use. TWAIN is the universal programming standard that the scanner and scanning programs use to communicate commands and images between each other.

TIP

If you have an old scanner and are using the drivers that came with it, you may have some accuracy problems. If this is the case, you will need the latest driver for your scanner. Go to the Web site of your scanner manufacturer and download the latest drivers.

As there are many scanner manufacturers, each installation process will be different. There are too many to list step-by-step instructions for installing every kind of driver. It is self-explanatory once you start the installation process.

1. Make sure your scanner is connected to your PC and switched on.

2. After placing the scanner software CD-ROM in your CD-ROM drive, the installation process should start. Follow the on-screen prompts for your scanner installation.

NOTE

The installation program should start automatically. If it does not, go to Windows Explorer. Locate your CD-ROM drive and click it. There in the top-level directory will be a program named Setup.exe or Install.exe or Autorun.exe. Double-click to start the program and the installation process.

The scanner driver installation will create a program folder in the Programs menu. For example, HP scanners create an HP DeskScanII or HP Precision Scan folder. Canon scanners create the CanoScan folder. Epson Scanner creates the Epson Smart Panel for its software.

After you have installed your scanner and scanner drivers, conduct a test using the TWAIN interface you have just installed. We have used the Epson TWAIN interface (Figure 1.14).

Every scanner manufacturer's TWAIN interface will be different. To test the Epson TWAIN interface, we selected Start > Programs > Epson Smart Panel, then clicked on Preview. When you click Preview, and most TWAIN interfaces have a preview button, it does a quick scan. If it

Figure 1.14
A simple way to do a test scan

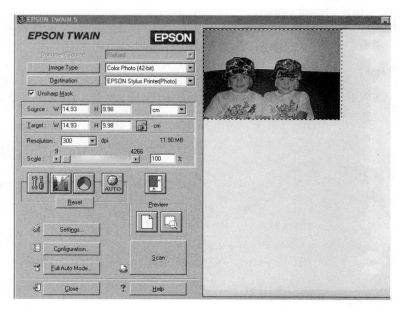

doesn't, there could be something wrong with the scanner or the cable, or the TWAIN drivers may not have been installed correctly. Consult the manual that comes with your scanner.

CAUTION

OmniPage supports scanners capable of scanning from 200 dpi to 600 dpi and is controlled by TWAIN or WIA (Windows Image Acquisition) scanner drivers. Scanners, scanner drivers, and programs are all made and released on the market at different times. It is important to ensure your scanner, scanner driver, scanning program, and application programs are compatible.

Please see the Scanner Guide at ScanSoft's Web site http://www.scansoft.com for a list of supported scanners.

Installing OmniPage 11

Make sure your scanner is connected to your PC and switched on. Have you done a test scan to make sure your PC can talk to the scanner? If not, do this first.

For Windows 98 users, make sure you have only Systray and Explorer running. Check this by holding down CTL+ALT keys and then press the Delete key once to select the Task Manager. There, you will see what programs are running. Close all but these two files. Always make sure you switch off your virus checker. It is important to do this; otherwise, you may get an incomplete installation.

All OmniPage files are copied automatically during installation. Follow these steps.

1. Make sure you've closed your anti-virus programs. This will avoid any possible conflicts when installing drivers and programs.
2. If you are installing on Windows 2000, Windows NT, or Windows XP, log on to your computer with administrator privileges.
3. Place the OmniPage 11 CD-ROM into the CD-ROM Drive. The installation program should start automatically.

NOTE

If the installation does not begin, go to Windows Explorer. Locate your CD-ROM drive and double-click it. In the top-level is Autorun.exe. Double-click this program. It starts the installation process.

4. The first screen asks you to choose a language. This language will be used for the Text-to-Speech system and as the program's interface language. The program interface language is used for displays such as menu items, dialog boxes, and warning messages. You can change the interface language later in Tools Options. Your choice determines which Text-to-Speech system will be installed with the program.

5.   If you own a previous version of OmniPage, or if you are upgrading from OmniPage Limited Edition, the installer will ask for your consent to uninstall that product first. You can leave the previous versions on your system.

6.   Accept the License Agreement.

7.   Enter your user name and company name if required.

8.   You will be asked to enter OmniPage 11's serial number. This appears on a sticky label at the back of the CD sleeve.

TIP

OmniPage 11's CD-ROM is in a paper sleeve. At the back of the cover, you will find the serial number on several removable sticky labels. To avoid losing your serial number, remove the label and place on the OmniPage Software CD-ROM. **You will need this serial number when installing or reinstalling OmniPage 11.**

Figure 1.15
Serial number on back
of CD-ROM sleeve

Follow the self-explanatory instructions on each screen to install the software. Next, you will be asked to register OmniPage. If you have an earlier version of OmniPage, register your software at http://www.mylearningsystems.com.

CHAPTER 1

Registration of OmniPage

ScanSoft's registration Wizard runs at the end of installation. You will be asked to fill out an electronic form to register your copy of OmniPage. You will be asked to enter OmniPage 11's serial number.

1. Fill out the online form.
2. To register online, click Send.

The program will search for an Internet connection. If it does not find an Internet connection, you will be given some offline registration choices.

This will happen if you install OmniPage on a computer where an Internet connection has not yet been set up. In this case, the Internet Connection Wizard starts when the OmniPage online registration starts. You can register OmniPage at another time. Reminders are displayed periodically.

NOTE

If you do not register the software during installation, you will be invited periodically to register. You do not need to register to run OmniPage. If you wish to receive details on upgrades and special promotions at discounted prices, however, it is worth it for you to register.

For registrations for Australia, New Zealand, and Asia Pacific, log on to http://www.mylearningsystems.com.

For registrations in the U.S., Canada, and Europe, log on to http://www.scansoft.com.

Setting Up Your Scanner with the OmniPage Scanner Wizard

The Scanner Wizard is used to get OmniPage and your scanner working together. Scanners send images to the computer as numbers. These numbers denote the color of each dot (pixel). But there are differences; for example, some scanners send white as a 1 and other scanners send white as a 0. The Scanner Wizard, with your input, checks and makes changes so that the scanned images are the same as the original.

The scanner takes you through several test scans: a plain text document, a black and white scan, a grayscale scan, and a color scan.

The Scanner Wizard will appear when you begin your first scan with OmniPage (Figure 1.16). It does not automatically pop up after installing OmniPage. The instructions are self-explanatory. If the Scanner Wizard does not appear, you should follow steps 1-3 below. Otherwise, start at step 4.

To use the Scanner Wizard:

1.   Choose Start > Programs > ScanSoft OmniPage 11.0.

2.   Click Scanner Wizard.

3.   Click the Setup button on the right-hand side of the Scanner Wizard dialog box.

4.   Choose Select Scanning Source, then click Next. If you have more than one scanner installed, select the current scanner you are using.

Figure 1.16
Scanner Wizard for setting up your scanner to work with OmniPage

NOTE

The drop-down box of Scanning Source will display all the scanner drivers you have installed. If, for example, you have upgraded to a new scanner, the old scanner driver will still be there. The drivers are stored in the folders C:\Windows\Twain32 and C:\Windows\Twain and have the file extension .ds. The folder Twain will contain the older 16- bit drivers. The folder Twain32 contains the newer 32bit drivers for Windows 98, ME 2000, and NT. The older drivers will still work in the new Windows environment. Remember, if you do have difficulty, go to the scanner manufacturer's Web site for the latest driver.

5. Click your scanner's driver to select it, then click Next.

6. Choose Yes to test your scanner configuration, then click Next.

7. The Wizard will now test the connection from the computer to your scanner. Click Next.

8. Place a test page with text but no pictures into your scanner.

9. The Wizard is now prepared to do a basic scan using your scanner manufacturer's software. Click Next.

10. Click Scan to begin the sample scan. Your scanner's "native" user-interface will appear. There will be a Scan button or similar button to start a scan. Click the button to start the scan.

11. When the image appears in the window, check that it displays correctly; i.e., black text on a white background. If it does not appear correctly, you may need to click "Inverse Image" or "Missing Image" and follow the prompts. Click the button that most appropriately describes the problem.

12. Click Next. This screen will show the type of scanner the wizard has detected. If this is not correct, select the appropriate scanner type and then click Next.

13. This screen shows additional information about your scanner.

14. Click Next to proceed to Page Size. The page sizes that the Wizard believes your scanner supports are listed in the window. To make any changes to the page sizes, click Advanced, make the changes, and then click Next.

15. The wizard displays another dialog box that says: "The first phase of optimizing your scanner is now complete. The next phase will test these settings by doing a series of scans without using your scanner's user interface." Leave the test page in the scanner from step 8. Click Next to begin a scan in black and white mode. If necessary, click "Inverse Image" or "Missing Image" and follow the prompts.

16. Click Next.

17. Now, test a color scan. Place into your scanner a color photograph or a page with a color picture. Click Next to scan in color mode. If necessary, click "Inverse Image" or "Missing Image" and follow the prompts.

18. Once the image appears correctly in the window, click Next.

19. Now, test a grayscale scan. Place a photograph or a page containing a grayscale picture into your scanner, or leave the color photograph or page and expect to see it come out as a grayscale image.

20. Click Next to begin a scan in grayscale mode. If necessary, click "Inverse Image" or "Missing Image" and follow the prompts. Once the image appears correctly in the window, click Next.

21. You have successfully set up your scanner to work with OmniPage 11!

22. Click Finish.

To change the scanner settings at a later time, or to add or set up another scanner, run through all the steps of the Scanner Wizard again. If you are already working in OmniPage, on the menu select Tools > Options > Scanner > Setup.

NOTE

Previous versions of OmniPage use Caere ScanManager. This program performs functions similar to the Scanner Setup Wizard. The Caere ScanManager is found in the Windows Control Panel.

The Caere ScanManager window displays the options to select your scanner driver and the settings to invert the scanned image—i.e., change the black background to white, etc. If you're using a previous version of OmniPage, you can download the latest version of ScanManager—version 5.0—from the Scansoft Web site: http://www.scansoft.com.

TIP

Where to look for more help:

► The first place to check when you are having difficulty is the Help menu on the OmniPage Menu bar.

► OmniPage User's Guide on the OmniPage CD-ROM. It is also installed in your OmniPage Pro 11 folder. In the Manuals folder are manuals in English, French, and German in Adobe Acrobat PDF format. You can read and search this guide with Adobe Acrobat Reader 3.0 or higher. Acrobat Reader 4.05 is included on the OmniPage CD-ROM.

► OmniPage Release Notes. On the OmniPage CD-ROM, in the Readme folder, are the latest release notes and useful tips in English, French, and German.

► Web sites for more information on OmniPage, related products, and training:

    http://www.mylearningsystems.com

    http://www.omnipagetraining.biz

    http://support.scansoft.com/OmniPage

OmniPage Pro 11 Recommended System Requirements

OmniPage may run with less than the minimum requirements; however, the results and performance may not be optimal. The faster the processor, the more memory, and the greater the amount of available disk space, the quicker the OCR process runs. Here are recommended requirements:

- ► A computer with a Pentium or higher processor.
- ► Microsoft Windows 95, Windows 98, Windows ME, Windows 2000, Windows NT 4.0, or Windows XP.
- ► 32 MB of memory (RAM); 64 MB recommended.
- ► 75 MB of free hard disk space for the application files, plus 10 MB working space during installation.
- ► 9 MB for Microsoft Installer (MSI) if not present, and 44 MB for Internet Explorer if not present. (These are present as part of the operating systems in Windows 98, Windows ME, Windows 2000, and Windows XP.)
- ► SVGA monitor with 256 colors and 800 × 600 pixel resolution.
- ► Windows-compatible pointing device.
- ► CD-ROM drive for installation.
- ► A compatible scanner. Please see the Scanner Guide at ScanSoft's Web site: http://www.scansoft.com for a list of supported scanners.

CAUTION

Scanning is reproducing existing material. Before you scan anything, whether it is for individual or company purposes, there are legal requirements of which to be aware. Often, a courtesy phone call, letter, or e-mail asking for permission to use other people's material is all that is required. Failure to get permission is an infringement of copyright. Make sure you know the legalities of reproducing material and/or intellectual property.

For your legal requirements:

U.S.A.—http://www.loc.gov/copyright

Australia—http://www.copyright.org.au

Canada—http://www.cb-cda.gc.ca/info/index-e.html

United Kingdom—http://www.patent.gov.uk/copy

CHAPTER 1

2

Navigating OmniPage

Now that your scanner is attached and working correctly with OmniPage, and you know how OCR works and what document scanning means, we are going to take a thorough look at the OmniPage desktop (the main screen). We'll consider each of the program's main views and work through its menus and wizards. This chapter may be a refresher for you. It is a good idea, however, to go through it so you will know your way around the screen and can easily identify the screen components when we refer to them. Moreover, there are important tips and formatting and layout tools that you need to know to get yourself out of difficulty.

The best way to navigate this chapter is to read about each component first. Then, locate the component on the screen and practice with it. Where there are lists of steps, follow through each step.

CHAPTER 2

NOTE
Always make sure your scanner is switched on before scanning. Otherwise, you will get a scanner error when attempting to scan.

Launch OmniPage by clicking on Start > Programs > ScanSoft OmniPage Pro 11 > OmniPage Pro 11 or by double-clicking on the OmniPage icon on your desktop.

When you launch OmniPage, the desktop displays the Tip of the Day (Figure 2.1). This can be a good resource for learning about the various applications of OmniPage. Click through each tip by clicking on Next Tip. If you do not want to show the Tip of the Day, deselect the small checkbox beside Show Tips at Start Up in the bottom left-hand corner.

TIP
Does your scanner have a button you can press to scan and OCR? Have you found when you do this the document does not come out like the original? If you have, then you are probably not using OmniPage. Your system is probably defaulting to your scanner's OCR program. To use OmniPage, you *must* launch it as stated above.

Figure 2.1
Tip of the Day
popup box

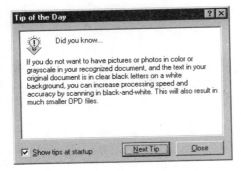

OmniPage Views

When you scan a document and view your work on the screen, you'll see that the OmniPage desktop interface is divided into three main views: the Document Manager, the Original Image, and the Text Editor. Let's consider each of these three views in turn.

1. **Document Manager:** The Document Manager is the left-hand window, which is itself divided into two views: Thumbnail and Details. The Thumbnail gives you a small picture of each page of the scanned document. You can rearrange the order of the pages or delete them. The Details tab displays information about each page, its status, the number of suspect words, accuracy, and OCR speed in words per minute. You can display eighteen other details.

2. **Original Image:** The Original Image view is the middle window. It displays the page selected in the Document Manager view. This is the scanned image of the original document, with automatic zones drawn around the text and any graphics or photos. This is where you can manually draw and edit zones.

3. **Text Editor:** The Text Editor view is the right-hand window. It displays the recognized text. You can reformat and edit the text and view the location of the text in the original image. More importantly, this is where you determine the layout before you save the document.

TIP

Display the function of each button by moving your mouse pointer over the button in question. To learn more about each button, click the help button at the end of the standard toolbar (the question mark). Move the mouse pointer over the button and click. A more detailed description of the button will display.

Figure 2.2
OmniPage desktop and
screen components

Formatting
toolbar

Standard toolbar

OmniPage:
AutoOCR,
Manual OCR,
and OCR

Document
Manager view

The current
page has a pale
border.

This page has
been resized.

This page has
zones drawn.
They are still to
be recognized.

The thumbnail
view shows a
small picture of
each page.

Page navigation buttons.

Buttons to show or
hide the three views.
Also rearrange the
text and image
windows.

Image toolbar,
used for drawing
zones, and
editing tables.

Original Image Window.
This displays the image of
the currently selected
page. It displays the
zones that have been
drawn automatically and
manually.

The Text Editor view
layout buttons. These are
very important buttons, as
they define the layout of
the saved text.

Drag the window dividers to
resize any of the three views.

Text Editor: This window displays
the recognized text of the currently
selected page. By default the
format is True Page. It is difficult to
edit a document saved in True
Page. When you open in a word
processor, you will find frames
around the paragraphs, making
editing difficult. Use True Page
(see page 34) when you do not
want to edit the scanned document.

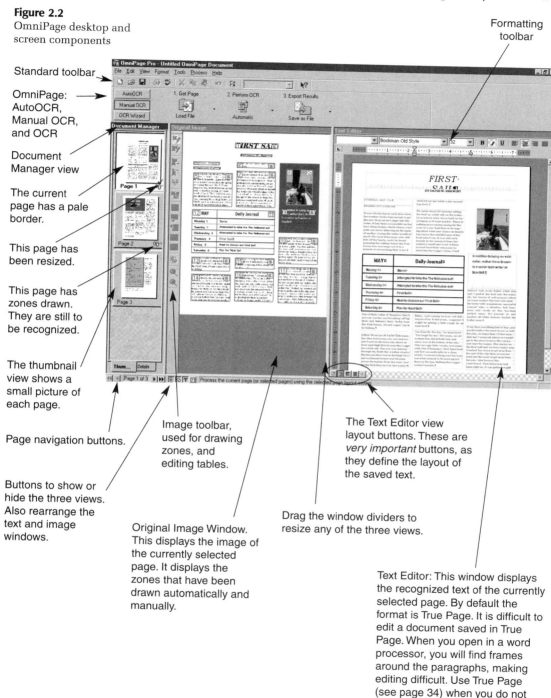

CHAPTER 2

Document Manager View

When you scan a document, all the pages of the document will be displayed in the Document Manager view. Access the Document Manager's two views from the tabs at the bottom of the window. (See Figure 2.3.)

Figure 2.3
Document Manager view with Thumbnail and Details

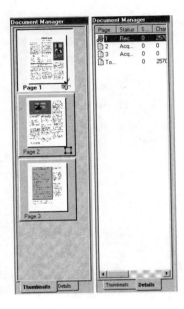

Thumbnail View

This view shows the scanned pages. The currently selected page is on a light yellow background and looks pushed in. There is a small icon in the bottom right-hand side of each page. A small blue box icon shows if the page has been "zoned." A pair of glasses and a check mark means it has been recognized and verified.

In Thumbnail view you can:

▶ Jump to a page of a multi-page document by clicking the icon of the desired page.

▶ Reorder a page by clicking the thumbnail of the page you want to move and dragging it above the desired page number. Pages are renumbered automatically. A yellow horizontal line will show its new location.

▶ Delete a page by selecting the thumbnail of the page you want to delete and pressing the Delete key on your keyboard.

► Select multiple pages by holding down the Shift key and clicking two thumbnails to select all pages between and including them. To add pages to a selection, hold down the Ctrl key as you click thumbnails one by one. Then you can move or delete the selected pages as a group.

► When multiple pages are being selected, the page set as current does not change. All selected pages are highlighted.

► Change or rearrange the order and column size of the Document Manager by clicking on the OmniPage menu and selecting View > Customize Details.

Details View

This view shows an overview of your document in a table format. There are a total of eighteen different details and statistics you can choose to display. By default, it shows the status (acquired, recognized, and proofed), the number of suspect words, the number of characters on the page, and the total of all of these for the document. In addition, accuracy and the speed of recognition in words per minute are displayed. The details acquired, recognized, and proofed refer to the status of the page. The image has been acquired; that is, it has completed the scan of the page or loaded the image file. Recognized means the page has been "zoned" and the "zoned" areas of the page have been through the OCR process and the recognized text displayed in the Text Editor view. Proofed mean that the Proofreader, with your input, has spell-checked the document and checked for any unrecognizable characters.

Each row represents one page. Columns present statistical or status information for each page and the current page is shown with a highlight. You can move pages in the Details view the same way as in the Thumbnail view

The Thumbnail and Details views both summarize the pages in the document, and they are synchronized; i.e., the current and selected pages remain the same when you switch views. The Thumbnail view also shows a small icon in the lower right-hand side of each page showing the status of that page (Figure 2.4).

Figure 2.4
Document Manager's page status icon—a scanned document of four pages, each with a different status

Page	Status	Thumb-nail icon	Detail icon	Page image has been...
1	Acquired	—	📄	Acquired with no manual or template zones and has not yet been recognized.
2	Zoned	⬚	—	Acquired and manual or template zones have been placed; not yet recognized.
3	Recognized	👓	📄	Recognized, but not proofread, or proofing was interrupted on the page.
4	Proofed	✓	📄	Recognized, and proofing has reached the end of the page.

CHAPTER 2

Original Image View

When you click on a page in the Document Manager Thumbnail view, the selected page will appear in the Original Image view (see Figure 2.5). This is where the zones are drawn and the text is recognized (OCR). The zones are drawn either automatically or manually, depending on the selection in the OmniPage toolbox and the selection of the Perform OCR Process. You will discover more about the toolboxes later in this chapter. A later chapter is entirely devoted to zones; they are that important. Zones are the "boxes" OmniPage draws around text and graphics it identifies on the page. OmniPage runs its OCR processes only on what is contained within those zones. Sometimes when OmniPage automatically draws the zones they are not as you want them; in these cases, you can manually draw zones to identify what parts of the page you want recognized.

Figure 2.5
Original Image view

Zones can be manually deleted, resized, redefined, and redrawn using the zone tools on the Image toolbar on the left-hand side of this window.

You will also discover on this toolbar two tools for making the windows bigger or smaller—Zoom In and Zoom Out. It is a good idea to zoom in when redrawing zones. It makes it easier to see what you are doing. There also is a tool for rotating the image. You do not need to rescan the page, as OmniPage can rotate the entire scanned image in the Original Image view. If your original document has text both ways on the page—landscape and portrait—OmniPage will recognize text in one direction only. If you rotate the image, do this before redrawing any zones, as any previous zones will be lost. OmniPage automatically straightens crooked images before the recognition process. You need to have the page in the correct orientation before beginning the recognition process.

The Image View toolbar also has tools for formatting tables and spreadsheets. We will go into more detail in Chapter 7, "Tables and Spreadsheets."

Sometimes you may need to find out the name of the image, its width, height, and resolution. To see the details of the scanned image:

1. Place the mouse in the Original Image view on the image.
2. Wait a few seconds; the details will display in a pop-up box.

NOTE

In Original Image view, the text is never very clear unless you use the Zoom option. The reason the text is not very clear is because it is an image of only 300 dpi. An A4 page is 2,480 pixels wide. A letter-size page is 2,550 pixels wide. The image is being displayed in the Original Image view in an area about 430 pixels wide. That is why it is fuzzy. As you zoom into the image, it becomes clearer.

Text Editor View

Once the text is recognized in the Original Image view, it appears in the Text Editor view (Figure 2.6). You can proofread the text and make changes using the Text Editor Formatting toolbar. Again, use the zoom function on the menu to clearly see the text.

Figure 2.6
Full view of Text Editor view for formatting

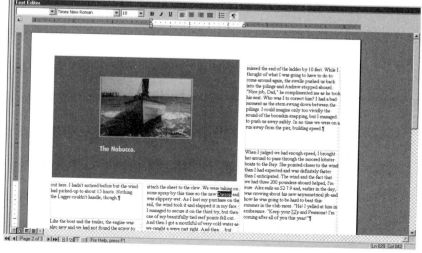

NOTE

You will notice that in the Text Editor view, the text is clean and sharp. This is because the text is no longer an image, but is composed of actual characters that can be edited.

CHAPTER 2

The Text Editor can display text layout in any of four views, using the buttons at the left of the scroll bar (Figure 2.7). You can also change the layout via the menu bar. The Text Editor views are very important! This is where many users have problems with their saved documents and will say things such as, "The format is all wrong," or, "The text is all over the place." The Text Editor view determines the layout or format of your saved document. It is easy to miss these little buttons at the bottom of the Text Editor.

Figure 2.7
The four Text Editor
layout views

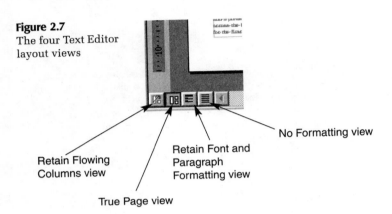

No Formatting view

Retain Font and
Paragraph
Formatting view

Retain Flowing
Columns view

True Page view

▶ **Retain Flowing Columns.** This view is identical to True Page view, except that arrows show the reading order of zones. The text flow between columns can be changed using the Page outline window. The document is saved with the view (formatting level) set at export time if the file type supports that. It is therefore possible to export the same document more than once, with different formatting levels.

▶ **True Page.** This view tries to conserve as much of the formatting of the original document as possible. Character and paragraph styling is retained. All page elements, including pictures, titles, tables, and columns, are placed in frames. It can be more difficult to verify and edit text in this view; you may need to scroll within a frame to see all the frame contents. Rows of arrows denote contents extending beyond frame borders.

▶ **Retain Font and Paragraph.** This displays text, no columns, with font and paragraph styling. The horizontal ruler is displayed. Text will be wrapped if selected. You may find this view convenient for verifying, editing, and modifying the text together with its styling.

▶ **No Formatting.** This displays plain left-aligned text, no columns, in a single font and font size, with the same line breaks as in the original document. Most formatting buttons and dialog boxes are disabled. Rulers are not displayed. You may find this view convenient for verifying and editing the text.

NOTE

When you switch to the No Formatting view, the different fonts and their sizes, styles, and attributes, as well as paragraph formatting, all disappear. However, they are not lost. When you switch back to a higher-level view, they are all restored. In No Formatting view you can set a single font and size for the whole text. These values are applied only in No Formatting view and are dropped when you switch to another view. In all other cases, the font and paragraph formatting is transferred from one view to another.

OmniPage 11 uses a formatting toolbar and ruler just like the formatting tools in Microsoft Word. It is located at the top of the Text Editor view window (Figure 2.8). This toolbar only becomes active when there is text in the Text Editor view. Using the toolbar, you can change tabs, paragraph styles, fonts, margins, and indents. You can format columns, change the alignment of the text, even bullet lists. With these tools, you can format your document before exporting to another application, if you wish.

Figure 2.8
Formatting toolbar in the Text Editor view

OmniPage Menu

Below the OmniPage title bar is the menu (Figure 2.9). This provides access to all commands in OmniPage. The mouse or the keyboard can be used to access the menu commands.

Figure 2.9
OmniPage menu

Point to the appropriate menu and click the left mouse button. A drop-down list of commands will display. Click the command required. To display the drop-down list of commands via the keyboard, hold down the Alt key and press the underlined letter of the menu you require. Use the arrow keys to highlight the command required, then press Enter to execute that command. Alternatively, once the drop-down list of commands is displayed, press the underlined letter of the command you wish to execute. Some of the commands have keyboard shortcuts; these are listed on the right-hand side of the menu in the drop-down list.

The menu commands are also covered below in the standard toolbar. However, there are some commands that are available only from the menu. We will cover the differences here.

CHAPTER 2

File

Saving, printing, and sending can be done from the File menu.

Table 2.1
Menu items

Command	Result
Save and Save As	Refers to saving the recognized text.
Save Image	Saves the scanned image in various image file formats.
Print	Gives two options: to print either the recognized text or the scanned image.
Send	This is the same as saving the recognized text as an e-mail. It will create a file attachment in the file format you choose.

You can save images of whole pages only, not graphic zones within a page. On the menu, select File > Save Image. The Save As dialog box gives you the option to save the images in thirteen different image file formats. OmniPage will save black and white images at their original scanned resolution to 600 dpi; 300 dpi is recommended for best OCR results.

Grayscale and color images are saved at 150 dpi, or less if scanned at a lower resolution. This is to reduce the file size and maintain the image quality.

Images are saved as displayed whenever possible. If you try to save a black and white image to JPG, a prompt to convert to grayscale will be displayed. This is because JPG does not support black and white images. If you try to save a grayscale or color image to TIFF G3 or G4, you will be prompted to convert to black and white. This is because TIFF G3 and G4 do not support color images

You cannot save original images to PDF format, because the PDF format is not really an image format. You can save recognition results to four different styles of PDF. All of these save the OCR recognition results as viewable PDF pages. See Chapter 10 for more on PDF.

Edit

The commands Select All and Clear function in different ways, depending on which view is active:

▶ In the Document Manager view, all the pages will be selected and the selected page(s) cleared.

▶ In the Original Image view, all the zones will be selected and the selected zone(s) cleared.

▶ In the Text Editor view, all the text and graphics will be selected and the selected text and/or graphics cleared.

View

This is where you can change what you view and how you view it on the OmniPage desktop. There are fourteen options to select in the drop-down list (Figure 2.10). OmniPage remembers the last option selected until you change it. If someone has switched off the toolbars, they won't display the next time you use OmniPage.

The Toolbars view is listed separately, as it is one with additional options and one that can catch users off guard. The rest of the options are listed in the bulleted list below; the view options are in seven different sections.

Figure 2.10
The view
drop-down list

Toolbars

This is where you can turn on or off the toolbars and views. When you select the option Toolbars, another dialog box displays (Figure 2.11) with a pick list of toolbars to turn on and off and options to be displayed with the toolbar buttons.

It is a good idea to click With Shortcut Keys. Then, when you run the mouse over the toolbars on the standard toolbar, you will see the function key to use as the shortcut; this is very handy.

Figure 2.11
View Toolbars
dialog box

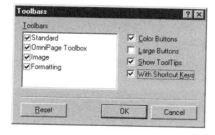

NOTE

Sometimes the toolbars or views are accidentally turned off.

To turn them back on, on the menu bar select View > Toolbars and click in the appropriate boxes. Clicking the Reset button will reset *all* OmniPage options to their default settings.

Other View Options

The remaining view options are:

▶ **OmniPage Toolbox.** Select the Auto OCR Wizard, Manual OCR, or Auto OCR.

▶ **Ruler.** Displays the ruler bar in the Text Editor view; this is available only when the Text Editor view is the active view.

▶ **Show or hide the views** to be displayed on the desktop: Document Manager, Original Image, and Text Editor. They will have a check next to them when selected.

▶ **Change Location** of the Original Image and Text Editor views: Side By Side, Above and Below, or Swap Text and Image. A small bullet displays alongside the selection.

▶ **Rotate Image.** You can rotate the image through 90, 180, and 270 degrees. You can also resize or rotate the original image with a shortcut menu. And, you can right-click in the Original Image area outside a zone and select a zoom or a rotation value.

▶ **Text Editor Views.** As mentioned earlier, this determines the layout of your scanned document.

▶ **Page Outline.** Only active when the Text Editor view is the active view. It allows you to move blocks of text around using a "Windows Explorer" style hierarchy.

▶ **Zoom.** Show more or less of the view: 25 percent, 50 percent, 100 percent, Page Width, Whole Page.

NOTE
When drawing zones, you will be more accurate if you switch off the Text Editor view and zoom in on the Original Image view.

The Standard Toolbar

The standard toolbar buttons across the top of the desktop (Figure 2.12) provide quick shortcuts for OmniPage's most frequently used functions.

The first nine buttons are the standard Windows buttons.

Figure 2.12
OmniPage standard toolbar

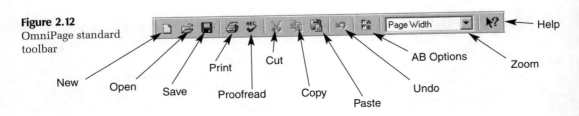

New   Open   Save   Print   Proofread   Cut   Copy   Paste   Undo   AB Options   Zoom   Help

Create a New Document

1. Click the New button in the standard toolbar or choose New in the File menu. This button is only active when a document is currently open. The New button really should be called the "Close Current Document" button, as it closes the current document and prepares to create a new one by scanning or loading an image file.

2. You are prompted to close or save the active document.

The OmniPage screen is then cleared and ready to scan or load a new document using the current settings.

Open a Document

Open (or Ctrl+O) opens an OmniPage 10, 11 (*.opd) or OmniPage 9 (*.met) file. This is *only* used for opening OmniPage files. OmniPage files are saved in a proprietary format that contains scanned or loaded images, zones, recognized text, and other information. An error screen will pop up if you attempt to open a non-OmniPage file. An OmniPage document opens with its original image in the Original Image view. The recognized text, if any, displays in the Text Editor view. When you want to continue the processing later or save what you have done to date, you save the file as an OmniPage file.

Save Changes in the Current Document

1. Click the Save button in the standard toolbar or choose Save in the File menu.

NOTE

If the document has not already been saved, the Save As dialog box appears the first time you choose Save. The default file type is an OmniPage Document (*.opd) file.

2. In the Save As dialog box, click the down-pointing arrow for Save as Type.

3. Select the file type you want the document to be saved as. If the document has already been saved, all the changes you make in the open document are saved in the currently selected file type. For example, suppose you save a recognized document as a .doc file called "Sample.doc." If you continue working with the text in OmniPage, choosing Save will save any text changes to "Sample.doc." To save the file with another file name and file type, use Save As in the File menu. The reason you may want to save as an OmniPage document is that it contains the images and zone information of the scanned pages. So, if you need to reprocess that document, you don't need to rescan all the pages.

CHAPTER 2

Print

Using the Print function, you can either print the image of the scanned page(s) or the recognized text as formatted in the Text Editor view.

1. Select Print in the File menu.
2. Choose Image to print original page images or Text to print recognized text.

Proofread OCR

Click Proofread in the standard toolbar, or in the Tools menu choose Proofread OCR. By default, proofreading starts automatically when the recognition is finished. You can manually select the proofreader if you had switched off the option to automatically proofread after recognition, wanted to rerun the proofreader to add new words to your dictionary, or simply wanted to recheck for any errors. Proofreading also updates the IntelliTrain files (more on this in Chapter 13) if selected. With IntelliTrain you can train OmniPage to recognize difficult characters and remember them for use in future recognition processes. The suspect words are underlined with color markers and are removed from the words that have been proofread.

The OCR Proofreader dialog box displays the reason for the proofread error and a picture of how the character or word originally looked in the image. You select how you want OmniPage to treat the word. After you choose an option for the word, the OCR Proofreader looks for the next possible error. Click Close to stop proofreading OCR.

NOTE
The reason OmniPage stops on a word will be displayed in the top left-hand corner of the Proofreader dialog box alongside the word in error.

The Proofreader displays one of three recognition errors:

1. **Suspect characters**: A character is suspect if OmniPage has recognized the character but it does not exactly match the pattern of dots that make up the character from OmniPage's map. These words are underlined in blue.
2. **Not in Dictionary**: These are words not in the standard Windows proofing dictionary or in the custom dictionary. These words are underlined in red.
3. **Reject Character**. If OmniPage cannot recognize the character, the character position is marked with a tilde (~).

Cut, Copy, and Paste

These allow you to copy or cut text to the clipboard and paste it to another location. This is handy when you only need a portion of the text from a page and do not want to save the whole document.

AB Options

The AB Options button opens the OmniPage Options panel, where you can get your hands on the controls and levers to make OmniPage do what you want it to do. Here, you change the settings for: OCR, Language, Scanner, Direct OCR, Process, Proofing, Custom Layout, Text Editor, Headers and Footers, Colored Text, Where to Insert Pages, Set the Scanner Interface to Pop Up, and Prompt for More Pages. There are seven different options panels covering each function of OmniPage. In the Options Panel, you have direct control over how OmniPage handles your documents. Once a setting is changed, it remains set until changed again. You can save specific settings for recall later. Reset to the default if things do not go the way you want.

While, most of the time, OmniPage will do a good job without changing these options, using them and other functions allows you to get excellent results all the time (when using appropriate documents).

Zoom

This zoom control is in the drop-down field at the end of the standard toolbar. Use the zoom control when in the Original Image or Text Editor views. In the Original Image view, it makes it easier to draw zones around text and graphics, especially if they are small or irregularly shaped. In the Text Editor view, it makes it easier to read the text. Click the drop-down arrow for the various zoom options (see Figure 2.13).

Figure 2.13
Zoom control

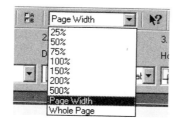

Help

The Help button is a great way to find out a little information about toolbar buttons and objects within the OmniPage desktop. Click the Help button and the mouse changes to a question mark. Move the mouse to the Text Editor buttons and a small pop-up tells you about the button and how it is used.

1.   On the standard toolbar, click the Help button.
2.   Move the mouse pointer over the button or area you want more information on and click. A pop-up box will give you more information.

You can drag and reposition the standard toolbar just as you do in other Windows applications.

The OmniPage Toolbox

By default, the OmniPage toolbox is located along the top of the OmniPage desktop—it is the toolbar of large buttons just below the standard toolbar. The toolbox can be floated and docked anywhere on the desktop. To reposition, simply point your mouse in a gray area of the toolbox, hold down the left mouse button, and drag to a new location. Release the mouse button at the new location.

The OmniPage toolbox consists of three processing buttons:

1. Auto OCR
2. Manual OCR
3. OCR Wizard

Click one of the buttons to select it; it will expand to display all available functions.

Auto OCR

Using the Auto OCR (Figure 2.14) is a little like driving your car in automatic. You select the desired gear and put your foot down on the gas pedal. The car accelerates and changes gears depending on what you have selected.

With Auto OCR, you make the selection of where and how OmniPage is to:

▶ Get the page
▶ Perform the OCR
▶ Export results

The gas pedal is the Start button, telling OmniPage to go ahead and process the document based on these settings. After you have saved the document, the Start button will toggle between Additional and Finish. You may want to add more pages, redraw the zones, re-recognize the pages, and save the document again.

Figure 2.14
Auto OCR toolbox

Each of the three processing buttons in the Auto OCR toolbar has its own drop-down submenu of parameters that modify the action of that process.

Get Page Menu

The Get Page menu contains the options to tell OmniPage how to scan the page(s) or load an image file with which to work (Figure 2.15).

Figure 2.15
Get Page
drop-down box

▶ **Load File**. This tells OmniPage where to get the image files of the pages to process. It can load an existing scanned document that has been saved as an image file, or it can load a PDF file. OmniPage can open and recognize twelve different image file formats.

TIP

One use of the Load File option is to OCR a fax that has come in via modem. Many fax programs have the option to save or export the received fax as a file. Save the fax in a TIF format. Then use the Load File option to perform the OCR.

▶ **Scan B&W (Black & White)**. Use this option for sharp, clear originals, line art, and drawings. Using Scan B&W is also much faster than the other two options. The scanner has much less information to send to the PC—eight times less than grayscale and twenty-four times less than color. To see how color affects scan times and file size, see Chapter 8.

TIP

If the quality of the original document is substandard—some characters are joined, some characters are missing or too light—the OCR result may have more errors than you like. If this is the case, try rescanning the document using the grayscale option.

CHAPTER 2

▶ **Scan Grayscale**. Use for pages with colored or shaded backgrounds and for black and white photos or graphics. Grayscale also gives better recognition on poor quality documents and run-together or broken text characters.

TIP

Use grayscale if the document has black and white photos or graphics. If you use black and white, you will end up with solid black and white blobs, as if you had faxed it.

Here is a trick when sending faxes: If you can send a fax from Word, change any photos or graphics to watermarks. The receiver of your fax will see the photos or graphics clearly and not as black and white blobs.

Always scan a poor-quality fax in grayscale, especially if there are photos. If you have color photos or graphics and you do not want to retain the color, scan in grayscale.

When scanning line art drawings or diagrams, the lines of the drawing will not be as sharp and clear when scanned in grayscale. You will get much sharper and clearer lines scanning in black and white.

▶ **Scan Color**. When you want to retain the color in documents with photos and color backgrounds, scan in color. This will be the slowest of all scans because of the amount of information being sent to the PC.

Perform OCR Menu

In the "Perform OCR" drop-down (Figure 2.16), you "describe the Original document" by telling OmniPage the layout format of the original document. This determines how OmniPage draws the zones around the text and graphics. Once the zones are drawn, OmniPage starts the OCR process. Remember from Chapter 1 how OmniPage looks at the page and compares the spacing between words and lines and how it determines tables and columns? Well, this is where you can modify the way OmniPage looks at each page. This setting will be applied to all the pages of the document.

Figure 2.16
Perform OCR
drop-down menu

NOTE

This is only half of the process of getting the scanned document to look like the original. The rest of the work is done in the Text Editor view, using the view layout icons to determine the layout for the output document. If you bypass that portion of the process, you may get unpredictable results when you open the document, for example, in Word.

▶ **Automatic**. It's usually best to leave this option set on Automatic. If the pages of your original document have different layouts, select Automatic. If it doesn't produce the result you want, you can change the setting and re-recognize the page.

▶ **Single Column, no Table**. This option tells OmniPage to look at every page as though it is a single column or block of text, like a page from a book. Use for documents with no columns or tables. Use for books, letters, or documents with no layouts. If you use Single Column, no Table on a page or document that has multiple columns or a table, the recognized text in the Text Editor view may look like the original. However, the columns will actually be lines of text with tabs to separate the text, to make it look like columns. Imagine trying to edit that!

▶ **Multiple Column, no Table**. This setting looks for columns of text where there is a common separation on successive lines or where the end of a gap is the same distance from the edge of the page. The recognized text can be saved to retain the column layout.

CAUTION

Beware the rivers of white space. On some block-justified text pages, where the gaps between the words are spread out to fill the whole line, the alignment of the gaps on successive lines can give the appearance of a column. OmniPage thinks it is a multiple column, so the page is incorrectly broken up into columns. This can happen when using the Perform OCR setting Automatic and Multi-Column.

The simple fix is to change the Perform OCR button to Single Column or redraw a zone over the incorrect area and specify as Single Column Text.

▶ **Single Column with Table**. This is the same as Single Column except the function to look for tables is switched on. OmniPage looks for table formats, where successive lines have text starting or finishing in the same place, like a spreadsheet. It also detects tables that have borders and grid lines. It reproduces them in the recognized text.

CHAPTER 2

▶ **Spreadsheet**. Use this option if the entire page is laid out like a spreadsheet. This option is great when scanning parts lists, price lists, itemized bills, and documents that need to be loaded into databases. Some of the samples we will use later in this book focus on scanning a telephone bill and a parts list, then saving as an Excel spreadsheet.

▶ **Custom**. Use this option when none of the preset options adequately describes your original document layout. To create your own custom layout, click the Options button and select the Custom Layout panel. It lets you specify the number of columns and the presence of tables and graphics in the original document. The values you set in the Options panel, Custom Layout, only take effect when you set the Perform OCR option to Custom. Custom Layout is not a template. Use it when there is no preset option for your document layout— for example, on a document where all the pages are single column and some pages may contain tables. See Chapter 13 for more details on this setting.

▶ **Template**. This option saves the layout of the zones drawn on a page. The zones can then be re-applied to other documents. This is great when scanning a document such as a telephone bill. You may only be interested in certain parts of each page. It's also great for a document like a spiral-bound book that shows the binding holes, interfering with the recognition process.

CAUTION

When selecting any setting other than Automatic, OmniPage evaluates *every page* in the entire document based on what you have selected. If you select Single Column, for example, all pages are evaluated as though they were single columns of text. Your layout will be all over the place. You must consider the layout of the original document as a very important step. We will talk more about zoning correctly in Chapter 4.

Export Results Menu

This is where you actually save the recognized text and graphics in a document, specifying the file type and location. You can elect to save to a file, copy to the clipboard to paste into another document, or link to your e-mail program and send the recognized document as an e-mail attachment. The e-mail attachment file type can be specified the same as when saving to a file (Figure 2.17).

Figure 2.17
Export Results
drop-down box

What do you want done with the recognized results?

▶ **Save as File**. As what file type do you want to save your scanned document? This option gives you thirty-two different file formats to choose from—everything from plain unformatted ASCII text to Word, Excel, WordPerfect, HTML, PDF, and, of course, the OmniPage file format.

▶ **Send as Mail**. This will automatically create an attachment in the file formats available in the Save As dialog box. It asks whether you want to create one attachment for all the pages, an attachment for each page, or a separate attachment each time it finds a blank page. OmniPage will then link to your mail client and create a blank e-mail with the attachments ready for a cover note and address.

TIP

This is a great, easy way to send lots of photos all in one go. See Chapter 10 for more about e-mailing photographs.

▶ **Copy to Clipboard**. The recognized text is copied to the clipboard to paste in another application. No formatting is retained.

Start, Additional, Finish, and Stop

These buttons are only found on the Auto OCR toolbar. Start, Additional, and Finish are the same button. The function of the button changes depending on where you are in the OCR process.

▶ **Start**. You click the Start button to start the OCR process; OmniPage automatically processes the document through each step according to what you have selected. When the export is complete, the Start button automatically changes to Additional.

▶ **Additional**. When you click the Additional button, you are prompted with three options: Export Document Again, Add More Pages to the existing document based on the current selected settings, and Re-process All Pages. You can change the settings before adding more pages or reprocessing all the pages. For example, if you have drawn new zones, deleted some zones, or respecified the contents of the zones, choose the Re-process All Pages option. This option reprocesses all pages based on the new zones. The Re-process All Pages option will bring up another dialog box, with the following options: Use only current zones, Discard current zones and find new zones, and Keep current zones and find additional zones. In the example above, you would choose Use only current zones.

CHAPTER 2

> ► **Finish**. This option becomes active if any of the processes are interrupted using the Stop button. Clicking on the Finish button will give the same option prompt as in the Additional, Automatic Processing box.

> ► **Stop**. Use this button to interrupt the processing at any stage. When the processing is stopped, the Start button automatically changes to Finish to resume processing.

Manual OCR

Using Manual OCR is like driving a manual car. You have to change gears depending on what you want to do. With Manual OCR, you still make the same selections of Get Page, Process OCR, and Export results. The difference between this toolbar and AutoOCR is that the process options are active buttons, and you need to click them to perform that process. (See Figure 2.18.) When you move the mouse on the icons, they show as buttons with a down arrow selector on the right.

Figure 2.18
Manual OCR toolbox

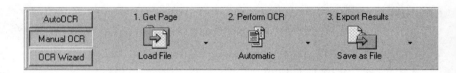

Each button has a narrow drop-down box on the right-hand side with a small down-pointing arrow. Click the drop-down arrow and select the function. All the buttons have the same options and functions as described for the AutoOCR toolbox.

Get Page

When you click the Get Page button, OmniPage will get the page either from the scanner or from the disk and that's all (Figure 2.19). It will stop there until you click the Perform OCR or Export Results button. Click the down arrow and select the function. There is an additional option: Scanner Settings. Selecting Scanner Settings takes you directly to the OmniPage Options panel and opens the Scanner tab. Here, you can change the brightness and contrast of the scanned image just like on a photocopier. This is very handy when dealing with documents that are too light or too dark. You can also run the Scanner Wizard to make changes.

Figure 2.19
Get Page
drop-down box

Perform OCR

Perform OCR has an extra option: OCR Settings (Figure 2.20). This takes you directly to the OmniPage Options panel and opens the OCR tab. Here, you can select the language character sets. There are 114 different languages, from Afrikaans to Zulu. You can select additional dictionaries to be used to assist in the recognition and in the proofreader, spell checking, the OCR method, font matching, and reject character. You may need to use this if your document has foreign languages. OmniPage will not translate the text for you. You will need the language character set installed in Windows setup. The text will then display in the Text Editor view in the language selected. It will also display in Word or Excel.

Figure 2.20
Perform OCR
drop-down box

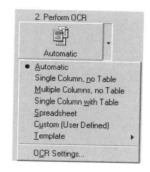

Export Results

The recognized document will not be saved until you click the Export Results button. Before you save the document, click the down arrow and choose from Save as file, Send as Mail, and Copy to Clipboard (Figure 2.21).

Figure 2.21
Export Results
drop-down box

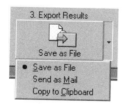

Summary: Using the Manual OCR Toolbox

1. On the Get Page button, click the down arrow. Select where the pages are coming from.

2. On the Perform OCR button, click the down arrow. Select the layout of the document.

3. On the Export Results button, click the down arrow. Select what you want to do with the recognized text.

4. Click the Get Page button icon (document source) to get the page.

5. Click the Perform OCR button icon (original layout). OmniPage will draw zones based on the layout that describes the original document, and recognize the document.

6. Click the Export Results button icon to save, send, or copy to the clipboard.

We find it better to use the Manual OCR toolbox, especially when scanning documents that need new zones drawn. This way, you do not need to wait for OmniPage to finish processing the pages. You draw zones around the text and graphics you want. Click Perform OCR, check the results, and make further changes if required. Then, click Perform OCR again. When you have the results you want, use Export results to save in the file type you need.

OCR Wizard

There is only one button to click to start the OCR Wizard, and there are no options to choose. The OCR Wizard guides you through the entire OCR process by asking you six questions about your document (Figure 2.22).

1. Where to get the image

2. What it looks like

3. Which languages are in it

4. What you want the saved appearance to look like

5. Whether you want to proofread the recognized results and use IntelliTrain

6. How you want to save the document

The OCR Wizard then sets all the options based on your answers and starts the process.

Figure 2.22
The first of six screens in the OCR Wizard toolbox

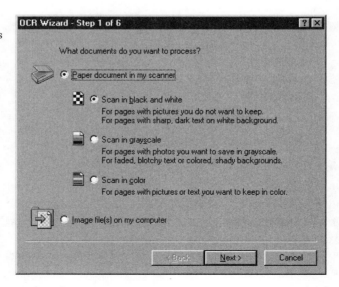

NOTE

The Wizard panels present the settings as they were previously set with the other toolboxes. OmniPage also remembers the settings you make in the OCR Wizard panels and applies them to future automatic or manual processing, until you change them. If you have more documents where the OCR Wizard settings are suitable, just switch to the Auto OCR toolbar and click Start.

Applicable settings not offered by the OCR Wizard take the options last set in the program. This concerns mainly scanner settings, a user dictionary, or a training file. Zone templates cannot be used with the OCR Wizard. Starting the OCR Wizard unloads any previously loaded template file and sets Describe Original Document to Automatic. You cannot export a recognized document as a mail attachment. Use the automatic or manual processing for this.

The Navigation Bar

The Navigation bar (Figure 2.23) is at the bottom left-hand side of the Document Manager view. It displays the page number of the document and allows you to navigate through the pages by pressing the left or right arrows. To the right of the page navigation buttons are the Show or Hide View buttons. These buttons are a quick way to hide and show the three views: Document Manager, Original Image, and Text Editor. You can also change the way the desktop is split between the Original Image and Text Editor from a vertical split, the default, to a horizontal split.

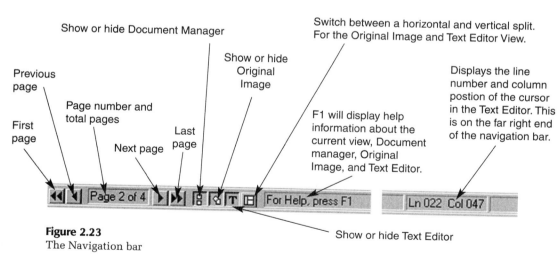

Figure 2.23
The Navigation bar

You should now feel comfortable moving around the OmniPage desktop with no hidden surprises. Remember the Text Editor view buttons at the bottom of the Text Editor View. They govern the format or layout of your saved document.

3

Basic Document Scanning

In Chapter 2, you learned your way around the OmniPage desktop: the menus, toolbars, and the three viewers. In this chapter, we will begin focusing on scanning itself. There are important questions to ask yourself before you begin scanning. These questions will help you to avoid layout and formatting mishaps when editing in other software applications. We'll go through the basic scanning process with the OCR Wizard toolbox, using as an example a page of text with no layout or pictures. At the end of this chapter, we'll also explore in more detail OmniPage's proofing tools: Proofreader and dictionary, Verify, and Text to Speech.

Before scanning a document, determine the results you need. What does your document look like? Is it black and white? Grayscale? Color? What is its quality? What is the layout and content of the document? Does it have tables, multiple columns, or pictures? What do you want to do with the document once it has been recognized? For instance, do you want to save it as a Word document or spreadsheet? Is it going on the Web or into a desktop publishing project?

By asking these questions before scanning and setting the appropriate options, you will have great success using OmniPage. If you follow our recommended scanning process sequence, you will avoid formatting problems and gobbledygook like this:

> ~~~~~~~~; proclucec' In Ausiralia ln 1:7:1J, `~ ~.- -. 11111 ~~ ~~ total"farmgate"marketvaluetoabout$A1 1 thr~ ~ ~ 1 ~I I I ~ million. Raw oil at the farm gate sells for I I I ~1' between $A50 and $A55 per kilo. The -15—- —— ——————— — Marketing consultant b :; - ~ ~~; - ~~ present prices being paid fortea tree oil c ~ ~ ~~~ ~ ~ be maintained on an inflation adjusted basis j~ in the future" - page 96,'.,,.il:t<P: - -:::~~ ~ ~ independent marketing consultants exp~hat the tea tree oil produced from:. ~ specific -es by

If you are not getting the results you want, more than likely you have missed one of the steps in the scanning process. At this point, we will walk through a simple example to introduce you to the process.

The Scanning Process

There are three basic steps to the scanning process, which are represented in the AutoOCR and in the Manual OCR toolbox by these functions: Get Page, Perform OCR, and Export Results.

Each of these basic steps has options associated with it that are selected from drop-down selection boxes. Always make sure your scanner is connected to your computer and switched on before you start scanning, otherwise you will get a scanner error message.

1. **Get Page**. This determines how the page is loaded into OmniPage for processing. You can scan a paper document in black and white, grayscale, or color. You can load one or more image files. The Get Page options are used to select the method of loading the pages. Once the pages are loaded, the images appear in miniature in the Document Manager's Thumbnail view and the page information is summarized in its Detail view. The image of the current page is displayed in the Original Image window.

2. **Perform OCR**. This is the actual OCR (Optical Character Recognition) process that generates editable text. During OCR, OmniPage first creates zones around elements on the page that will be processed and then interprets text characters or graphics in each zone. These zones are automatically drawn based on the Perform OCR option selected. You can also draw your own zones and save zones as a template to reuse at another time. When the OCR has finished, you can check and correct errors in the document using the OCR Proofreader and edit the recognized text in the Text Editor.

3. **Export Results**. Once the OCR is complete and you have proofread the text and made any necessary corrections, use this step to save your document. You can save it to a specified location, file name, and type; place it on the clipboard; or send it as a mail attachment. You can save the same document repeatedly to different locations, as different file types, and with different settings and levels of formatting.

Using OmniPage really is as simple as 1, 2, 3, as you will see when we walk through our first scanning exercise later in this chapter. Before you scan, you will need to make some decisions based on the results you hope to attain. The questions that follow will help you determine what options to use, depending on your goals.

Before You Scan

As discussed earlier, always evaluate your document and set the options before beginning your scan.

Scanning and Loading Options

Evaluate your document before scanning to determine the scanner setting to use. Once the pages are scanned into OmniPage, you can reprocess and resave as many times as you like without having to rescan the pages. However, if you choose the incorrect scan option, you will need to rescan the pages.

Table 3.1
Scanning settings

Goals	Appropriate setting
Do I want to Scan in black and white?	Use the AutoOCR or ManualOCR toolbox
Is my original document of good quality?	AutoOCR > Get Page > Scan B&W
Does my document have line art drawings?	ManualOCR > Get Page > Scan B&W
Do I want to scan in grayscale?	Use the AutoOCR or ManualOCR toolbox
Is my original document of poor quality?	AutoOCR > Get Page > Scan Grayscale
Does my document have images I want to retain as grayscale images?	ManualOCR > Get Page > Scan Grayscale
Do I want to scan in color?	Use the AutoOCR or ManualOCR toolbox
Does my document have color images or color backgrounds I want preserved in my saved document?	AutoOCR > Get Page > Scan Color or ManualOCR > Get Page > Scan Color
Am I loading an existing image file to OCR?	AutoOCR > Get Page > Load file or ManualOCR > Get Page > Load file

Document Elements

Listed below are some elements you will find in your documents, like logos, columns, pictures, and tables. Beside them are the appropriate Scan and Perform OCR settings to achieve the best results. OCR is not an exact science. Sometimes, you may need to experiment with different settings in OmniPage to improve your results. In some cases it may not be possible to get a good result; for example, good results can be hard to obtain if the original is of very poor quality, has a patterned background, has handwriting over it, or has a very complex layout.

Table 3.2
Document elements and Scan and Perform OCR settings

If your document has:	Use this setting:
Columns	AutoOCR *or* ManualOCR toolbox > Perform OCR >, select Multiple column, no table or Automatic. If the document has tables, use Automatic.
Tables such as price lists, schedules, parts lists, telephone bills	AutoOCR *or* ManualOCR toolbox > Perform OCR >, select Automatic or Single Column with Table or Spreadsheet
Lines around a table	In the Text Editor View, position the cursor in the table, click some text in the table. Select Menu > Format > Borders and Background. Here you can change the thickness and color of the grid lines. Apply colored background to the table.
Signatures (To retain signatures in documents. To create an electronic signature for future use in documents, use a thick felt pen.)	AutoOCR *or* ManualOCR toolbox > Get Page > Scan B&W. Clear any zones around the signature. Manually redraw a zone around the signature. Set the properties to Graphic Zone. Use the Manual OCR toolbox to re-OCR to get the correct result.
Pictures	AutoOCR *or* ManualOCR toolbox > Perform OCR > Automatic. Make sure the zone is drawn around the picture and is set to Graphic. Redraw the zone(s) if necessary and scan using the appropriate Get Page option: black and white, grayscale, or color.

Table 3.2
(continued)

A logo or a letterhead	AutoOCR *or* ManualOCR toolbox > Get Page. If the logo or letterhead is black and white, Scan B&W. If the logo or letterhead is color or gray, scan as grayscale or color. You will probably need to manually redraw a zone around the logo. See Chapter 4 for more about working with zones. Use the Manual OCR toolbox to Scan, OCR, and re-OCR to get the correct result.
A document with headers and footers that you want to retain	On the Standard Toolbar, click the AB Options button. Select the Text Editor Tab. Set on the Option Headers and Footers to show header and footer indicators. When saving the document, click the advanced button and select the header and footer option you want.
Colored text	AutoOCR *or* ManualOCR toolbox > Get Page > Scan Color. On the standard toolbar, click the AB Options button. Select the Process tab. Set on the option Retain text and background color.
Colored background or boxes around text or graphics	AutoOCR *or* ManualOCR toolbox > Get Page > Scan Color. On the Standard Toolbar, Click the AB Options button. Select the Process tab. Set on the Option Retain text and background color.
Pictures (cartoons, black and white line art)	AutoOCR *or* ManualOCR toolbox > Get Page > Scan B&W. Check that the zone includes the entire cartoon or drawing and the properties are set to a graphic zone.
A line art plan drawing	AutoOCR *or* Manual OCR toolbox > Get Page > Scan B&W. Check to be sure the zone includes the entire drawing and set the properties to Graphic Zone.
A form type layout, like a tax form or application	Best results will be obtained with another program, such as OmniForm. OmniForm is specially designed to scan and create OCR forms. You may have some success by manually drawing table zones around the Form Fill in field, then saving it in True Page Layout.

CHAPTER 3

End Uses of the Saved Document

The last step, Export Results, is how you save the OCR results of your documents. There are three options: Save as File, Send as E-mail, or Copy to Clipboard. Save as File has thirty-three different file types to choose from. Send as E-mail creates a file attachment of the document—you can choose from among the same file types that are available under the Save as File option. Copy to Clipboard does just that—you can then switch to the application into which you want to paste the recognized text.

Your purposes for the saved document will determine the option and file type you choose. For example, you may have scanned a price list and want to import it into your database, then save it as an Excel spreadsheet. From there, it is very easy to import it into a wide range of database applications. You may be using it for desktop publishing using Microsoft Publisher. If so, save it as Publisher 98 (RTF) file type.

Some options and settings for exporting the results are shown in Table 3.3.

Table 3.3
End uses and editing the saved document

Desired end result:	Appropriate setting or process:
I just want to save as a Word document.	AutoOCR > Export Results > Save as File. In the Save as dialog box, select Word 97 2000.
I want to save as an Excel spreadsheet.	AutoOCR > Export Results > Save as File. In the Save as dialog box, select Excel 97 2000.
I want to e-mail the saved document.	AutoOCR > Export Results > Send as Mail. In the Attachment dialog box, select the file type you wish to create as an attachment to the e-mail.
I want to edit a photo in my document.	You can edit the scanned photo or graphic in OmniPage. The format for a photo in the Text Editor view is BMP. In the Text Editor view, double-click the graphic. OmniPage will open the program you have set in Windows to automatically open BMP files (by default, that's Microsoft Paint). You then edit the photo in your image-editing program and save it in the appropriate file format.

Table 3.3
(continued)

I want to send the document out to a print shop to turn into a brochure.	First, check with the print shop; ask them what file format and resolution they require for the images. OmniPage embeds the colored images as 150 dpi BMP format into Word and RTF (Rich Text Format) document types. It's best to scan the images separately using an image editing program and submit the text and pictures separately.
I want to e-mail the document or use it on the Web.	Use Save as HTML. OmniPage automatically saves the document as HTML text and any pictures as Web-ready image files in JPG format, reduced to 75 dpi. You will find HTML file format in the Save as Type field in the Save dialog box.

Scanning a Plain Text Document with No Layouts

In this exercise, you will be using the OCR Wizard. The Wizard is one of three OCR toolboxes. It will ask you questions about your document, including: where you are getting it from, what it looks like, and what you want to do with the results. In response to your answers, the Wizard sets the options both of the ManualOCR and AutoOCR, and some of the options accessible from Tools > Options. These same questions are the ones you should ask yourself before scanning. You can then make the changes and use the ManualOCR or AutoOCR toolbox. The document used in this exercise is "test.tif." You will find it in the appendix. It consists of a single page of text without pictures, tables, or columns. When the OCR process is complete, you will use the Proofreader to check the errors, then save it as a Word document. We will see how to copy the document to another application using Copy to Clipboard. At the end of the chapter, we will use some really cool features, like having OmniPage read the text out loud, using the Text Verifier to locate the original scanned word, and using dictionaries to assist with the recognition process.

Quick Automatic Scan with the OCR Wizard Toolbox

For this exercise, you will scan the document named "test.tif." Here are the steps:

1. Create a directory for your training documents. Using Windows Explorer, create a directory named "Training" off your drive's top-level directory (for example, C:\training).

2. Make sure the scanner is switched on.

CHAPTER 3

3. Place the document "test.tif" in the scanner (Figure 3.1). You will locate this file in the appendix or it can be downloaded from the Web site (see Introduction).

4. If you closed OmniPage, launch it.

Figure 3.1
Test document

BUSINESS

Caere designs, develops, manufactures and markets information recognition software and systems products. The Company's products provide a low cost, accurate means of converting text, numeric and bar code data into computer usable form. For many applications, the Company's products are an attractive alternative to manual data entry, which is slow, tedious and error prone. Caere currently offers two families of information recognition products. OmniPage, which was first shipped in September 1988, is a page recognition software product with versions for the Apple Macintosh II and SE/30, the IBM PC AT and compatibles (with a coprocessor card) and 80386-based computers. The Company also markets a line of OCR and bar code data entry products. Caere introduced its OCR products in 1977 and its bar code products in 1983. As a pioneer in the OCR market, the Company believes that information recognition markets, whether OCR, bar code or page recognition, are technology driven, cost sensitive and often slow to develop. Building upon its extensive experience in OCR, the Company's strategy is to identify and pursue markets in which manual entry of information can be cost effectively automated.

Desktop Recognition Products

The earliest information recognition systems required proprietary hardware and were expensive. Lower cost recognition systems were subsequently introduced, but these systems were only capable of recognizing a few type styles and sizes and were unable to recognize typeset pages or pages organized in columnar format. As a result, these lower cost systems met with limited market acceptance.

OmniPage is a software product that uses widely available, powerful personal computers and low cost scanners to bring capabilities to the user's desktop previously available only on expensive, dedicated recognition systems. A user can scan a page of text or numeric data and then use OmniPage software to capture, edit, save and load the scanned image into popular word processing, spreadsheet and database programs running on industry standard personal computers. The desktop recognition market encompasses a wide range of document processing applications, including general office, desktop publishing, legal, educational and governmental.

OmniPage is currently available in three versions: a software-only version that runs on Apple Macintosh II and SE/30 computers; a version for the IBM PC AT and compatibles that requires a coprocessor card to supply additional computing power and memory; and a software-only version for computers utilizing the Intel 80386 microprocessor. Both of the PC versions run under Microsoft Windows. The Macintosh version was first shipped in September 1988, the AT version in December 1988 and the 386 version in July 1989.

The three versions of OmniPage are virtually identical in features and functions. OmniPage recognizes text which has been scanned from a printed or typed page and captures the text in a computer usable form. The speed with which a page is recognized is dependent upon the type and speed of processor, the quality of the scanned image and the graphical elements, headers and variety of fonts included on the scanned page. On a 386-based 20 megahertz personal computer, the page you are now reading takes approximately one minute to be scanned and converted by OmniPage into a text file. OmniPage is capable of recognizing letters and numbers in many different layouts and presentations including landscape, single and multiple columns and financial (spreadsheet) forms.

OmniPage is "omnifont"—it recognizes virtually all nonstylized fonts in sizes ranging from 8 to 72 points without training or programming. In addition, OmniPage accelerates when reading a consistent font, achieving speeds in excess of 100 characters per second (about 25 seconds per typical typed page). During page recognition, OmniPage displays sample characters from the scanned document in a character window, allowing the user to monitor and improve the recognition process, primarily by adjusting the scanner contrast settings. Once scanned and recognized, text may be edited within the OmniPage transitional editor prior to transferring it to an application file.

15

5. Click the OCR Wizard toolbox button (Figure 3.2), then the Wizard button, the one with the wand in it, to the right.

Figure 3.2
OCR Wizard toolbox

OCR Wizard, Step 1

The Wizard dialog box appears. The OCR Wizard will present six steps to complete. Each step will ask a question about a process or option, and, in response to your answer, the program will make the change in the process or option. Each of the questions has a description and reason why you may choose the option. The first screen asks you where you are getting the image from and whether you want to scan in black and white, grayscale, or color. See Figure 3.3.

Figure 3.3
Determine how you
will get your image

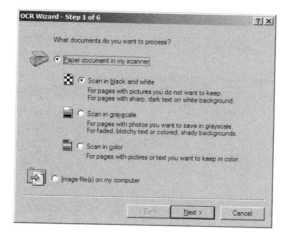

1. If the radio button next to Paper Document in my Scanner is not selected, click to select it. This tells OmniPage you will be scanning the page.
2. Select Scan in Black and White, as the page you are scanning is text only and is of reasonable quality.
3. Click Next.

OCR Wizard, Step 2

What does your original document look like? (Figure 3.4)

Figure 3.4
Describe the original
document layout

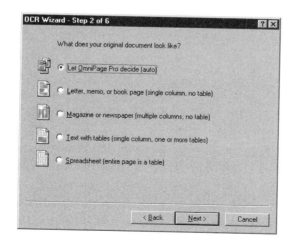

CHAPTER 3

1. Click the radio button for Letter, Memo, or Book Page (single column, no table). This document has no layouts. The text goes from the left to the right margin and there is no picture or table. As you can see, there are five options from which you can choose. You can also use the Let OmniPage decide (Auto) option and OmniPage will automatically work out the best way it sees to divide the document into zones.

2. Click Next.

OCR Wizard, Step 3

What languages does your document contain? (Figure 3.5)

Figure 3.5

Choose the language and accuracy

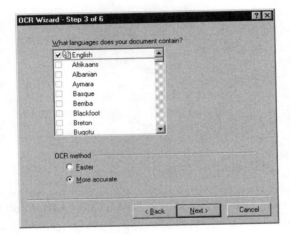

1. Make sure you check the box beside your preferred language. In this case, English, the default. If your document contains other languages, select them here. The languages at the top of the list are your recent choices. Below are listed the languages in alphabetical order. Type a letter to jump to it.

2. Under OCR Method, if the radio button More Accurate is not selected, click it to select.

3. Click Next.

OCR Wizard, Step 4

How much of the original document's appearance do you want to retain? This sets the Text Editor view option. It is the Text Editor view that determines the layout when the document is saved. (See Figure 3.6.)

Figure 3.6
How much of the
original document's
appearance do you
want to retain?

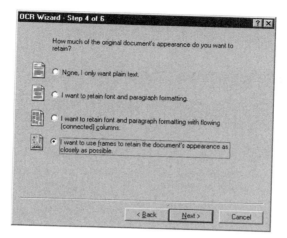

To scan the document and make changes to it in your word processor or spreadsheet application, click "I want to retain font and paragraph formatting." Table 3.4 gives some of the reasons for choosing the various options, as does the Wizard screen.

Table 3.4
Options in OCR Wizard Screen 4 (These options are applicable even if you use the AutoOCR and Manual OCR toolboxes).

Option	Why you would choose this option
None, I only want plain text.	You may want to copy text to the clipboard to paste in another application. You do not want to retain any formats. You are going to save as a spreadsheet to import into a database.
I want to retain font and paragraph formatting.	You are just interested in getting the text, but you want each paragraph separate, and you want to keep the font size and style. You also want to do extensive editing.
I want to retain font and paragraph formatting with flowing (connected) columns.	You want the saved document to have the same layout as the original, and you want to edit the text and move pictures around.
I want to use frames to retain the document's appearance as closely as possible (default).	You want the saved document to have exactly the same layout as the original, and you want to do only minimal editing.

After making your choice, click Next.

CHAPTER 3

OCR Wizard, Step 5

Proofread the recognized text and apply IntelliTrain (Figure 3.7).

Figure 3.7
Wizard proofread
questions

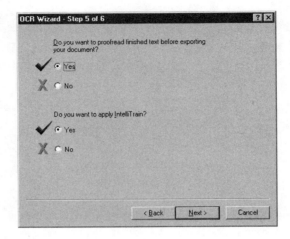

If you select the options to proofread and run IntelliTrain in step 5, OmniPage launches the Proofreader as soon as the OCR process has finished and turns on the "intelligent" trainer, IntelliTrain. The Proofreader does a spell check using OmniPage's built in dictionaries and any user dictionary you have created. It also stops on any word that OmniPage was unsure about. When you correct a character that was incorrectly recognized, the IntelliTrain will add it to its training file. This is a training file for characters that are not in OmniPage's Standard Character Maps. It is like a user dictionary of characters OmniPage does not recognize and is used in the future recognition of documents.

You can launch the Proofreader at any time by clicking the Proofread OCR button on the toolbar, or on Tools > Proofread OCR, or simply by pressing F7. However, once you have completed the proofreading you cannot proofread your document again without re-recognizing it, that is, redoing the Perform OCR.

Set both of these options to Yes and click Next. We will discuss IntelliTrain in more detail in Chapter 13.

OCR Wizard, Step 6

How do you want to export your document? (Figure 3.8)

Figure 3.8
How do you want to
export your document?

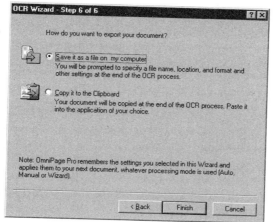

This final step tells OmniPage what option to set for Export Results. There are only two options: Save as File and Copy to Clipboard. The option Send as Mail is only available in the Manual OCR and Auto OCR.

1. Click the radio button Save it as a File on my Computer. At the end of the process, the Save As dialog box will display for you to choose the location and file type for saving the recognized text.

2. Click Finish. This starts the scanning and OCR process. The Scanning Progress Meter (Figure 3.9) displays on the status bar at the bottom of the OmniPage desktop.

Figure 3.9
Scanning Progress
Meter and Cancel
button

NOTE

If you want to cancel the scanning, click Cancel above the navigation bar, in the bottom left-hand corner of the OmniPage desktop. You may want to stop the export and rezone the document or verify the text with the original image. If you want to restart the scanning process, click the Wizard icon and the warning dialog box (Figure 3.10) will display. You will need to finish the scanning processing with either the AutoOCR or Manual OCR toolbox.

Figure 3.10
Message to restart
processing after
canceling the OCR
Wizard

CHAPTER 3

Proofreading Your Results

What happens once the OCR Wizard process starts? A bitmap image of the original document will be displayed in the Original Image view. It will also appear in the Document Manager view when you click the Thumbnail tab. Zones (blue boxes) are automatically drawn around the text in the Original Image view, based on your response to step 4. The Single column, no table icon appears in the top right-hand corner of the zone. The scan and OCR are performed.

The recognized text from the image is displayed in the Text Editor view for proofing. After the recognition process is complete, OmniPage will begin an automatic proofread of the results of your recognized text. The OCR Proofreader dialog box displays the first word that either has suspect characters, is not in the dictionaries, or is an unrecognized character. The reason OmniPage stopped on that word is displayed in the top left-hand corner of the Proofreader dialog box, beside the word in question. The Proofreader also suggests words from the dictionaries.

Suspect characters. If a character does not exactly match the pattern of dots that make up the character from OmniPage's Map, it is a suspect character. These words will be underlined in blue in the Text Editor view and highlighted in yellow in the Proofreader dialog box. When the Proofreader selects the word in the Text Editor view, the black text will appear white and the blue underline will appear yellow. To show the selected word, the Text Editor inverts the color.

Not in dictionaries. These are words that are not in the OmniPage Proofing Dictionary or in either the user or custom dictionary. These words will appear underlined in red.

Reject Character. If OmniPage cannot recognize the character, the character position is marked with a red tilde (~).

Figure 3.11 shows the Proofreader dialog box stopped on a word that contains a suspect character.

Figure 3.11
Proofreader dialog box with suspect word

Look in the Text Editor view. The word it has found is "office," and it is underlined in blue.

The OCR Proofreader dialog box displays, "Contains suspect character:" in the top left-hand corner. The word "office" is displayed in both the recognized character field and in the suggested words field. As this is correct, click Ignore.

NOTE
You may not get exactly the same errors in this exercise. OmniPage can give slightly different results on different PCs and even on the same PC. It may flag more or fewer errors in the Proofreader, depending on your computer's available system resources and how many other programs are open at the time. The Proofreader has nothing to do with the OCR process. The OCR process creates text. The Proofreader checks the text against the dictionaries.

The proofreading continues, bringing up suspect characters and words not found in the dictionaries.

The next phrase is "'omnifont'—it." Notice that "'omnifont'—it" is underlined in red in the Text Editor view. This is because the word is not in any dictionaries. As this is correct, click Ignore. The red underline marking in the Text Editor disappears when you answer the Proofreading questions.

Figure 3.12
Word not found in
Dictionaries
Proofread box

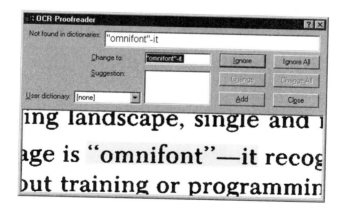

The OCR Proofreading is complete, and the dialog box (Figure 3.13) displays. Click OK.

Figure 3.13
Dialog box displays
when OCR
Proofreading is
complete

CHAPTER 3

Saving Your Scan

Once the proofreading is complete, the Save As dialog box (Figure 3.14) displays. This is where you indicate where you want to save your scanned document and what file type you want it saved as—Word, Excel, HTML, etc. If you like, OmniPage can automatically launch the program for your saved file so you can see what it looks like and start your editing.

The Save As dialog box has six other options you can use when saving your file. Clicking on the Advanced button accesses these options. As discussed previously, there are thirty-three different file types you can use and four format levels. These format levels are the four Text Editor views that determine the way the text is formatted when saved. They are:

- ▶ True Page (TP)
- ▶ Retain Flowing Columns (RFC)
- ▶ Retain Font and Paragraph (RFP)
- ▶ No Formatting (NF)

The format level/Text Editor view was set in response to step 4 (page 62). You can change them at any time by clicking on the Text Editor view buttons at the bottom of the Text Editor window, or by clicking on View > Text Editor views. Some of the file formats only work with certain format levels. Table 3.5 details the file types and compatible format levels. If you choose a file type and an incompatible format level, OmniPage will prompt you and make the necessary changes.

Figure 3.14
Save As dialog box for saving text, graphics, and photos from the Text Editor view

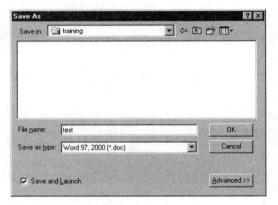

Now select the drive and directory to save the file.

1. Click the down-pointing arrow of the Save in field.
2. Select the drive and directory. Locate the training directory you created before starting this exercise.
3. Click the down-pointing arrow of the Save as Type box. Select the format appropriate for your word processing application.
4. Type the name of document in the File name box. Name it "Test."
5. Make sure Save and Launch is checked in the bottom left-hand corner of the Save As dialog box.

Notice the Advanced button on the right-hand side. When clicked, more options become available (see Chapter 10). The Advanced setting is where you select how OmniPage saves the file and more. We will go into this in more detail later in this book.

OmniPage saves the file and launches the application appropriate to the file type you chose in the Save As step. The scanned text is displayed. The layout formats are fine, because you followed the scanning process with the OCR Wizard toolbox and selected settings appropriate for this document layout.

Now, you can edit the document in Word (if that's the application you chose).

See Table 3.5 for the different file types and compatible format levels.

Table 3.5
Save as File types—their compatible format levels and graphic support

File type	File extension	Text format levels (Text Editor Views)	Supports graphics
ASCII text	txt /csv	No Formatting view (NFV)	No
Adobe PDF, normal	pdf	True Page	Yes
Adobe PDF with image substitutes	pdf	True Page	Yes
Adobe PDF with image on text	pdf	True Page	Yes
Adobe PDF, image only	pdf	True Page	Yes
Excel (3.0 to 7.0, 97, 2000)	xls	NFV, RFP (Spreadsheet)	Yes
FrameMaker (5.5.3)	mif	All	Yes
Freelance Graphics	txt	No Formatting view (NFV)	No
Harvard Graphics	txt	No Formatting view (NFV)	No
HTML (3.0 or 4.0)	htm	All	Yes
PowerPoint 97	rtf	All	Yes
Microsoft Publisher 98	rtf	All	Yes
Word for Windows (6.0, 97, 2000)	doc	All	Yes
PageMaker 6.5.2	doc	All	Yes
Quattro Pro for Windows 4.0, 8	xls	NFV, RFP (Spreadsheet)	No
Rich Text Format (RTF) 6.0, 95	rtf	All	Yes
Unicode Text	txt / csv	No Formatting view (NFV)	No
Ventura Publisher	doc	All	Yes
WordPad	rtf	NFV, RFP	Yes
WordPerfect (5.0, 5.1, 5.2, 6.1, 8)	wpd	All	Yes
OmniPage Document	opd	All	Yes

CHAPTER 3

Copying to Another Application

As you have used the OCR Wizard to process the page, any further changes or reprocessing will need to be done using the AutoOCR or Manual OCR toolbox. If you just want a portion of the saved text, you can use the Windows copy and paste to select some of the text in the Text Editor view and paste it into another document. This is not the same as using the Export results option of Copy to Clipboard, where the entire document (all pages) is copied to the clipboard.

Read through the steps and practice with the document "Test," now scanned in OmniPage.

Text formatting, such as bold and italics, is retained when you paste into an application that supports RTF information. Otherwise, only plain text will be pasted. Graphics are retained if the application supports insertion of images.

1. In the Text Editor view, zoom in or make the Text Editor view larger by dragging the window divider bar.
2. Select an area of the text by clicking and dragging the mouse.
3. Right-click in the selected text and select Copy. This copies the text and any pictures, if selected, to the clipboard.
4. Switch to your word processor and paste the copied text.

Additional Tools for Proofing Recognized Text

There are three additional tools for proofing recognized text. They are:

1. User dictionaries
2. Verify Text window
3. Speech to Text

User dictionaries are used in conjunction with OmniPage's built in dictionaries and assist in the recognition process. Verify Text is a great way to find out what the original scanned word was. Instead of trying to locate the word in the Original Image view, double-click the word or area in the Text Editor, and the Verify Text window displays the original scanned image of the word. Text to Speech is a cool feature—OmniPage reads your recognized text out loud. Read through the steps below and practice with the document "Test."

The Dictionaries

OmniPage has built-in dictionaries for many languages. It offers recognition of 114 languages using three alphabets: Latin, Greek, and Cyrillic.

Languages with dictionary support include: Catalan, Czech, Danish, Dutch, English, Finnish, French, German, Greek, Hungarian, Italian, Norwegian, Polish, Portuguese, Russian, Spanish, and Swedish. These dictionaries are used, along with user dictionaries, to assist in the recognition process and to provide suggestions during proofing.

User dictionaries will contain proper nouns, such as your name and the name of your company and its products. They are also useful for storing technical terms and abbreviations from your particular field, which may not appear in standard dictionaries. You can save any number of user dictionaries, but only one can be loaded at a time. Your user dictionaries from Microsoft Word are also available; a dictionary called Custom is the default user dictionary for Microsoft Word. By using the Microsoft Word Custom dictionary, you really only need to maintain the one dictionary for both OmniPage and Word.

When you first start using OmniPage, there is no user dictionary. The first time you add a word to the user dictionary, OmniPage will create a user dictionary for you and prompt you for a file name for it.

To Add a Word to the User Dictionary from the Proofreader Dialog Box

In the OCR Proofreader dialog box, with no user dictionary loaded, click Add. OmniPage creates a new user dictionary and prompts for a file name (Figure 3.15).

Figure 3.15
Prompt for new
dictionary file name

To Select a User Dictionary before Proofreading

1. On the menu, click Tools.
2. Click User Dictionary to select it.
3. Click the Set as Current button or double-click the required user dictionary (Figure 3.16).

Figure 3.16
Creating, selecting,
deleting, and editing
user dictionaries

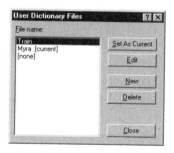

To Create a New User Dictionary

1. On the menu, click Tools.
2. Click User Dictionary.
3. Click New.
4. Give the dictionary a name.
5. Click OK.
6. Click Close.

To Add Your Own Words to a User Dictionary

1. On the menu, click Tools.
2. Click User Dictionary.
3. Double-click the required dictionary.
4. Click Edit.
5. In the User word field, type in a word (Figure 3.17).
6. Click Add.
7. Click Close.

Words can be imported to a user dictionary from a word list, but they must be in a plain text file and each entry must be on a new line.

Figure 3.17
Adding and deleting words in the user dictionary

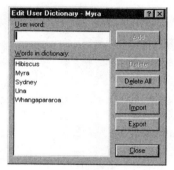

NOTE

Words cannot be added to a user dictionary if there are punctuation characters at the beginning or end of the word, or if there is white space or a reject character.

Deleting Words in a User Dictionary

1. On the menu, click Tools.
2. Click User Dictionary.
3. Double-click the required dictionary.
4. Click Edit.
5. In the Words in Dictionary field, click the word. Use Ctrl+click to select multiple words.
6. Click Delete.
7. Click Close.

Using the Microsoft Word Custom Dictionary

OmniPage will automatically detect if the Microsoft Word Custom dictionary is installed. When selecting the user dictionary from Tools > User Dictionary, the Options panel, or the Proofreader, the dictionary [Custom] will be displayed.

Verifying Text

After performing the OCR, you can compare any part of the recognized text in the Text Editor view against its corresponding part of the original image to verify that the text was recognized correctly. This is a very useful function, as it is often difficult to locate a word in the original scanned image.

The Proofreader window that displays the original scanned image is similar to the Verify Text function.

To verify text against its original image in OmniPage Pro:

1. In the Text Editor, double-click or select a word, and on the menu select Tool > Verify Text.
2. The Verify Text window opens and shows a picture of the scanned original word and its surrounding area (Figure 3.18).

Figure 3.18
The Verify Text
window

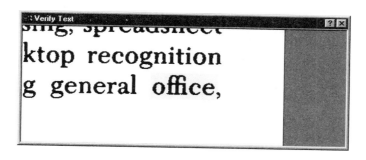

3. To enlarge or reduce the picture, click inside the window. The mouse pointer changes to a magnifying glass; by clicking the mouse button, the image cycles through magnifying and reducing the image. You can resize the window to see more of the surrounding original image or move the window to another area of the desktop.
4. Modify the recognized word in the Text Editor as necessary.
5. Continue double-clicking words that you want to verify, correcting them as you go. Look especially for the underlined suspect words and for unrecognized characters, denoted by a red reject symbol. By default, this is a tilde (~).
6. Click the Close button to close the verifier window when finished.

CHAPTER 3

Converting Text to Speech

OmniPage's speech facility is a useful feature during text checking and verification. It converts your recognized text into speech and reads it aloud, allowing you to listen to your document. It's also a great aid for the visually impaired. Movements of the insertion point in the Text Editor view control where the reading will start.

Hearing the Recognized Text Read Out Loud

1. On the menu, click Tools.
2. Click Speech Mode, or press F5.
3. On the menu, click Tools.
4. Click Speech Settings to select a voice, a reading speed, and the volume.

Now, movements of the insertion point in the Text Editor will cause text to be read aloud. Make selections with the mouse or use keyboard keys as shown in Table 3.6.

Table 3.6
Keys for controlling Text to Speech

To hear the recognized text	Use these keys
One character at a time forward or back	Right or left arrow
Current word	Ctrl+Numpad 1
One word to the right	Ctrl+right arrow
One word to the left	Ctrl+left arrow
A single line	Place the insertion point in the line
Next line	Down arrow
Previous line	Up arrow
Current sentence	Ctrl+Numpad 2
From insertion point to end of sentence	Ctrl+Numpad 6
From start of sentence to insertion point	Ctrl+Numpad 4
Current page	Ctrl+Numpad 3
From top of current page to insertion point	Ctrl+Home
From insertion point to end of current page	Ctrl+End
Previous, next, or any page	Ctrl+PgUp, PgDn or navigation buttons
Typed characters	Each typed character is pronounced, one by one, including punctuation

If you begin with the cursor in the middle of a word, you will first hear a word fragment. From the second keystroke, you will hear whole words.

TIP

The three basic keyboard speech keys are:

Ctrl+Numpad 1 - read current word

Ctrl+Numpad 2 - read current sentence

Ctrl+Numpad 3 - read current page

Set Speed, Pause, and Resume for Speech Proofreading

Use the controls outlined in Table 3.7.

Table 3.7 Keyboard Controls for Speed, Pause, and Resume	To do this	Use these controls
	Pause/Resume	Ctrl+Numpad 5
	Set speed higher	Ctrl+Numpad plus (+)
	Set speed lower	Ctrl+Numpad minus (–)
	Restore speed	Ctrl+Numpad asterisk (*)

As you can see, using OmniPage is fundamentally a three-step process. You can leave all the options to the default (Automatic) and generally get good results. But when you understand and use the correct settings for your documents, you consistently get very good results. The OCR Wizard has introduced you to important questions for evaluating your documents. Using those questions to make your own changes in the Manual OCR and AutoOCR is quicker than using the Wizard, and it gives you more control over the scanning and OCR process. You can set up your own dictionaries and use Verify Text to find the original scanned word. The Speech to Text feature is a great way to hear what your document sounds like.

CHAPTER 3

4

Working with Zones

Now that you have studied the OmniPage desktop and are familiar with using the OCR Wizard toolbox to scan a plain text document, let's turn our attention to zones. As you recall, zones are the blue and green "boxes" that OmniPage automatically draws around the text and pictures of the document image in the Original Image window. OmniPage will only recognize elements of the page that are contained within a zone.

When using OmniPage, you can either let it determine where and what type of zones to draw, or you can draw your own zones. Most of the time, OmniPage will accurately identify and draw the zones when you use the OCR Wizard or the AutoOCR option. However, there are times when scanning complex pages and pages with pictures that you will want to override the zones OmniPage has drawn. You may find that OmniPage has broken the scanned image into too many zones and the saved document is not what you wanted. You can manually redraw all the zones, or you can use some of the zones OmniPage has drawn and ones you have drawn or modified.

When using AutoOCR and Manual OCR, it is the option of the Perform OCR button that determines how OmniPage will divide the scanned page into zones and their properties.

A time when you would manually draw your own zones is when scanning the example image "Skeleton.tif" in the appendix. When using the AutoOCR option, OmniPage identifies only some of the text and parts of the picture. In this case, you need to redraw the zones around the parts of the page you want kept as an image—the "skeleton"—and redraw zones around the text elements of the page. See "Skeleton.tif" and "Skeleton zones.tif" in the appendix for the image, position, and type of zones to draw.

Zones determine and identify which parts of the page will be processed and how they will be processed. Zones cannot overlap each other. Each has a zone number in the top left corner and a zone type icon in the top right. Left-click in a zone to select it. Current and selected zones are shaded. Any areas not enclosed by zones are ignored during the OCR process, so if there are no zones on the page, nothing from that page will be recognized

Zone Properties

Every zone on a page has a zone type and a zone content setting. To make it easy for you to recognize the type of zones drawn, OmniPage has a small zone identifier (icon) in the top right-hand corner of each zone. The blue zone borders are text zones and the green zone borders are graphic zones.

Zone Types

There are six types of zones; the contents of each zone can be defined as alphanumeric or numeric. The following table describes each of the zone types.

Table 4.1

The icon for each zone type is shown in the table below

Icon	Zone type
	Single-column text zone: For text zones that contain a single column, such as a letter or memo. Blue zone border.
	Multicolumn text zone: Multiple columns of text contained within the same zone, such as magazines or newspaper pages. Blue zone border.
	Table zone includes tables and spreadsheets: This is for a table zone within a text document or a single table zone over the entire page, for spreadsheets, for example. These zones can only be a rectangular shape. Blue zone border.
	Auto-detect zone: Use this when you are unsure of how to specify the zone. OmniPage will use its expertise and rules to identify and process the zone. When you choose this zone, auto-zoning runs, which may result in the zone order being changed on the page. After recognition, you see the type of zone that is applied. If you use an auto-detect zone to cover a page area that has varied contents, OmniPage may replace the auto-detect zone with a number of smaller zones. Blue zone border.
	Graphic zone: Use this to capture graphics, pictures, logos, signatures, or any part of the page that is not text that you want to include in the saved document. OCR is not performed on graphic zones. The graphic is embedded as an image and can be exported with the document to applications that support graphics. The graphics are embedded in BMP format and at 300 dpi resolution for black and white and not more than 150 dpi for grayscale and color. Green zone border.
	Ignore zone: Use this to define areas on a page that you do not want processed. The Auto-zoning will not place zones here. To exclude a given area of a page from many pages—headers or page numbers, for example—place ignore zones in a template. Then, in the Options dialog box, in the Process tab, select "Find zones in addition to template/current zones." A good use of "Ignore zones" would be if you were scanning a spiral bound book. The image of the binding can interfere with the zoning and recognition process. Create an Ignore zone to cover the binding area, and save the zone as a template. Select the template in the Perform OCR process. This has a blue zone border.

Zone Contents

The zone contents property specifies whether the text in the zone is alphanumeric or numeric. The zone contents are set using the Properties button on the toolbar or by right-clicking on the zone. The zone contents property only applies to text zones.

- ▶ **Alphanumeric** is for text zones that contain letters and numbers.
- ▶ **Numeric** is for text zones that contain only numbers. Use this if the zone has only numbers—for example, a spreadsheet. It helps prevent numbers like 1, 0, and 8 from being recognized as I, O, and B, respectively.

Zone Tool Buttons

The zone tool buttons are used for modifying existing zones and drawing new zones; they are located on the Image toolbar (Figure 4.1), which is inside the Original Image Window on the left-hand side. You can click and drag this toolbar to another location, but the toolbar is active only when there is an image in the Original Image view and that view is the active window.

Figure 4.1
The Image toolbar

> **TIP**
> Click a zone tool button to use it, but remember to always deselect zone buttons after you use them, to avoid mishaps. To deselect the current function, click the Draw Rectangular Zone button. This will save you from accidentally applying the function of a previously clicked button.

The Image toolbar is divided into three sections. The first six buttons are for drawing and modifying zones; the next five are tools just for table zones; and the last three buttons are for rotating the page and zooming in and out. In this chapter, we are going to concentrate on the zone tool buttons only (Figure 4.2). We will cover the table buttons in Chapter 7.

Figure 4.2
Zone tool buttons

> **TIP**
> When drawing zones, OmniPage remembers the properties of the last zone drawn and will draw the next zone with the same properties. For example, if the first zone you draw is single column text, the next zone will also be single column text, or if the last zone drawn was a graphic, the next zone will also be drawn as a graphic zone. This can be very handy if you have a number of graphic and text zones.

When using any of the draw zones tools, the mouse pointer will change to cross hairs. This makes it easy to draw your zones accurately. The cross hairs pointer will also have a small graphic identifying the type of zone you are drawing.

Draw Rectangular Zone

This tool (Figure 4.3) draws square and rectangular zones. Click and drag to select the area to be included in the OCR process. Always click this button when you have finished using other zone tool buttons to avoid drawing mishaps.

Figure 4.3
Draw Rectangular
Zone tool

When you click the Draw Rectangular Zone button and position the mouse pointer on the image, the mouse pointer changes to cross hairs. When using any of the draw zones tools, the mouse pointer will change to cross hairs. This makes it easy to accurately draw your zones. The cross hairs pointer will also have a small graphic identifying the type of zone you are drawing. See Figure 4.4.

The mouse pointer changes to a cross with:

Figure 4.4
The Draw Rectangular
Zone mouse pointers

▶ Letter A to denote an alphanumeric text zone
▶ 123 for a numeric-only zone
▶ A small picture to denote a graphic zone

Steps for drawing rectangular zones:

1. Click on the top left-hand corner of the text or graphic to be zoned and hold down the left mouse button, dragging to the bottom right-hand corner of the area to be zoned.

2. Release the mouse button.

3. Keep the mouse pointer in the zone and right-click to set the zone properties, such as single column text or graphic. (The zone properties button is discussed in detail later in this chapter.) The zone turns gray, with a zone type identifier in the top right-hand corner. The number in the top left-hand corner identifies the sequence in which OmniPage will recognize and export the zones. The zone sequence numbers are used in the saving options. Depending on the save option you choose, the text can be saved in the zone order. The Text Editor views Retain Font and Paragraph and No Formatting use the zone order when saving the recognized text.

Again, make sure you always click this button when you have finished using other zone tool buttons to avoid drawing mishaps.

Use the Draw Rectangular Zones button to select a zone to resize or move. When a zone is selected, there are small black squares—handles—on each corner. Use these handles to resize or change the shape of the selected zone:

Figure 4.5
Using handles to
resize a zone

1. Click on the zone to select it.
2. Move the mouse pointer to a corner handle, where it will change to a diagonal double arrow (Figure 4.5).
3. Click and hold the mouse button down.
4. Drag to change the size of the zone.
5. Release the mouse button to complete.

Moving a zone:

Figure 4.6
Moving a zone

1. Click on the zone to select it.
2. Move the mouse pointer inside the zone, where it changes to a cross with arrows (Figure 4.6).
3. Click and hold the mouse button down.
4. Drag to move the zone to a new position.
5. Release the mouse button to complete.

Draw Irregular Zones

Use the Irregular Zones button (Figure 4.7) to trace around irregularly shaped blocks of text or pictures. This button *does not* work like the click and drag of the other zone buttons.

The mouse pointer has a small "irregular zone" graphic (Figure 4.8) in the top left-hand corner to let you know it is set to draw irregular zones. The zone contents graphics in the lower right-hand corner are the same as for regular zones.

Figure 4.7
The Draw Irregular
Zone button

Figure 4.8
Draw Irregular Zone
mouse pointer

It is one of the trickier buttons initially, but it becomes easy to master once you have used it a few times.

Click to anchor the first point of the zone, then take your finger *off* the mouse button. Then, when you move the mouse, a line is automatically shown on the screen from the first anchor point to the mouse. As you move the mouse, the line follows the mouse pointer. This can be a bit disconcerting, especially if you want to scroll up or down the screen or move the mouse to another location on the desktop.

Just move the mouse to the next anchor point of the text or graphic you are zoning. Click to lock that point in, then continue moving and clicking around the area you want.

Finish with a double-click to join up to the starting point.

Sometimes the lines can go all over the place. If this happens, just double-click. OmniPage will automatically connect from where the pointer is now to the original starting point. It may not be the shape you want, however, so just press Delete on the keyboard, or right-click and select Clear to remove the zone. Then, simply start again.

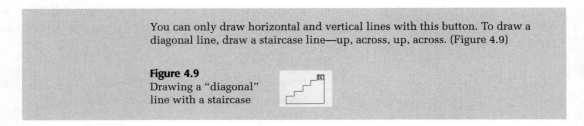

You can only draw horizontal and vertical lines with this button. To draw a diagonal line, draw a staircase line—up, across, up, across. (Figure 4.9)

Figure 4.9
Drawing a "diagonal" line with a staircase

Steps for drawing irregular zones:

1. Position the mouse pointer close to the area of text or graphic you want, then click. Take your finger off the mouse. This is the anchor point of the zone

2. Move the mouse to the next point and click. The line will only be drawn horizontally or vertically.
    (Try this: Keep your finger off the mouse button, and move the mouse around in a circle. Notice how the line will only draw horizontal and vertical directions.)

3. Repeat step 2 until you have completed drawing your irregular zone.

4. Double-click to complete the zone. The zone will be joined up to the starting point.

5. If the zone shape is not correct, double-click to finish the zone, then press Delete on the keyboard. Start again.

Add to Zone

Use this button (Figure 4.10) to extend or join two or more zones together. This is useful if the automatic zones have not captured all of the image or text in the one zone.

Steps to extend an area of a zone:

Figure 4.10
Add to Zone button

Figure 4.11
The Add to Zone mouse pointer

1. Click the Add to Zone button.

2. The mouse pointer in the image viewer becomes cross hairs with a plus sign (Figure 4.11).

3. Position the mouse inside the zone and at the point where you want to start extending.

4. Hold down the left mouse button and drag around the area you want to include (extend) in the zone.

5. Release the mouse button when you have completed extending the zone.

The zone border changes to display the modified zone area.

Steps to connect two or more zones:

1. Click the Add to Zone button.
2. Position the mouse inside the zone you want to join. Click and hold down the left mouse button and drag the drawing tool into the zones to be connected.
3. Release the mouse button when completed.
4. The properties of the first zone are transferred to the second zone.
5. The zone border changes to display the modified zone area.

TIP
Start inside the zone you want to add to or extend.

Subtract from Zone

You can reduce an area or divide a zone into two zones using the Subtract tool (Figures 4.12 and 4.13). Click and drag to remove portions of a zone or to divide a zone into two separate zones. This is useful if the automatic zones have captured all of the image or text in the one zone.

Figure 4.12
Subtract from
Zone button

Figure 4.13
Subtract from Zone
mouse pointer

Steps to subtract an area of a zone:

1. Click the Subtract button.
2. The mouse pointer in the image viewer becomes a drawing tool with a minus sign.
3. Position the drawing tool outside the zone close to the point where you want to start subtracting.
4. Hold down the mouse button and drag the drawing tool over the area that you want to remove.
5. Release the mouse button when you have completed subtracting.

The zone border changes to display the modified zone area.

Steps to divide a zone:

1. Click the Subtract button.
2. The mouse pointer in the image viewer becomes a drawing tool with a minus sign.
3. Position the mouse outside the zone to divide.
4. Hold the mouse button down and drag the drawing tool through the area you want to divide, finishing outside the zone, on the other side.
5. Release the mouse button when completed.

Two separate zones are now created, both with the same zone type and contents.

TIP
Start outside the zone you want to subtract from.

CAUTION
You cannot subtract an area inside a zone; i.e., you can't make a hole inside a zone. This would create an invalid zone shape. OmniPage can simulate the hole in the middle of a zone by creating two zones. One zone will be an elongated C shape that contains the top, side, and bottom of the C shape. The other will be a small rectangular zone that will close the C shape and leave the appearance of a hole in the zoned area. This is not recommended—the saved layout of the text will be difficult to edit, as it will be placed into two separate text frames in Word.

Figure 4.14
A zone with an area "subtracted" from the center.

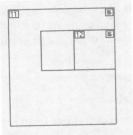

In the example in Figure 4.14, a "subtract from" zone was drawn in the center of zone 11. OmniPage has created a new zone, zone 12.

Reorder Zones

The Reorder Zones button (Figure 4.15) will change the order of the zones when the text is saved. This only works when the Text Editor view options are: No Formatting or Retain Font and Paragraph. The top left-hand corner of every zone is numbered in sequence. This is the same as cutting and pasting paragraphs of text in Word; it is far easier and safer to change the order of the blocks of text in Word than in OmniPage.

Steps for reordering zones:

Figure 4.15
The Reorder
Zone button

1.   Click the Reorder Zones button.

Figure 4.16
Reorder Zone
mouse pointer

2.   The mouse pointer changes to a pretzel shape (Figure 4.16) and the existing sequence numbering is removed from the zones. Click on each zone in the order you want each zone to be recognized.

3. Click within the first zone you want recognized. The number 1 appears in the zone.

4. Click in the next zone you want recognized. The number 2 appears in the zone.

5. Repeat step 3 until all the zones are appropriately reordered.

The reordering of the zones determines the order in which the zones are saved in the saved file. This only applies when the Text Editor view options Retain Font and Paragraph Formatting or No Formatting are selected. You can check the order of zones before saving by changing the Text Editor view to Retain Font and Paragraph Formatting.

If you do not number all the zones, they are automatically numbered for you when you start Perform OCR.

Zone Properties

Each zone on a page image is assigned properties, a zone type, and zone contents. OmniPage assigns zone properties to each zone when it creates zones automatically. You do not need to change the zone properties unless you want to modify the way zones will be processed during OCR. For example, you may be scanning a table of numbers, in which case changing the zone contents to numeric will reduce the recognition errors. OmniPage may have identified a zone as text and you want it as a graphic. Use the Zone Properties button (Figure 4.17) to change the properties.

Figure 4.17
The Zone Properties button

To change the properties of a zone:

1. Click on the zone you want to change.

2. Hold down the Shift key and click to select multiple zones.

3. Selected zones are shaded.

4. Click the Zone Properties button to open the Zone Properties dialog box.

You can also use the shortcut menu to change a zone's properties—right-click on the zone and select the properties from the quick menu.

The Zone Properties dialog box (Figure 4.18) displays the settings for the selected zone. If you selected multiple zones, the Zone Properties dialog box shows only settings that the zones have in common. Other settings are blank.

Figure 4.18
Zone Properties dialog box

Setting properties for multiple zones:

1. Select a zone type for the selected zones.

2. Select a zone content option for the selected zones.

3. Click the close button (x) when you are done.

If you had selected more than one zone, all zones are changed to the selected zone properties.

Erasing a Zone

There is no button for erasing a zone or erasing multiple zones. Here's how you can do it:

1. In the Original Document View, position the mouse pointer on a zone and click the right mouse button to select the zone and pop up the shortcut menu.

2. Click Clear or press Delete on the keyboard to delete the selected zone.

3. To delete multiple zones, hold down the Shift key and click on the zones to select, then right-click and click Clear or press Delete on the keyboard.

4. To delete all zones, right-click on any zone, and in the shortcut menu click Select all, press Delete on the keyboard, or right-click again and select Clear.

You may want to zoom in on the Original Image view when redrawing zones, as it makes it easier to see what you are doing. Here is a refresher on the View tools.

View Tools

These buttons affect the scanned image (Figure 4.19). They allow you to rotate the image—for example, to reorient a landscape document that was scanned on portrait setting. You can use the zoom buttons to zoom in to the scanned image to more accurately draw your zones.

Figure 4.19
Rotate, Zoom in, and Zoom out, the last three buttons on the Image toolbar

Rotate the Image

If your original document has text both ways on the page—in landscape and in portrait orientation—OmniPage will rotate the page several times in an attempt to recognize the most text in one direction only. The text in the other direction will probably come out as a mix of garbage characters and graphics. If this is the case, you will need to delete the incorrect zones. If you need the text from the other direction, you can rotate the image and reprocess. On the other hand, if you need all the text as an integral unit, it is best to draw a manual zone over the entire area and set to a graphic. OmniPage automatically straightens crooked images during the recognition process. (This is the default setting in the Options > Process tab.)

CHAPTER 4

TIP

If you need to rotate a page, be sure to do so before zones are created, because all zones are deleted when the page is rotated.

To rotate a page image:

1. Click on the page image to make the Original Image view active.
2. Click the Rotate Image button on the Image toolbar to rotate the image 90, 180, or 270 degrees, *or*
3. Select View on the menu and click Rotate Image. Then, select 90, 180, or 270 degrees.

Zoom In and Out

The zoom in and zoom out buttons work only in the Original Image view.

To zoom in or out in a view using the standard toolbar and the menu bar:

Figure 4.20
Zoom from the toolbar

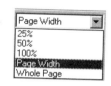

1. Make the view active by clicking in the view Original Image or Text Editor.
2. In the zoom drop-down list on the standard toolbar, choose a zoom option (Figure 4.20) *or*
3. On the menu, click Zoom and select a zoom option in the drop-down list.
The view resizes as specified.

Zone Templates

Imagine if you had a long document that required you to manually draw zones each time you scanned the document, or if every month you had to scan a document with a particular, specific layout. You would not want to have to redraw the zones each time. In this case, you can create a zone template file of the zones so that you can reapply those same zones at a later date.

A zone template is a set of zones, their properties, and their order—all stored in a template file. After you have created at least one zone template, Load Template will appear as another option in the Perform OCR drop-down list or from the Tools menu.

When you load a template with the Manual OCR toolbar, its zones appear immediately on the current page, replacing any already there. Existing pages are not affected. The template zones are placed on all subsequent pages until the template is unloaded. You can modify the template zones and add new zones before performing recognition.

When you load a template with the AutoOCR toolbar, it does not affect the current or existing pages. The template zones are placed on all subsequent pages until the template is unloaded.

If the option "Find zones in addition to template/current zones" is turned on, the OCR process will look for text and graphics on the page in areas outside the template zones. This option is turned on in the Options panel, under Tools > Options. Alternatively, click the AB options button on the toolbar. Select the Process tab and select the option "Find zones in addition to template/current zones."

Save a Zone Template

Manually draw zones on a page for the areas you want recognized. Check their locations, properties, and order. Perform the OCR process and check the results in the Text Editor view. If you are satisfied with the results, click Tools > Zone Template. In the dialog box, select [zones on page] and click Save. Give the template a file name that describes the use for this template. See Figure 4.21.

Figure 4.21
Save zone template

Modify a Zone Template

To make changes to an existing zone template:

1. Load the template you want to modify.
2. Load or scan a suitable document using Manual OCR. The template zones appear.
3. Modify the zones and/or properties to suit the new document.
4. On the menu, select Tools > Zone Template. This opens the Zone Template File dialog box. The current template is selected; this is the one you have just modified.
5. Click Save.
6. Click Close. This will overwrite the original zone.

How Perform OCR Evaluates a Page

How does the choice of Perform OCR options change the zones and the way a page is recognized? Remember that *every* page in your document is evaluated based on the Perform OCR setting. Once the page is scanned or loaded, you can change the Perform OCR setting, manually draw zones, change the text layout, and save in different file formats as many times as you like, without having to rescan or load the original document.

The only time you would need to rescan is when you want to change the original image—for example, if you want to change a black and white image to grayscale or color. Another good reason why you may want to rescan is if the OCR results from a black and white scan had several errors in the proofreader. This could be because the document is of poor quality. In this case, rescan using grayscale for improved results.

The example document used here consists of multiple columns, a table, and a picture.

Perform OCR Setting: Automatic

With this setting, OmniPage evaluates each page of the document separately for columns, tables, and graphics. All the blocks of text are correctly zoned, as are the picture and table. The text has the correct layout in the Text Editor (Figure 4.22). The text will be saved with this layout *only*, because the selected Text Editor view is set to True Page.

Remember, the selected "view" option in the Text Editor view determines the layout of your saved document.

If you want the text saved as Flowing Columns or Retain Font and Paragraph Formatting, choose the appropriate view in the Text Editor view. You would choose either of these two options if you want to do extensive editing in your application.

Figure 4.22
Perform OCR setting:
Automatic Zones

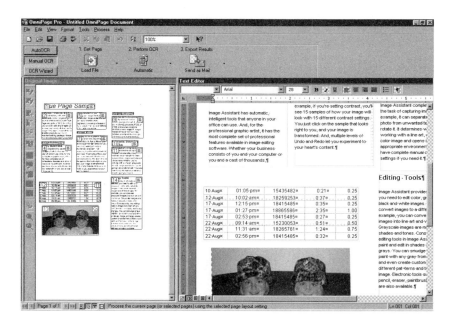

Generally, Automatic is the best Perform OCR setting, as OmniPage is very good at working out the page layout, especially if your document has different page layouts throughout.

For this particular page and pages like it, Automatic is the right setting. It evaluates each page separately and saves you a lot of rezoning.

Perform OCR Setting: Single Column No Table

When using this setting, OmniPage will evaluate *every* page of your document as though it is a single column with no tables.

In the Original Image view (Figure 4.23), you will see OmniPage has drawn zones around the three columns of text and another around the table and the column of text to the right of the table. The photo is recognized correctly.

In the Text Editor view, the text looks like columns and the table like a table. However, the lines of each column of text are actually in one line across the page, with tabs to create the column look. Imagine trying to edit this.

Figure 4.23
Perform OCR setting:
Single Column
No Table

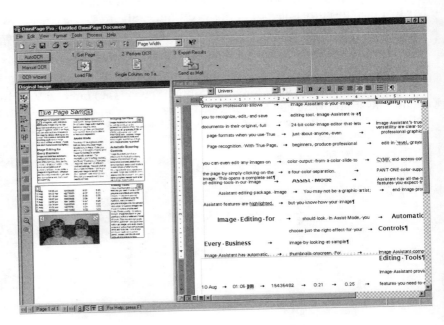

Perform OCR Setting: Multiple Column No Table

When using this setting, OmniPage will evaluate *every* page of your document as a multiple column with no tables.

In Figure 4.24, we see that OmniPage has correctly identified the columns and picture and reproduced them correctly in the Text Editor. However, the table has been broken into separate columns of text (Figure 4.24).

Figure 4.24
Perform OCR setting:
Multiple Column
No Table

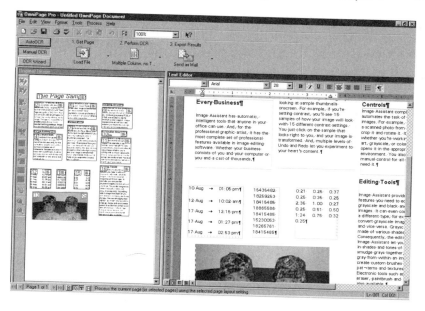

CHAPTER 4

Perform OCR Setting: Single Column with Table

When using this setting, OmniPage will evaluate *every* page of your document as single column with tables.

In Figure 4.25, we see that OmniPage has drawn a single zone around the three columns of text on the top of the page and correctly identified the table zone. It created a separate zone around the column of text to the right. The picture is recognized correctly.

Figure 4.25
Perform OCR setting:
Single Column
With Table

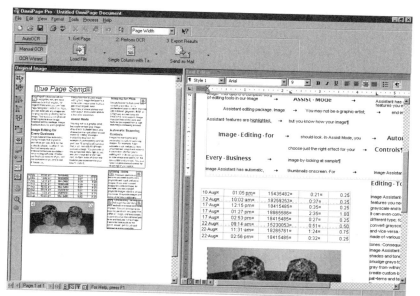

Again, in the Text Editor view, the text looks like columns. However, it is actually on one line with tabs to create the column look.

Perform OCR Setting: Spreadsheet

In Figure 4.26, we see that OmniPage has drawn a single zone over the whole page and zoned it as a table zone. The entire zone has been split into table cells at each line and column.

The picture is not recognized. In fact, parts of the picture have been interpreted as text and appear as small garbage characters in some of the table cells.

Figure 4.26
Perform OCR setting:
Spreadsheet

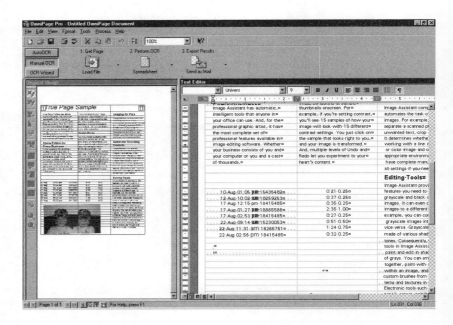

This should give you a good idea of how each of the OCR Process settings can handle the pages of your document. Always be aware that when selecting any setting other than Automatic, every page of your document will be processed using that setting.

Practice Drawing Zones

This is a bit of fun. You can now experiment with all the zone tools on a blank page.

First, let's set up a blank page:

1. Set the OCR toolbox to Manual OCR.

2. Set the Get Page step to Scan Black and White.

3. Scan a blank page.

Make sure the scanned and "blank" image is in the Original Image view. Now, let's experiment.

Draw Zones

1. Click Draw Regular Zones.
2. Place the mouse pointer in the Original Image view.
3. Click and drag to draw a zone.
4. Right-click and change the properties to Graphic.
5. Draw another zone; notice that it is drawn as a graphic zone. This is because the previous zone was a graphic.
6. Change this new zone to multiple column.
7. Draw four more zones and change the properties to one of each of the different property types and content (alphanumeric and numeric).

Draw Irregular Zones

1. Move the mouse to a clear area of the image.
2. Click to anchor the point. Take your finger off the mouse button.
3. Move the mouse around in a circle; see how the line follows the mouse in only the horizontal and vertical directions.
4. Use mouse clicks to anchor different points; double-click to complete. Press Delete on the keyboard to delete the zone you have just drawn.

Figure 4.27
Irregular zone in the shape of the letter E

5. Move to a clear area again and draw the letter E by clicking and locking in the points. Then, double-click to complete. See Figure 4.27.
6. Try to draw a zone like the letter G. You will find you can't, as you can't draw a zone that "doubles back" on itself, like on the bottom of the letter G.

Figure 4.28
A staircase zone where a diagonal line is required

7. Now, draw a staircase zone. You may need to draw zones like this when you have text or a graphic that needs a "diagonal" line to capture (Figure 4.28).

You will find that you can't have an irregular zone shape as a table zone.

Move Some Zones Around

1. Make sure you have deselected Draw Irregular Zone by clicking on the Draw Regular Zone button. Otherwise, if you click anywhere in a blank area, you will start drawing lines as if to draw another irregular zone.
2. Click on a zone to select it.
3. Make sure the mouse pointer is a cross.
4. Click and hold the mouse button down and drag the zone to a new position.
5. Try dragging the zone on top of another. Notice how you can only drag it adjacent to another zone and not overlap.

Resize a Zone

1. Click on a zone to select it.

2. Move the mouse pointer to a corner; when the pointer changes to a diagonal pointer, click and hold the mouse button and drag to resize or change the shape of the zone.

Change the Properties of Several Zones at Once

1. Click on one zone to select it.

2. Hold down the Shift key and click on other zones to select.

3. With the mouse pointer inside one of the zones, right-click to pop up the quick menu and select an option to change all the zones, or click the Zone Properties button.

Add to a Zone

1. Click the Add To zone button.

2. Move the mouse pointer to inside a zone; click and drag to outside the zone to create an extension of the zone. Release the mouse button.

Join Two Zones Together

1. Click on one zone and hold the mouse button down, then drag to another zone. Release the mouse button. The properties of the first zone are transferred to the second zone.

2. Try joining two table zones together; you will find you can't because it would create a nonrectangular zone. All table zones must be rectangular.

Subtract from a Zone

1. Click outside a zone. Hold the mouse button down and drag into a zone to delete a portion of that zone. Release the mouse button to complete. You can use this method to remove an entire zone by drawing a Subtract from zone over the whole zone you want to delete

2. To divide a zone in two, start outside the zone; click and hold the mouse button and drag through and out the other side. Release the mouse button to complete.

3. Try using the Subtract from tool to make a hole inside a zone. Place the mouse inside a zone and draw a small zone. Notice how OmniPage draws another zone to plug the gap.

Reorder the Zones

1. Make sure you still have some zones in the image view; if not, now that you are an expert at drawing zones, draw some more.
2. Click the Reorder zones button. All the numbering is removed and the mouse pointer has changed to a pretzel shape.
3. Click on the zones in the order you would want them saved in a document. Remember that the zone order only applies to the text when it is saved as Retain Font and Paragraph format or No Formatting.

Create and Use a Zone Template

Let's for the moment assume the zones you currently have on this blank image are the ones you need to apply to documents like this in the future. Let's create a template.

1. On the menu, click Tools > Zone Template > [zones on page]. Click Save.
2. Save the new zone template as file name "Test" then click Close.
3. Let's now use the new zone template test. Close the document. Click No to not save the current document.
4. Click on the down arrow to the right of the OCR Process button and select Template > Test.
5. Click the Get Page process button and rescan the blank page. Notice how OmniPage has drawn the zones as saved in the template.
6. Set the option "Find zones in addition to template/current zones."
7. On the toolbar, click the AB options button and select the Process tab. Check that the option "Find zones in addition to template/current zones" is not selected.
8. Click OK to close the options box.
9. Click the OCR Process button. The text window will probably display numerous paragraph markers and no text, which is what we expected.
10. Now, go back to the options panel and select the option "Find zones in addition to template/current ones."
11. Click the OCR Process button. The Zoning Instructions dialog box displays, asking if you want to use the current zones (your template), discard the template zones and find new ones, or use your template zones and find more. Select "Use your template zones and find additional." The text window will probably display the same as before, although if there were other items on the page, OmniPage would find them, draw additional zones around them, and then OCR your template zones and the new ones.

Delete a Zone Template

1. To delete the zone template, select Tools > Zone Template.
2. Select the template "Test" and click the Delete button.

Once you have the hang of drawing zones and changing the contents, it is very easy to cope with tricky pages and improve the results you get with OmniPage.

5

Multi-Column Documents

You can use OmniPage to scan newspaper articles, magazines, or any text layout in columns. You select the columns and areas of text to be recognized by manually drawing zones, or by letting OmniPage automatically determine the zones. OmniPage reproduces the saved document like the original, or in other layouts you select.

OmniPage's Multi-Column Choices

We know when a document is laid out in columns or a table just by looking at the hard copy; however, OmniPage looks at the gaps between words on each line.

The simplest definition of multiple columns from OmniPage's point of view is this: If the text on the same line, in the adjacent column, is *not* related, then it is a column. If the text *is* related, then treat it as a table. For example, a price list has a product in one column and a price for that product in the next column. The product and price are on the same line and are "related." A newspaper, on the other hand, is laid out in columns, but text on one line is not related to the text in the next column on that same line.

When scanning multiple-column documents, select the setting Multiple Columns, no Table, or Automatic. Just remember, if you use the Multiple Columns setting, any tables will be broken up into unrelated columns.

You have the option of scanning on Automatic and letting OmniPage make its own decisions about how to handle multi-column documents, or you can switch to manual Multiple Column mode. Automatic mode is by far the quickest and easiest, especially when scanning multi-page documents with different page layouts. Sometimes, though, if you're scanning a multi-page document in Automatic mode, you may come across some pages that have multiple columns, and, due to the layout and closeness of the columns, OmniPage will zone the text as a single "wide" column, rather than as two separate narrow columns. In this case, Multiple Columns may give a better result. The alternative is to redraw the zones manually.

Table 5.1
When to use zone settings

Type of zone	When to use
Draw Manual Zones	Only want a part of a page.
	Need to respecify the contents of a zone.
	Add or remove parts of a zone.
	Want to create a zone template file.
	When using Automatic, some of the text was zoned incorrectly.
Automatic Zones	You want to process your document quickly.
	Your document contains pages with different or unknown layouts.
	You have a page with multiple columns and a table.
	You have many pages containing more than one table.
Multi-column, no table	All the pages of your document are multi-column and none of the pages contain a table.
	When using Automatic, some of the text was zoned incorrectly.

Scanning a Multi-Column Document

In this exercise, you will scan the document "Tpexmple." It is in the appendix, and it can be downloaded from the Web site (see Introduction). If you download from our Web site, save the file in the training folder. You can print it and scan it, or you can use Load Image to load the file.

You will be using the Manual OCR toolbox to manually control the three scanning and OCR steps: 1) Get the Page, 2) Perform the OCR, and 3) Save the results. The first thing to do is set the options for the three process steps.

If you have any documents open in OmniPage, close them.

Scan the Document

1. Click the Manual OCR toolbox.
2. Click the down-pointing arrow of Get Page.
3. Select Scan B&W. Use this option if you are going to scan the page at the back of the book. Otherwise, use Load Image if you have downloaded the file "Tpexmple.tif" from the Web site. You will be presented with the Load Image dialog box; locate the file in the training folder.
4. Click the down-pointing arrow of Perform OCR.

5.   Select Automatic; OmniPage determines where to draw the zones.

6.   Click the down-pointing arrow of Export Results.

7.   Select Save as File.

8.   Place the page "Tpexmple" in the scanner.

9.   Click Get Page button. The page will be scanned or loaded.

The image appears in the Document Manager and Original Image view with no zones. This is because we used the Manual OCR toolbox. OmniPage is now waiting for you to start the next process, which is Perform OCR.

Perform OCR

To OCR the page:

1.   Click Perform OCR. The zones are drawn.

2.   The Proofreader dialog box pops up.

3.   For now, close the Proofreader; click Close.

Look at the zones OmniPage has drawn and the text layout in the Text Editor window. Your screen should look like Figure 5.1.

Figure 5.1
Auto-Zone OCR result with Retain Flowing Columns view

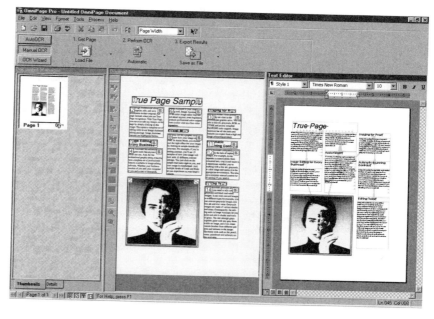

The light gray arrows in the Text Editor view show the flow of the text. These only show when you save the document, using the Retain Flowing Columns layout. Remember, these views are selected using the View buttons in the bottom left-hand corner of the Text Editor view.

Setting Up the Zoning Instructions

When drawing manual zones, turn on the Zoning Instruction option. This gives you more control over the OCR processing of the zones you draw. The processing of your manual zones will still work without the zoning instruction switched on. Let's turn it on, then zoom into the Original Image view to make drawing zones easy.

To switch on the zoning instruction:

1. On the standard toolbar, click the AB Options button.
2. Select the Process tab.
3. Click in the checkbox for "Find zones in addition to template/current zones" to select it.
4. Click OK.

Draw a Manual Zone

If you were to scan this document with Perform OCR set to Automatic, the results would export to Word as per the original. There would be no need to draw manual zones. However, for this exercise, we need a document with different elements on the page and this is a good one with which to work. We are going to change the way OmniPage has drawn the zones. So, we will clear all the zones, draw manual zones, and, finally, reprocess the document.

We will draw zones around the following areas:

- The title at the top of the page.
- The two columns of text above the picture.
- A part of the picture.
- The last paragraph of text to the right of the picture.

Let's hide the Text Editor view so you can see more of the Original Image view, as it makes it easier to draw zones. On the OmniPage desktop navigation bar at the bottom of the screen, click the T. Show or hide the Text Editor. Alternatively, drag the window divider bar between the Original Image view and the Text Editor view, to the right.

If you need to see more of the image, use the Zoom tool to enlarge the view. Zooming into the Original Image makes the job of drawing zones much easier. OmniPage works better when there is white space around the text, so don't draw your zone borders right next to the text.

1. On the Image toolbar, click the Zoom tool with the plus symbol in the magnifying glass.
2. Select 25%.

First, let's clear all the zones OmniPage drew, and then we will draw our own.

1. Position the mouse pointer on a zone.
2. Click the right mouse button to pop up the quick-select menu for zones.
3. Click Select All.
4. Click Clear, or press Delete on the keyboard. All zones are removed, and you are ready to redraw new zones.

Draw a Rectangular Zone

Next, draw a rectangular zone around the title "True Page Sample."

Figure 5.2
Draw Rectangular
button

1. Click the Rectangular Zone button (Figure 5.2).
2. Position the pointer above and to the left of the title at the top of the page.
3. Click and hold the left mouse button, dragging to the bottom right-hand corner of the title to be zoned. Make sure you have not drawn the zone touching or cutting off any of the characters. Always make sure you have some white space around the text.
4. Release the mouse button.

TIP

Always make sure you have plenty of white space around the text. It's easy to accidentally cut off descending characters: See figures 5.3 and 5.4 below. In the first figure, the zone has cut off the bottom of the "g" and "p". The next figure shows the results once the zone has been recognized. Remember, OmniPage recognizes only what is in the zone.

Figure 5.3
The zone cutting off
the descending
characters

> True Page Sample

Figure 5.4
The recognized text

> True·Paae·SaMDle¶

CHAPTER 5

We need to repeat the above steps for drawing manual zones to draw zones around the following:

▶ The two columns of text above the picture.

▶ The last paragraph of text to the right of the picture.

▶ The part of the picture that shows only the model's eye and part of the camera.

If you make a mistake, clear the zone and start drawing again.

When you have finished, your zones should look like those in Figure 5.5.

Figure 5.5
The four new zones

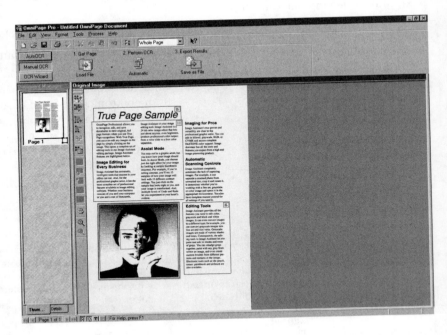

You will notice the zones are numbered automatically and they are all single column text. OmniPage remembers the zone type and content of the previous zone you drew and assumes the next zone you draw will be the same. You can change the properties and contents as you draw them.

In order to tell OmniPage the content of the zone, we need to set the properties of each zone.

Change the Properties for Each Zone

We will select each zone and set the zone type and content for each new zone. Let's do that now.

Zone 1: The Title

1. Position the mouse pointer in zone 1 (the title) and right-click. The zone turns gray.
2. Click Properties, the selection at the bottom of the list.
3. Click the down-pointing arrow of Zone Type.
4. Click Single column flowing text.
5. Click the down-pointing arrow of Zone Content.
6. Click Alphanumeric. This is first in the list, so it should already be selected.
7. Close the Zone Properties box. Click the x on the top right-hand corner.

Notice the icon in the top right-hand corner of the zone shows a single column in blue. The border is also blue.

Zone 2: The Two Columns of Text

1. Position the mouse pointer in zone 2 (the two columns) and right-click. The zone turns gray.
2. This time, we will use the shortcut menu to select the zone contents. Point to the top option in this shortcut. It currently shows Single Column Text. Click with the left mouse button; another menu pops up.
3. Click Multiple column flowing text.
4. Right-click the zone again.
5. Move the mouse down to Alphanumeric, second on the list. Click with the left mouse button. Another menu pops up. Alphanumeric should already be selected. Click Alphanumeric to close.

Notice the icon in the top right-hand corner of the zone shows a multiple column in blue. The border is also blue. Notice also that all the zone numbers have disappeared. This happens when selecting a block of text as multi-column. During the OCR process, OmniPage will have to break up the multi-column zone into the individual single columns and renumber them.

Zone 3: The Picture

1. Position the mouse pointer in zone 3 (the picture) and right-click. The zone turns gray.
2. Click Properties.
3. Click the down-pointing arrow of Zone Type.
4. Click Graphic. Notice the zone content is dimmed. There is no content setting for graphic.
5. Close the Zone Properties box. Click the x in the top right-hand corner.

Notice the icon in the top right-hand corner of the zone shows a graphic symbol in green. The border is also green.

Zone 4: Column Beside the Picture

1. Position the mouse pointer in zone 4 (the single column of text) and right-click. The zone turns gray.
2. Click Properties.
3. Click the down-pointing arrow of Zone Type.
4. Click Single column flowing text.
5. Click the down-pointing arrow of Zone Content.
6. Click Alphanumeric. It should already be selected.
7. Close the Zone Properties box. Click the x in the top right-hand corner.

Now that we have set the properties for each zone, we can recognize the image. First, we will switch on the Text Editor, so we can see the recognized text and proofread the results.

CHAPTER 5

Recognizing the Image

The recognition of the zoned text is done in the Perform OCR step. As you are using the Manual OCR toolbox, you need to tell OmniPage to do the next step, perform the OCR. The Text Editor view, which was turned off in the previous exercise, must be turned back on to see the recognized text.

Display the Text Editor View

Switch on the Text Editor view. On the navigation bar, in the bottom left-hand corner, click the T. Show or hide the Text Editor.

Perform OCR

1. Click the Perform OCR button.
2. The warning box (Figure 5.6) will display, asking if you want to replace the current recognized text in the Text Editor view. This is because the page has already been recognized. You have drawn new zones to recognize different parts of the page, and OmniPage is just making sure you want to replace the existing recognized text with that from the new zones.
3. Click Yes.
4. Click Use only current zones (Figure 5.7), the ones you have just drawn. As soon as you click the button, OmniPage starts the OCR process.

Figure 5.6
"This page has already been recognized" warning box

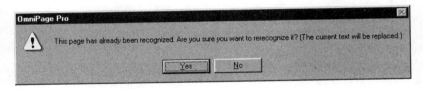

The Zoning Instructions box (Figure 5.7) displays, asking if you want to:

▶ Use only current zones—the ones you have just drawn.

▶ Discard current zones and find new zones.

▶ Keep current zones and find additional zones.

Figure 5.7
Zoning Instructions box

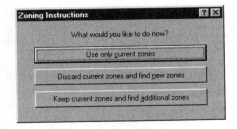

Remember, if you deselect the option to display the zoning instructions in the Options Process tab, the Zoning Instruction box, as displayed above, will not display and the OCR process will begin. You won't get the option to choose the other options. If you have not selected the zoning instructions, OmniPage will process only the zones present on the Original Image. It will not look for other zones, nor remove all existing zones and find new zones. Notice that new zones are drawn around the text inside the multiple column zone. This is because you selected that zone as Multiple Column. OmniPage turns on its multi-column zoning to break up the multi-column zone into individual single columns within that zone. This is done to make sure the text is recognized and positioned correctly. The placement of the columns and headings will not change. It will remain as multiple column flowing text.

When the OCR process is completed, the Proofreader dialog box displays. In the Proofreader dialog box, the first word to be found as suspect is "heart's." As this is correct, click Ignore. Go through the Proofreader until OCR proofreading is complete.

So now, let's save the results.

Saving the Results

Before you export—save any results—you need to set the format or layout for the saved document. Remember that there are four different format view options in the Text Editor. It is the view you have selected in the Text Editor that determines the format of the document when it is saved. Once your document has been recognized, you can save it as many times as you like and in the different formats. In OmniPage, "layout" refers to the layout of the original document, i.e., what it looks like. "Format" is used in saving results to describe the way the saved document is formatted. Is it formatted to look like the original, i.e., True Page, or formatted as plain text with a single font and size, i.e., No Formatting?

Let's look at how these various choices affect the saved results. The Format (layout) views are located at the bottom of the Text Editor view.

Flowing Columns View

The icon at the bottom of the Text Editor view should be set to Retain Flowing Columns view. If it is not, click Retain Flowing Columns view. It is the button on the left-hand end of the Text Editor view buttons.

The columns have maintained their original position. We zoned the two columns side by side and set the zone properties as multiple column flowing text zone. The graphic and single column to the right are in their correct locations. We zoned the graphic as a graphic and the zone around the last column as a single column. The recognized text format or layout in the Text Editor view will look like Figure 5.8.

Figure 5.8
Document format with
the Retain Flowing
Columns view

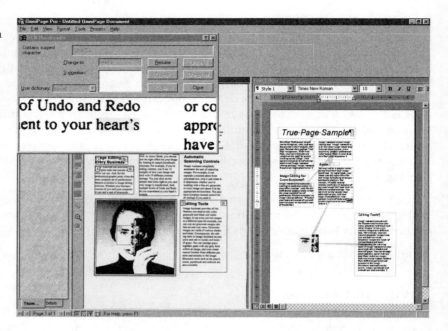

NOTE

To keep the original layout of the pages, including columns, select Retain
Flowing Columns before exporting. Use this setting when you want to edit the
text in your word processor. Text will then flow from one column to the other.
The light gray arrows show the text flow order.

Exporting the Results

Now that you have set the output format for the document, we can save the document.

1. Click the Export Results button.

2. In the Save as dialog box, click the down-pointing arrow of the Save in field.

3. Select drive and folder. Locate the "Training" folder.

4. In the file name field, enter "Multicol-RFC" for Retain Flowing Columns.

5. Click the down-pointing arrow of the Save as Type box. Select Word 97, 2000
   (*doc) or your appropriate application format.

6. Select the option to Save and Launch the application.

7. Click OK. Word launches and displays the document.

NOTE

Using the Automatic Setting on Perform OCR:
When saving the results as Retain Flowing Columns, the text is saved in text columns and not frames. If you only zone part of the page with manual zones, you will get some frames. OmniPage will flow the text from column to column, except when text spans two or more columns, and for graphics. When the text spans two or more columns, it will be placed in a frame. This is why the title of the page is in a frame.

Using Manual Zones:
The text from the multi-column zone is in flowing text columns. However, the last zone of text from the right-hand side is placed in a frame. If there are "orphaned" blocks of text—i.e., there is a gap between the zones—OmniPage will place them in a frame. It does this so it can reproduce a text layout similar to the original. The result is a mix of Flowing Columns and True Page. You will find that when using the option Retain Flowing Columns, there may be zones of text that are saved in frames. The best way to handle this is to let OmniPage Auto-zone the entire page and save the document as Flowing Columns. Then, in your word processor, delete the unwanted text and crop the picture.

Let's look at what happens when you choose the other Text Editor views. You can compare the results in the Text Editor view before saving. Then save in the format you want.

True Page View

You want the saved document to look as similar as possible to the original. You do not intend to do much editing or layout changes.

1. Switch to OmniPage.
2. Click True Page View and see what happens to the layout. The results will look like Figure 5.9 below.

Figure 5.9
True Page View maintains the original layout using frames

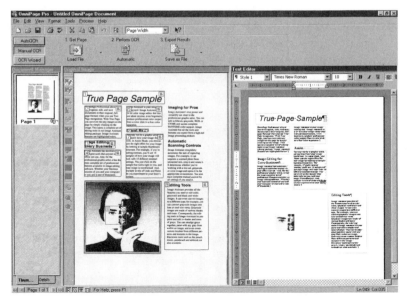

CHAPTER 5

Resave the document in Word, or your word processor format.

1. Click the Export Results button.

2. In the Save as dialog box, click the down-pointing arrow of the Save in field.

3. Ensure your training folder is still selected.

4. In the file name field, enter "Multicol-TP."

5. Click the down-pointing arrow of the Save as Type box. Select Word 97, 2000 (*doc) or your appropriate application format.

6. Select the option to Save and Launch the application.

7. Click OK. Word launches and displays the results.

Figure 5.10 shows how the result looks in Word.

Figure 5.10
Using True Page view, Word displays all elements in their original location

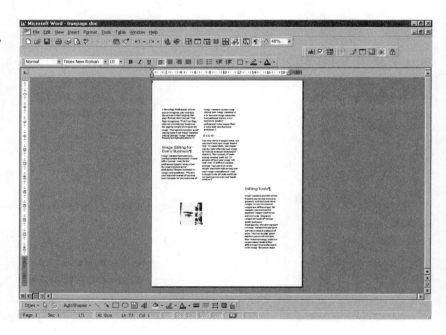

The True Page setting places every zone in a frame in your word processor. OmniPage then relocates each zone on the saved page. The frames usually are just big enough to hold the text in the zone; sometimes, however, they are not quite big enough. When this happens, not all the text displays in your saved document. The text is there, it's just that the frame OmniPage created in Word is not big enough to display it.

If the Zone Is Too Small

When the zones are too close to the text, the Text Editor view will show small gray arrows on the side or bottom of the zone. These arrows mean the text may extend past the edge of the frame and can't be displayed. This sometimes happens when OmniPage automatically draws the zones, because it puts the borders very close to the text. It doesn't tend to happen as much with manual zones, because users usually draw the zones a bit bigger than OmniPage does. If you draw the zones too close to the text, you will get the same results.

There are three ways you can fix this.

To Fix in OmniPage

1. In the Original Image view, click the zone.
2. Resize the zone so there is more white space around the text.
3. Then, reprocess the page by clicking the Perform OCR button.

To Fix in Your Word Processor by Resizing the Text Frame

1. Click in the text frame to select it.
2. Click the shaded frame border to select it.
3. Click and drag a frame handle to make it bigger to display the text. You may have to drag it horizontally to display the rest of a line, or vertically to display more lines.

Figure 5.11 is an enlarged portion of the saved text in a word document. On the left-hand side, you can see the frame and how it has cut off the bottom of the word "Assist" (the text should read "Assist Mode"). The right-hand side shows the text frame made larger, displaying all the text, "Assist Mode."

Figure 5.11
Rezising a frame

a·color·slide·to·a·tour·color·
separation.¶

| Assist· |

You·may·not·be·a·graphic·arti
you·know·how·your·image·sh

from·a·color·slide·to·a·four·
color·separation.¶

| **Assist·Mode¶** |

You·may·not·be·a·graphic·artist:
you·know·how·your·image·shou
look.·In·Assist·Mode,·you·choos

To Fix in Your Word Processor by Resizing the Font

1. Click in the text frame to select it.
2. Highlight the visible text.
3. Change to a smaller font. Once the selected text is a smaller font, the rest of the text will be visible.
4. Select the remaining text and change to the same smaller font. If most of the text in the frames is not displaying or the font sizes are incorrect, use Select all and change all the text on the page to the desired font size.

TIP

As the text is in frames, the text of one frame is not linked to the next frame. This makes editing difficult. If you want to add more text to the frame, you first must make the frame larger. Conversely, when you delete text from a frame, the frame doesn't get smaller, it just leaves blank space at the bottom. So, to close up the gaps, you have to resize the frame.

CHAPTER 5

With True Page selected, all the elements of the original are reproduced in the saved text format. The font size and style are maintained and the paragraphs are kept in their original locations. Just check that the frames are displaying all of their text, and that no zones in the Text Editor view have any little gray arrows.

Now, let's experiment with the next layout.

Retain Font and Paragraph View

1. Switch to OmniPage.
2. In the Text Editor view, click Retain Font and Paragraph and see what happens to the layout.

When you click the view buttons, the recognized text in the Text Editor window is formatted and displayed in the view you have selected.

Retain Font and Paragraph does not maintain the layout of the original document. Instead, all the zones are laid out in a single column in the order of their zone number. The display of the text in this view can be set to wrap to the page width setting of the ruler bar (Figure 5.12). Figure 5.13 shows the text layout with no wrap.

Figure 5.12
Retain Font and Paragraph view does not maintain columns—this view is with the OmniPage Word Wrap option set to Wrap to Ruler

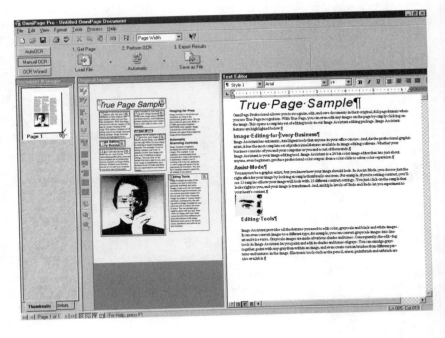

Figure 5.13
Retain Font and
Paragraph view with
the Word Wrap Option
set to No Wrap

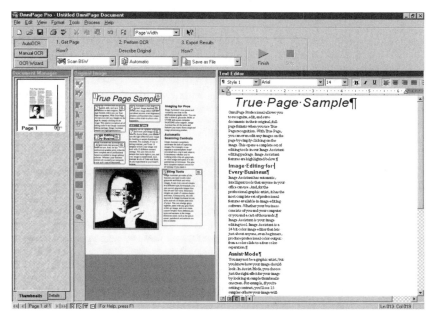

If your OmniPage desktop looks like Figure 5.13, it is because the Word Wrap setting is off. The setting is located in OmniPage Options (click the AB switch button to launch) under the Text Editor tab (Figure 5.14). The default is Wrap to Ruler. With the default set to Wrap to Ruler, you will get the screen as shown in figure 5.12. Word Wrap only affects the display of recognized text when Retain Font and Paragraph view is selected. It does not affect the layout of the saved text in your word processor.

Figure 5.14
Word Wrap option sets
the text display and
wrapping for the Retain
Font and Paragraph
view only

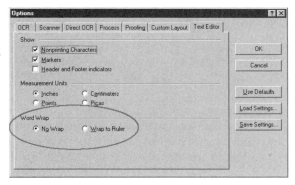

CHAPTER 5

Resave the document in Word or your word processor format.

1. Under Export Results, click Save as File.

2. In the Save as dialog box, click the down-pointing arrow of the Save in field.

3. Ensure the training folder is still selected.

4. In the file name field, enter "Multicol-RFP" for Retain Font and Paragraph.

5. Click the down-pointing arrow of the Save as Type box. Select Word 97, 2000 (*doc) or your appropriate application format.

6. Select the option to Save and Launch the application.

7. Click OK. Word launches and displays the results.

Figure 5.15 shows how the Retain Font and Paragraph view looks when saved as a Word document.

Figure 5.15
A Word document saved using the Retain Font and Paragraph view

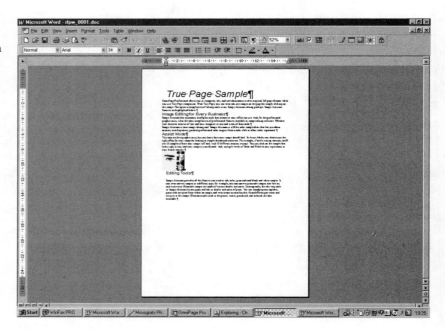

All elements are saved without any columns. The text flows from one paragraph to the other in the zone order. You lose the multiple column layout. The document has been changed to a single column, with all the paragraphs on the left margin under their appropriate headings. The font size and style is maintained and the paragraphs are kept together.

TIP

Use Retain Font and Paragraph on a multiple column document when you want to change the number of columns and layout in your word processor.

NOTE

Retain Font and Paragraph format is suitable for all file types except those with the TXT or PDF extensions. The TXT and PDF file types do not support this formatting.

Now, let's look at the last format.

No Formatting View

1. Switch to OmniPage.
2. Click the No Formatting button.

The No Formatting view removes all formatting from the recognized text. The text is exported based on the font and size set in the Text Editor toolbar. Figure 5.16 shows the Text Editor view with No Formatting selected.

Figure 5.16
No Formatting view displays all elements without any formatting or columns—all the text is in one font and size

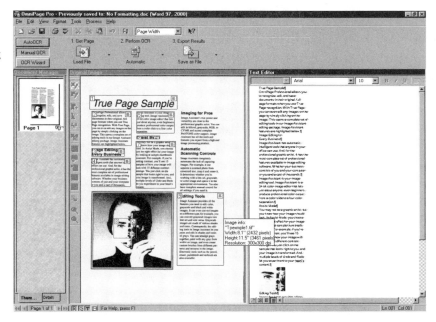

Resave the document in Word or your word processor format.

1. Under Export Results, click Save as File.
2. In the Save as dialog box, click the down-pointing arrow of the Save in field.
3. Ensure the training folder is still selected.
4. In the file name field, enter "Multicol-NF" for No Formatting.

5. Click the down-pointing arrow of the Save as Type box. Select Word 97, 2000 (*doc) or your appropriate application format.

6. Select the option to Save and Launch the application.

7. Click OK. Word launches and displays the results.

Figure 5.17 shows the saved Word document when the No Formatting view is selected when saving the document.

Figure 5.17
The No Formatting format in a Word document

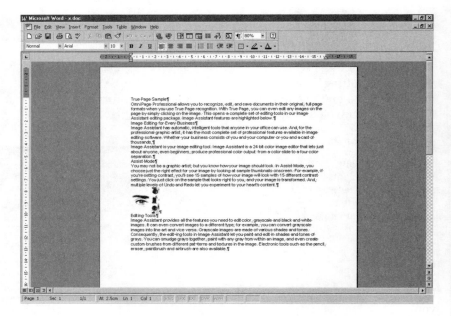

You lose the multiple column layout. The document has been changed to a single column, with all the paragraphs on the left margin under their appropriate headings. The paragraphs are kept together. All the text is the same font and size, as was selected in the Text Editor formatting toolbar.

TIP
This is a good format if you want to import the text or data into a database application. Save the document as an Excel spreadsheet; this makes it very easy to import into your database.

NOTE
Use the No Formatting view when exporting to ASCII, Unicode, or other formats with the extension .TXT. These file types do not accept graphics or tables. You can export plain text to any file type and target application.

6

Direct
OCR

Direct OCR is a feature installed with OmniPage that allows you to OCR pages while working in your word processor or other application. It lets you scan, recognize, and paste the results directly into your current file at the cursor position, without leaving the application. You don't have to launch OmniPage; your application communicates directly with OmniPage in the background. You can choose to acquire an entire page, or several pages if you have an ADF, or just draw a zone around the section you want. This is a handy feature, especially when you want to scan a document or part of a document into the one in which you are currently working. It works well in Excel when you want to insert a table from your scanned page. OmniPage also installs an OCR option in Windows Explorer. Using Windows Explorer, you can right-click any compatible image file to OCR and convert text or PDF.

Setting Up and Using Direct OCR

Direct OCR installs two additional options in the drop-down File menu of the application you are working in: Acquire Text and Acquire Text Settings. Before you can use Direct OCR with an application, the application must be registered in OmniPage's Option Direct OCR. The Direct OCR feature must also be enabled in OmniPage's Option Direct OCR.

The Direct OCR feature is accessed through the OmniPage Options dialog box (Tools > Options) or from the Options button (AB) on the standard toolbar.

Direct OCR works with applications such as word processors, spreadsheets, and desktop publishing applications—programs that have a File menu and that can paste text from the clipboard. In using Direct OCR, the OCR results are copied to the clipboard. These OCR results are then pasted into the application at the insertion point. If the application cannot accept text from the clipboard—for example, an image-editing program—Direct OCR will not work.

Register Your Applications for Direct OCR

When you open the Direct OCR panel from the Options dialog box, OmniPage searches your PC for open applications. There are two ways to register your applications. The easiest way is to have your application open before you open the Direct OCR panel. The other way is to open the Direct OCR panel and use the Browse button to locate and select your application.

CHAPTER 6

Steps to register your application(s) (see also Figures 6.1 and 6.2):

1. Launch Word and any other applications you want to use with the Direct OCR.
2. Switch to OmniPage as the active application.
3. On the OmniPage toolbar, click the Options button and select the Direct OCR tab. This opens the Direct OCR panel.
4. In the left-hand box labeled Unregistered are the applications you have open.
5. Select the applications by clicking their names.
6. Click the Add button to register.

Figure 6.1
Direct OCR Options
before registering
applications

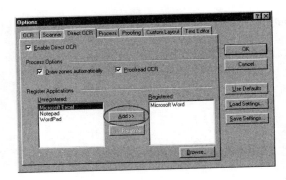

When you have registered your applications, they will be in the right-hand Registered box as shown in Figure 6.2.

Figure 6.2
Direct OCR options
with applications
registered

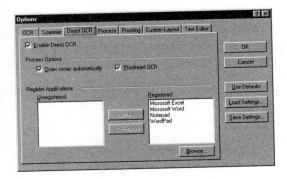

Direct OCR Options

Enable Direct OCR

The Enable Direct OCR setting enables or disables the Acquire Text options. When deselected, the options are removed from the File menu of applications like NotePad and WordPad. When using Word or applications that use templates and macros, the function is disabled, although the options still appear in the File menu.

In Word, the Acquire Text link to OmniPage is held in the global template. When deselecting the Direct OCR option, you will get a warning message as in Figure 6.3, saying the global template is about to be changed and asking if you want to save the changes. If you answer No, the Direct OCR function will still work. If you say Yes, the Acquire Text option will still appear in the File menu; it just doesn't do anything when selected.

Figure 6.3
Warning in Word when disabling the option Enable Direct OCR

Direct OCR Process Options

The Direct OCR Process options give you the choice to have OmniPage automatically draw zones and proofread the recognized text. By default, both options are selected. The options set in this Direct OCR panel are the default settings applied every time you use Acquire Text from the application's File menu. You can change these options before you acquire text by using the Acquire Text Settings selection from the application's File menu. Figure 6.4 shows the File menu of Microsoft Word with Direct OCR enabled.

Figure 6.4
The Acquire Text selections added to the File menu of Word

After you have registered the application you want to use with OmniPage, you can then scan directly into that application. Let's walk through an example:

The Stages of Direct OCR

1. Register the application you intend to use with Direct OCR.
2. Open your registered application and document.
3. Within your document, place the cursor in the position where you wish to import the recognized results.
4. Place the page to be scanned correctly in the scanner.

CHAPTER 6

5. From the application's File menu, select Acquire Text Settings to specify the settings to be used during this recognition session, the same as you do when using OmniPage. Acquire Text Settings displays four options: OCR, Scanner, Format, and Direct OCR. These are the same settings as in OmniPage; when you make a change here it is reflected in OmniPage the next time you use it, and vice versa. The Direct OCR option also specifies where the input document is coming from, either the scanner or a file. Any setting that is not displayed here uses the same value as was set the last time OmniPage was used.

6. From the application's File menu, select Acquire Text to acquire one or more images from your scanner or from a file. You can open a set of image files by adding to the selected files list in the Advanced file open option. You can open multi-page image files. To scan multiple pages for Direct OCR, you need an ADF (Automatic Document Feeder). If you do not have an ADF, you have to use Acquire Text for each page.

7. If you selected Draw Zones Automatically, recognition starts immediately. If not, each page image will allow you to draw zones manually. The Direct OCR zoning window looks just like the standard OmniPage desktop, but without the Text Editor view, menu, or standard toolbar. It has only the thumbnail and image views and the Perform OCR Process button. When you have drawn the zones, click the Perform OCR button to start the recognition.

8. If Proofread OCR was selected, the Proofreader dialog box displays if required when the recognition is complete.

9. The recognized text and graphics are inserted at the cursor position in your application, with the formatting as selected in the Format panel of the Direct OCR Options dialog box. If your application cannot support the formatting you specified (i.e., Graphics, True Page, Retain Flowing Columns, or Retain Font and Paragraph), plain text will be pasted. For example, when using Direct OCR into Notepad, only plain text will be inserted, as Notepad does not support different fonts, bolding, and text layout. WordPad will bring in the text with different fonts, bolding, paragraphs, and pictures, but it doesn't support multi-columns or frames for True Page. If there is no document open in your application, or your application doesn't support pasting text, the recognition results are sent to the clipboard.

Whew! Although it looks like many stages, it's actually easy to use. Once you've registered your applications with Direct OCR, the only steps required are: Put the page in your scanner, click Acquire Text, draw the zones around the areas you want, and click the OCR Process button (or just click OCR Process to AutoOCR the whole page). If it doesn't come out the way you want, use the Acquire Text Settings to change the settings of one or more of the four options. Most of the time, it is the format option that plays havoc with text in your document. If you use Direct OCR in your document and all of a sudden it looks like a dog's breakfast, *don't panic!* Bill Gates gave us a very useful button—the Undo button—so use it.

A case in point: We were writing this chapter and decided to use Direct OCR to bring in the example page "Tpexample.tif" from the back of this book, the one with the three columns of text and a picture. We placed the cursor right here and used Direct OCR. As we had used the format option Retain Flowing Columns, it brought in the text and part of the picture sort of OK, *but* it converted the entire document into three columns. What did we do? We thanked Bill Gates for the Undo button, erased our mistake, and moved on. You can quite often get caught on this if you don't check the format option before acquiring the text. This option is not in OmniPage's options; it is only in the Acquire Text Settings options.

TIP

As a precaution in Word, set a continuous section break before the point at which you want to insert the text. This stops the format of the OCR'd text from reformatting the entire document. It also allows you to Direct OCR multi-column text into a single column text document.

Set the Acquire Text > Format option to Retain Font and Paragraph formatting. This way, all the text you Direct OCR will come in in one column, with the fonts and paragraphs retained. You can then easily change the layout to suit your document.

NOTE

If you Direct OCR text and graphics, only part of the picture might be displayed. This is because the frame of the picture is incorrectly formatted, as seen in Figure 6.5. To fix this, the wrapping of the picture frame needs to be changed. In Word, right-click the picture frame and select Format Picture. The Format Picture dialog box will display (Figure 6.6). Click the Position tab and click the option Float over text, (it will be switched off). Once the Float over text option is set, click the Wrapping tab to indicate how you want the text wrapped around your picture. If you don't select Float over text, all the wrapping options will be grayed out.

Figure 6.5

Only part of the picture is displayed in the frame—the frame needs to be reformatted

Figure 6.6

The Format Picture options in Word—select "Float over text" and your wrapping option

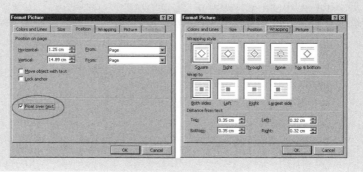

Let's have a quick look at Acquire Text Settings before we do an exercise.

Acquire Text Settings Options

Acquire Text Settings displays four options: OCR, Scanner, Format, and Direct OCR. These options are the same settings as in the Options dialog box of OmniPage, except for Format. If you change the settings here, they are reflected in OmniPage, and vice versa. Please see Chapter 13 on Advanced Configuration for more detail on the OmniPage options and settings.

The Acquire Text Settings option lets you set some of the OmniPage and Direct OCR options before you acquire text. The options panel that displays is similar to the one in OmniPage. To view it, you must be in one of your registered programs, click File, then Acquire Text Settings (Figure 6.7).

Figure 6.7
Acquire Text Settings, showing the format options

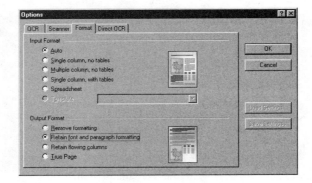

We've shown the Format tab here, as it is the one that will cause the most problems, especially if you are inserting text in the middle of a document. The format option is in two sections. The top half, Input Format, defines the layout of your original document. The lower half, Output Format, defines the format in which the recognized text (and pictures) will be pasted into your document. In each section, there is a graphic that changes when you change the selection of Input Format and Output Format. This is helpful in giving you an idea of what will happen with the recognized text and pictures

Input Format

Input Format defines the layout of the page to be scanned, telling OmniPage how to process the page. They are the same options as the Perform OCR Process options in OmniPage.

► Auto
► Single column, no tables
► Multiple column, no tables
► Single column, with table
► Spreadsheet
► Template

Using Auto is usually the best bet. When you click the other Input Format options, the graphic on the right changes to depict that format. The trick is to choose the correct input and output formats for the document in which you are working. Let's say you are working on a college assignment or management proposal. You are only interested in acquiring the text and headings, because you are going to incorporate them as part of the existing text in your document. In this, set Input Format to Auto and Output Format to Retain Font and Paragraph formatting. When you choose Remove formatting, all the text comes in in one font.

Output Format

Output Format defines the format of the text when it is pasted into your document.

- ▶ Remove formatting
- ▶ Retain Font and Paragraph formatting
- ▶ Retain Flowing Columns
- ▶ True Page

Most of the time, you will find Retain Font and Paragraph format works best, as it does just what it says. It also makes the editing easier in Word. Remove formatting pastes the text in one font, and it is difficult to see where the paragraphs were.

Retain Flowing Columns and True Page can give you problems. As these formats rely on creating columns and frames, they can affect the layout of the existing text and sometimes change the entire format of your document. If you need to keep the style and layout of the existing text, insert a continuous section break (if you're working in Word), before and after the Direct OCR inserted text. This effectively isolates the formatting of the Direct OCR text from the rest of your document. You will also find that when you use these two format settings, the resulting font style and size may not be the same as the original. The text and pictures are inserted in generic RTF (Rich Text Format) and plain text. If the document was scanned in OmniPage and saved as a Word document, it would be formatted as a Word document. You get the best results if the acquired page is the first page of your document. If the text is not how you want, you can use Undo in Word, change the Acquire Text Settings options, then reacquire, or select the acquired text and reformat in Word.

You can also Direct OCR into Excel or other spreadsheet applications. When using Acquire Text into a spreadsheet, manually draw table zones around the tables you want to insert. Always make sure you have enough empty cells in your spreadsheet to accommodate the acquired text table. If not, it will overwrite the contents of existing cells without warning, and with *no* Undo. Direct OCR does not bring in spreadsheet formulas, only the values you can see in the cells.

Try clicking different settings in both Input Formats and Output Formats to see how the graphics change to depict the results.

Other Acquire Text Settings Options:

▶ **OCR**. This has the same options as in OmniPage. They are the languages in your document, user dictionary to use, reject character, OCR method, and font matching. This setting will be the same as you have currently set in OmniPage.

▶ **Scanner**. This shows the same options as in OmniPage for paper size and orientation, ADF, flatbed options, and contrast and brightness.

▶ **Direct OCR**. This shows the process options: Draw Zones Automatically and Proofread. We prefer not to select Draw Zones Automatically, because you can then draw the zones manually before pressing the Perform OCR button. If you don't draw any zones, OmniPage will auto-zone the whole page. This area also has the Image Source option to say whether to load an image file or scan a page from the scanner.

You should have a good idea about Acquire Text now. Experiment with scanning and loading different pages using different Input and Output formats and compare the results. This is the best way to understand how to use it. Let's do an Acquire Text exercise.

Acquire Text Exercises

In these exercises, you will use the Acquire Text function twice on the same document using differing output formats. First, you will acquire text with the Output Format set to Retain Font and Paragraph. Then, you will reacquire the same text using Retain Flowing Columns. This way, you will have firsthand experience with the different output formats. The last part of the exercises shows you how to overcome the problems of Direct OCR reformatting your existing document by using section breaks in Word.

For this exercise, we will use one of the sample files installed with OmniPage: "Sample1_single.tif." It was loaded into C:\My Documents\My Pictures at the time of installation. You can also find it in the appendix. We will use Word as the application.

Make sure you have registered your application or Word (if you need to, go back to the beginning of this chapter to see how to register an application). Launch Word, and open a blank document.

Acquire Text Setting: Retain Font and Paragraph

1. On the Word menu, click File > Acquire Text Settings.
2. Click the Direct OCR tab and deselect Draw Zones Automatically. Click Image source and select image file.
3. Click the Format tab and select the Input Format as Auto and Output Format as Retain Font and Paragraph formatting.
4. Click OK to apply these settings.

Getting the Acquired Text into Your Document

1. On the Word menu, click File and select Acquire Text.

2. In the Load image dialog box, navigate to C:\My Documents\My Pictures and select the file "Sample1_single.tif." As you had deselected Draw Zones Automatically, this page is now loaded into the Direct OCR desktop. If Draw Zones Automatically was selected, this step is bypassed. Now, you can draw zones around the parts of the text you want inserted into your document. But for right now, don't draw any zones.

3. Click Perform OCR.

4. When the OCR Proofreader dialog box opens, just click Close. For this exercise, close the Proofreader each time it is displayed.

The whole page will now be auto-zoned and inserted into your Word document. The document should display as in Figure 6.8. Each paragraph is separated and occupies the width of the page. The headings are bold and the picture and table are in the same order in which OmniPage created the zones.

Figure 6.8
The result in Word
using the format
"Retain Font and
Paragraph"

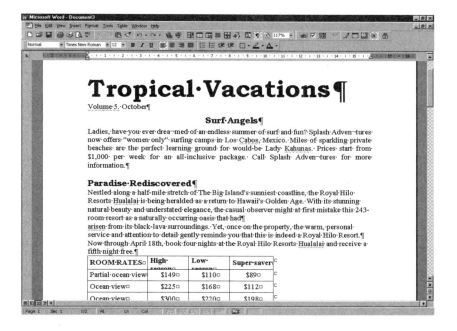

The text may need a bit of fixing up, such as changing the bolding and font size and removing the hyphens from some words. Since OmniPage recognizes characters, and a hyphen is a character, OmniPage reproduces the hyphen. The original document had hyphens on some words that were wrapped over two lines due to the text column width. The text that has just been pasted into your document doesn't need these hyphens.

CHAPTER 6

Notice that the layout is not like the original; this is because you chose Retain Font and Paragraph formatting. Let's now use this document to acquire some more text, and this time use the Retain Flowing Columns format to see what happens. Make sure your cursor is at the end of your document.

The Acquire Text Setting: Retain Flowing Columns

1. On the Word menu, click File, and select Acquire Text Settings.
2. Click the Format tab and select the Input Format as Auto and Output Format as Retain Flowing Columns.
3. Click OK to apply these settings.

Getting the Acquired Text into Your Document

Now, to acquire the text using the format setting Retain Flowing Columns:

1. On the Word menu, click File and select Acquire Text.
2. In the Load image dialog box, navigate to C:\My Documents\My Pictures and select the file "Sample1_single.tif."
3. Click the Perform OCR button.
4. The whole page will now be auto-zoned and inserted into your Word document. The document should display as in Figure 6.9. You may need to scroll up a little to get to the top of the page.

Figure 6.9
The result in Word using format "Retain Flowing Columns"

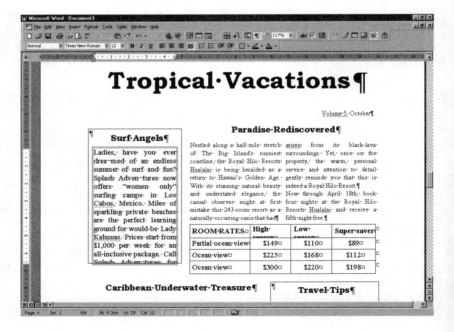

Click in the first paragraph under "Surf Angels;" notice how it has been placed in a frame and not all the text is displayed. Scroll through this page and compare the results with the first acquire. You will find that several paragraphs have been placed in frames. Remember, this can make editing a bit difficult.

Now, scroll to the top of your document and see what this last Acquire Text has done to the first page.

The original page had two columns in it, so the Retain Flowing Columns format has applied that format to the entire document. The beginning of your document should look like Figure 6.10. What a mess!

Figure 6.10
The beginning of the document after it has been reformatted with Acquire Text format "Retain Flowing Columns"

The way to fix it is to insert a section break in Word to isolate the formatting of this block of acquired text from the rest of the existing text.

This is where the Undo tool comes in handy. It works with acquired text in Word but not in Excel. Use the Undo button in Word to undo the pasted acquired text. Now, insert a continuous section break at the end of the first page you first acquired, then repaste the acquired text.

CHAPTER 6

If you are not sure how to insert a continuous section break, do the following:

1. On the Word menu, click Insert > Break.
2. Select Section Breaks, Continuous (Figure 6.11).
3. Click OK to insert.
4. Repaste the acquired text. Click Edit > Paste.

Figure 6.11
Inserting a continuous
section break in Word

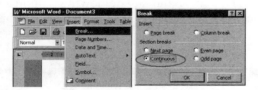

The document will display as shown in Figure 6.12.

The view in Word has been changed to two pages to show the separation of the formatting and to display the last page of the first Acquire Text and the first page of the second Acquire Text.

Notice the section break circled in red. To prevent the Retain Flowing Columns format from affecting the rest of your document, insert another section break at the end of the acquired text.

Figure 6.12
A two-page view in
Word showing the
separation of acquired
text formatting using
section breaks (section
break circled)

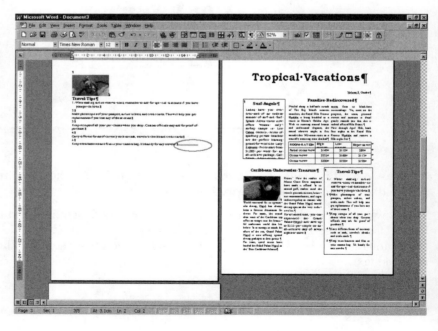

Now you can see how easy it is. Once you've learned how to set up and use Acquire Text, Direct OCR is a very easy and quick way to get the text into your documents. We typically set Direct OCR up with Automatically Draw Zones deselected, the Input Format as Auto, and the Output Format as Retain Font and Paragraph formatting. We rarely have to change these settings.

Now that you know how to use Acquire Text in Word, have a go at acquiring the table from the image file into Excel.

Getting the Acquired Text into Excel

Launch Excel and open a blank spreadsheet. On the Excel menu, click File Acquire Text Settings and set the Output Format back to Retain Font and Paragraph formatting. You will need to do this, since the last exercise left it as Retain Flowing Columns. Click Acquire Text and select the same image file, "Sample1_single.tif." When the page image appears in the Direct OCR desktop, manually draw a zone around the table and set the properties to Table zone. Click the Perform OCR Process button. The table will then be acquired into your Excel spreadsheet.

Did you know that you can OCR image files from within Windows Explorer? Let's take a look.

Using Windows Explorer to OCR Image Files

When OmniPage is installed, a Convert To option is added to the Windows Explorer File menu, shortcut menu, and File Properties. This option is displayed only when a valid OmniPage image file type is selected. This is an easy way to convert images of scanned documents and images, faxes sent by modem, or any image file into Word documents, Excel spreadsheets, and even PDF files.

To see how it works, launch Windows Explorer and navigate to the sample files in C:\My Documents\My Pictures folder, the same folder you used in the Acquire Text exercise. Right-click any of the image files to select the file and select Convert To (Figure 6.13). The conversion options are displayed. Right-click an image file again and select Properties and then the OCR tab. This time, it shows the registered file types to convert to and an Options button. The Options button just gives the OCR setting, language, dictionary, etc., as in Direct OCR, and the format for the input and output options. You can deselect the registered file types, but we leave them all set. The option Launch Application will launch the application associated with the saved file type. For example, utilizing Convert To Microsoft Word Document will launch Word; Adobe Acrobat Document will launch Adobe Acrobat if you have it installed; and Text Document launches Notepad.

When using the Windows Explorer OCR option, the OCR'd file is always saved in the same folder as the image file.

CHAPTER 6

Figure 6.13
The two Windows
Explorer OCR
options—Convert To
and OCR Settings
properties

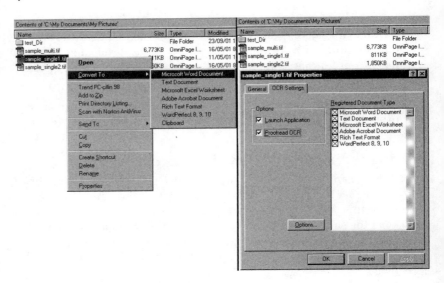

You will find these two features, Convert To and OCR Settings properties, very handy when you want to incorporate text, tables, and pictures from existing paper documents into your own documents.

Myra is currently working on one of her assignments for her diploma. She loves the Direct OCR feature for her assignments. She just scans in class papers from her lecturer in Word, then draws a zone around the text she wants, performs the OCR and, *voilà*, in comes the text. She says this has saved her at least an hour in preparation time, and she still has the skin on her fingers.

Myra says Direct OCR is like having her own personal typist on hand any time of the day or night. Have fun with Direct OCR; it sure saves you time.

7

Tables and Spreadsheets

OmniPage's table feature is great for scanning prices, product and parts lists, telephone bills, schedules, and documents containing tables—in fact, any documents that have tables or that look like a list. OmniPage has powerful table tools on the Image toolbar to handle those spreadsheets and tables and will automatically detect and recognize both. The Table buttons are used to edit the grid lines of tables and spreadsheets. You can also use the Table tool buttons to turn columns of text and numbers into a table, draw gridlines on a page of text that does not have a table, and change the layout and formats of columns and rows. The table feature makes it easy to get data into a database. After scanning the document, you save it as an Excel spreadsheet. From there, you can import straight into your database.

To show what a real difference scanning tables can make on a practical level, consider the experience of one of our clients, a police investigation department. This particular police department was in the habit of keying long lists of phone numbers into a spreadsheet in order to analyze the relationships among the numbers—to see who had called whom. After we taught them how to scan the lists of numbers and import them into their spreadsheet, one officer told us that it would save them over three weeks on one particular investigation.

In this chapter, we will first learn what OmniPage means by "table format." Next, we'll scan a sample document and look at the results. Then, we will look at the Table tools in detail and see how they are used within table zones to define rows and columns. We'll then save the document as an Excel spreadsheet and Word document. We'll also look at some ways to jazz up your tables in OmniPage by adding color and gridlines. Finally, we'll run through an exercise in Excel to replace the leading zeros that do not display when saved as an Excel file.

We will illustrate the concepts in this chapter using a telephone bill (Figure 7.1). The file name is "Phone.tif," and you will find it in the appendix or it can be downloaded from the Web site (see Introduction).

Figure 7.1
Document "phone"

10 Aug	01:05 pm	Mobile	015435482	Peak		0:21	0.25
12 Aug	10:02 am	Mobile	018259253	Peak		0:37	0.25
17 Aug	12:15 pm	Mobile	018415485	Peak		0:35	0.25
17 Aug	01:27 pm	Mobile	018865586	Peak		2:35	1.00
17 Aug	02:53 pm	Mobile	018415485	Peak		0:27	0.25
22 Aug	09:14 am	Mobile	015230053	Peak		0:51	0.50
22 Aug	11:31 am	Mobile	018265761	Peak		1:24	0.75
22 Aug	02:56 pm	Mobile	018415485	Peak		0:32	0.25
26 Aug	09:07 am	Mobile	018617249	Peak		0:44	0.50
26 Aug	01:34 pm	Mobile	018415866	Peak		0:42	0.50
29 Aug	10:11 am	Mobile	018969363	Peak		0:29	0.25
30 Aug	12:30 pm	Mobile	015431007	Peak		2:34	1.00
30 Aug	12:54 pm	Mobile	018044682	Peak		11:03	4.50
30 Aug	04:14 pm	Mobile	018153040	Peak		0:26	0.25
31 Aug	12:21 pm	Mobile	018256063	Peak		0:19	0.25
31 Aug	12:45 pm	Mobile	018256063	Peak		0:32	0.25
31 Aug	02:27 pm	Mobile	018617249	Peak		0:31	0.25
31 Aug	03:02 pm	Mobile	018617249	Peak		1:27	0.75
05 Sep	02:12 pm	Mobile	018969363	Peak		0:48	0.50
05 Sep	02:59 pm	Mobile	018212472	Peak		0:30	0.25
05 Sep	03:17 pm	Mobile	018212472	Peak		4:04	1.75
05 Sep	04:34 pm	Mobile	018617249	Peak		0:43	0.50
Telephone Service 02-957 2674							
10 Aug	12:08 pm	Mobile	015435482	Peak		1:00	0.50
23 Aug	10:23 am	Mobile	018617249	Peak		0:20	0.25
31 Aug	04:49 pm	Mobile	018293791	Peak		4:38	2.00
01 Sep	10:22 am	Mobile	018617249	Peak		1:35	0.75
05 Sep	03:06 pm	Mobile	018617249	Peak		0:23	0.25
Telephone Service 02-957 2713							
24 Aug	11:46 am	Mobile	018278366	Peak		0:44	0.50

Continued page 5

Working with Tables and Spreadsheets

To determine whether the document you are about to scan is in table format or contains a table, look to see whether an entry or text in one column is related to an entry or text on the same line(s) in an adjacent column. For example, in a price list, the product is "related" to the price on the same line in the adjacent column. Conversely, in a newspaper, the text in a column is not "related" to the text on the same line in the adjacent column. If the text is related, then this is a job for the table function. The table function works by identifying the layout of the text, ensuring that when OmniPage detects this layout (and you have selected a Perform OCR option that detects tables), the table is recognized and formatted correctly.

If, instead, you describe the original as Multiple column no table, or draw a multiple-column zone and set the view layout in the Text Editor view to Retain Flowing Columns, the data will be split into unrelated separate columns. Using the example "Phone," OmniPage would separate the first three columns with tabs and bring it into Word as one column. The next three columns are divided up and display in three separate frames in Word, making it a mess to edit (Figures 7.2 and 7.3). Exporting to an Excel spreadsheet is no better. So, with documents such as the ones shown in this chapter, you must always choose the Describe Original option setting as Spreadsheet, or use one of the Perform OCR settings that detects tables.

Figure 7.2
Results of choosing the incorrect Perform OCR option to scan a table

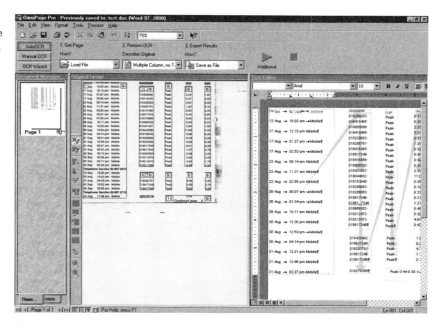

Figure 7.3
Results of choosing the incorrect Perform OCR option to scan a spreadsheet and export to Excel

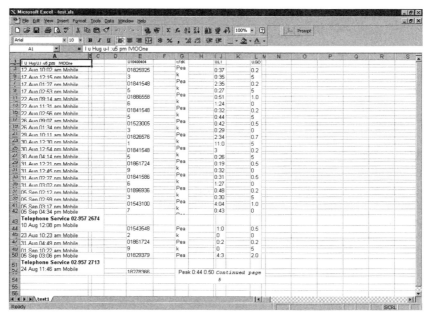

Two Ways to Scan a Table

There are basically two ways to set up scanning for a table.

Entire Document is a Spreadsheet

If all the pages within your document are tabulated or laid out like a spreadsheet, use the Spreadsheet setting in the Perform OCR option. OmniPage will automatically draw a table zone around the entire page. It places the Table Identifier icon in the top right-hand corner of the table zone. See Figure 7.4 below.

Figure 7.4
The file "phone" with Describe Original set to Spreadsheet using the AutoOCR toolbox

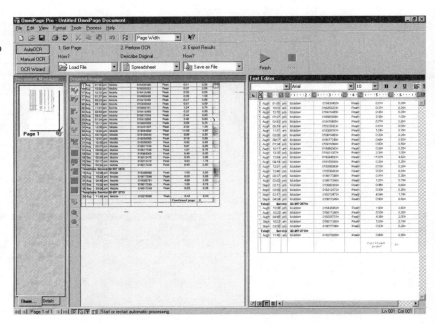

Multi-Layout Document with a Table

If your document is a multi-layout document—for example, if it has multiple columns or graphics or other text not in a table and contains a spreadsheet or table—set Perform OCR to Automatic or use a setting that detects tables. You may need to draw manual zones or use a template. Check that OmniPage has correctly identified the tables; see Figure 7.5.

NOTE
Table zones can only be rectangular and square. Attempting to modify the area of a table zone to an irregular shape is not permitted. If you change an irregular zone's type to Table, it will snap to a rectangle.

Figure 7.5

The file "tptable" with a table zone manually drawn around the table with Perform OCR set to Automatic

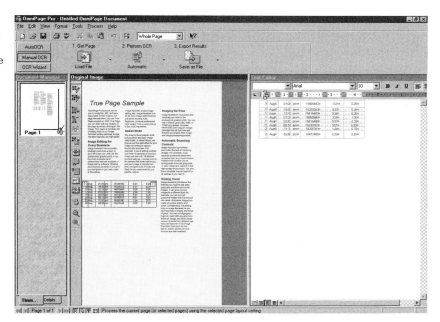

Let's scan the telephone bill and save it as a spreadsheet. This entire document can be treated as a spreadsheet, since it is only one page and the table occupies the whole page; i.e., there is no other text.

Setting Options for Document Type

Before you scan any document, always look at the document layout and change the OmniPage settings to best suit that document. Since the telephone bill takes up the entire page, you could call it a spreadsheet; set Perform OCR to Spreadsheet and you will get a good result. The telephone bill could also be scanned with the option Single Column Text with Table or as Auto, and you will get the same good result. The only difference will be the location in the saved document of the text "continued page 5" at the bottom of the table. Using the Spreadsheet option, it will be included in the table and appear on the right-hand side; with Automatic and Single Column Text with Table, it will be in a separate text zone and will appear on the left-hand side.

When you scan the telephone bill, use all three options of Perform OCR to see the difference. Remember, you do not need to rescan the page, just change the Perform OCR option and reprocess the page.

Select the Options in the Three Processing Buttons

1. Click AutoOCR button (Figure 7.6).
2. Click the down-pointing arrow of Get Page. Select Scan B&W (or Load Image).
3. Click the down-pointing arrow of Perform OCR. Describe original as Spreadsheet.
4. Click the down-pointing arrow of Export Results. Select Save As.

Figure 7.6
AutoOCR toolbox and
Perform OCR selected
as Spreadsheet

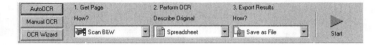

NOTE

Remember that choosing the Spreadsheet option will zone all pages in your document as a spreadsheet.

If you scan the same document every month and the only thing that changes is the data, you can create a template or custom layout to use again and again. This saves you going through and selecting all the settings each time.

TIP

Creating a custom layout is easy. Try out some of these options on some of your documents that contain tables or are spreadsheets. If you want more specific zoning and different types of zones, use zone templates.

After determining what your original document layout is, click the AB Options button. Then, click the Custom Layout tab (Figure 7.7). In Table, click one of the following for:

No Tables

Choose this to have all text areas treated as flowing text. Use it even if there is a table in the original and you want to keep its text, but you do not want it treated as a table. That means it will not be placed in a grid; the text may be kept in columns, or it may just flow, allowing you to reformat it as you wish.

One Table

The program will try to detect a table on each page. If it finds tabular data, in the Text Editor view, the data will be placed in a grid. You can choose whether it should be exported in the grid or transformed to columns separated by tabs by choosing the Layout view after processing.

Auto

Choose this to let the program auto-detect tables. Use it for pages with more than one table and for documents containing some tables, but not on all pages.

Finally, click Save Settings and give your OmniPage settings a name. Click OK. When you want to use the custom layout, simply click Load Settings and select the appropriate one.

Figure 7.7
Option Setting Custom
Layout for Tables

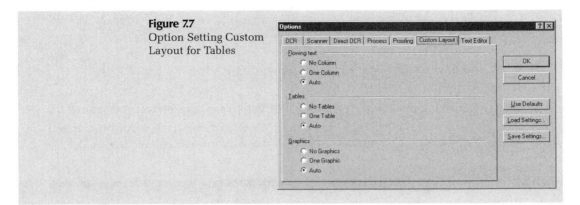

OmniPage is great at removing stray shading from photocopied documents or colored backgrounds from computer paper printouts. The document "Phone" you are using for this exercise has been photocopied and has shading down the right-hand side of the page. You will notice that when you scan it, the shading is not included in the table zone when using Auto or Single Column. It will be included in the Spreadsheet option, as OmniPage treats the entire page as a table zone and assumes that any black could be a character. The quality of the photocopy is good, so there is no need to scan in grayscale.

The Scanning Process

Now that you've set up the options, it's time to try scanning a spreadsheet. Save the results first as an Excel spreadsheet and then as a Word document. Remember to try using the other two Perform OCR option settings: Auto and Single Column Text with Table.

1. Click the Start button. The original image appears on the Original Image view and thumbnail.

2. The spreadsheet/table is identified, and a table zone is drawn around it. Notice the row and column dividers around the cells. You will see the table zone identifier in the top right-hand corner of the table zone.

3. There is no proofreading to be done on this document, as it did not find any errors.

4. The Save As dialog box pops up (Figure 7.8).

Figure 7.8
Save As dialog box
with Excel file format
selected

5. In the Save In field, click the down-pointing arrow and choose your training directory.
6. In the File name field, type "Phone."
7. In Save as Type, click the down-pointing arrow and select Excel 97.
8. Click OK.
9. Excel launches, and the phone bill displays as a spreadsheet (Figure 7.9).
10. Re-export the results and save as a Word document. Click Additional and select Export document. Again, save as a Word document: "phone.doc."

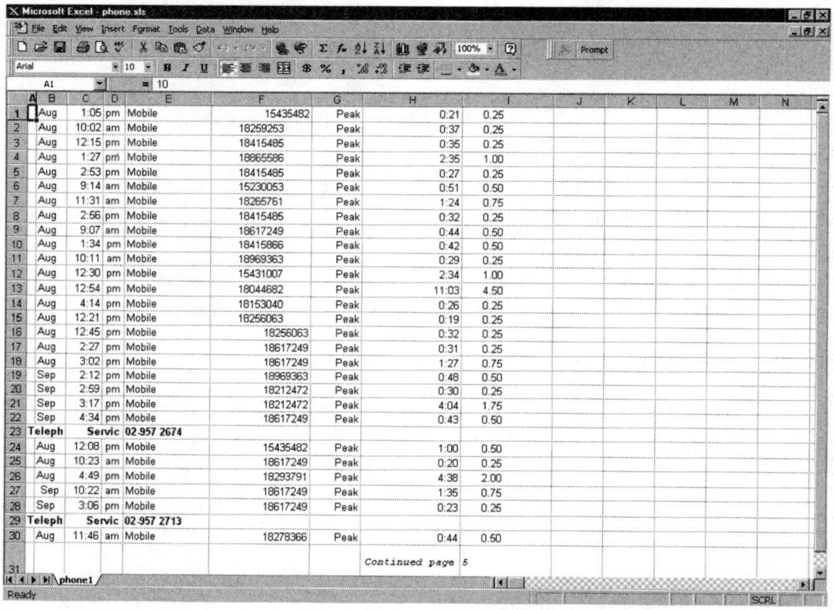

	A	B	C	D	E	F	G	H	I
1		Aug	1:05	pm	Mobile	15435482	Peak	0:21	0.25
2		Aug	10:02	am	Mobile	18259253	Peak	0:37	0.25
3		Aug	12:15	pm	Mobile	18415485	Peak	0:35	0.25
4		Aug	1:27	pm	Mobile	18865586	Peak	2:35	1.00
5		Aug	2:53	pm	Mobile	18415485	Peak	0:27	0.25
6		Aug	9:14	am	Mobile	15230053	Peak	0:51	0.50
7		Aug	11:31	am	Mobile	18265761	Peak	1:24	0.75
8		Aug	2:56	pm	Mobile	18415485	Peak	0:32	0.25
9		Aug	9:07	am	Mobile	18617249	Peak	0:44	0.50
10		Aug	1:34	pm	Mobile	18415866	Peak	0:42	0.50
11		Aug	10:11	am	Mobile	18969363	Peak	0:29	0.25
12		Aug	12:30	pm	Mobile	15431007	Peak	2:34	1.00
13		Aug	12:54	pm	Mobile	18044682	Peak	11:03	4.50
14		Aug	4:14	pm	Mobile	18153040	Peak	0:26	0.25
15		Aug	12:21	pm	Mobile	18256063	Peak	0:19	0.25
16		Aug	12:45	pm	Mobile	18256063	Peak	0:32	0.25
17		Aug	2:27	pm	Mobile	18617249	Peak	0:31	0.25
18		Aug	3:02	pm	Mobile	18617249	Peak	1:27	0.75
19		Sep	2:12	pm	Mobile	18969363	Peak	0:48	0.50
20		Sep	2:59	pm	Mobile	18212472	Peak	0:30	0.25
21		Sep	3:17	pm	Mobile	18212472	Peak	4:04	1.75
22		Sep	4:34	pm	Mobile	18617249	Peak	0:43	0.50
23	**Teleph**		**Servic**		**02 957 2674**				
24		Aug	12:08	pm	Mobile	15435482	Peak	1:00	0.50
25		Aug	10:23	am	Mobile	18617249	Peak	0:20	0.25
26		Aug	4:49	pm	Mobile	18293791	Peak	4:38	2.00
27		Sep	10:22	am	Mobile	18617249	Peak	1:35	0.75
28		Sep	3:06	pm	Mobile	18617249	Peak	0:23	0.25
29	**Teleph**		**Servic**		**02 957 2713**				
30		Aug	11:46	am	Mobile	18278366	Peak	0:44	0.50
31								Continued page	5

Figure 7.9
Saved Excel file, "Phone.xls," with Text Editor view set to "Retain Font and Paragraph"

Let's look at the saved results in the Excel spreadsheet. You will see that the alignment in Column E is off slightly, and the leading zeros have been dropped from the telephone numbers. The date and time fields have been split up and the text "Continued Page 5" is on the right. At the end of this chapter, we'll learn how to put the zeros back on the numbers. There are no borders around the cells. When we look at improving the look of the table later in this chapter, we'll go back to OmniPage and put them on. You can, of course, put them on in Excel.

Now, go back to OmniPage and try the other options. Change Perform OCR to Automatic and click the Additional button to reprocess the page. You will get a series of prompts. Select Reprocess All Pages, Discard Current Zones and Find New Zones, and save as an Excel file named "phone1." Then, repeat using the Single Column Text with Table option and save as "phone2."

Look at the differences in the three options. When using Spreadsheet, there is only one table zone on the page. The other two options have made the table zone smaller (not included the shading) and made a separate text zone for "Continued Page 5." The results in Excel are also slightly different, as the date and time fields have not been split, nor have the phone number headings, and the text "Continued Page 5" is on the left.

NOTE

Any formatting you do in OmniPage may not automatically transfer to the application you are exporting it to. This depends on that application's formatting capabilities.

Now that we have scanned and OCR'd our spreadsheet/table, let's look at the Table tools and how you can use them to redefine the row and column dividers.

The Table Toolbar

Now that we've scanned the telephone bill, let's take a look at how to spruce up your results using the Table toolbar. The purpose of the Table toolbar is to redraw and move the row and column dividers to reformat the table the way you want it. The Table tools will delete and insert individual row and column dividers, delete and replace all row and column dividers, move row and column dividers, and delete and insert individual cell column dividers. When using the Table tools, you don't have to place row dividers on every line. You could, for example, use the tools to place blocks of text into a table; i.e., to break up a report or tabulate survey results.

As you can see in Figure 7.10, when you used the Spreadsheet option, OmniPage drew column dividers between the day and month, the time, and a.m. and p.m. The text of the Telephone Service number has been split over several table cells. You fix this using the Table tools. You move, resize, join, or divide row and column dividers to determine where gridlines will appear. You should move, resize, or modify the table zone's shape before drawing dividers, because all dividers are removed if a table zone is altered in any way.

1. On the task bar, click Excel and close the application without saving any changes.

2. On the task bar, click OmniPage to make it the active window.

3. So that you can see more of the Original Image view to work with, switch off the Text Editor view using the toolbar. Click View > Text Editor or slide the window divider to the right.

Now you are ready to work with the Table tools. Before you do, however, let's look at the buttons and what they do.

Figure 7.10
The file "phone" with
cell dividers in the
wrong places in the
Original Image view

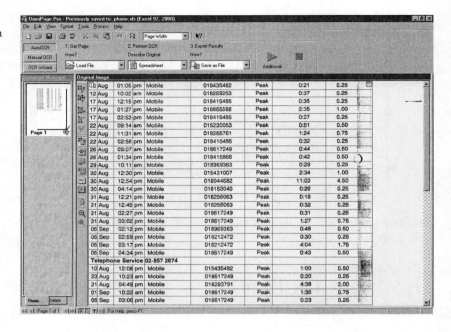

The Table Toolbar Buttons

The Table tools are located just below the Zone tools in the Original Image View on the Image toolbar. They remain grayed out until you have a document with a table zone. The Table buttons only work in table zones. Click the button to select the function you want. Remember to click the Draw Regular Zones button when you have finished. The toolbar is like a pushbutton radio that stays on the station until you manually change it. If you leave the Table tool button selected, you won't be able to select other zones on the page or draw zones, and you may accidentally draw or delete dividers.

TIP

If you have been manually drawing rows and columns and want to start again, use Remove/Replace All Row Column Dividers to quickly delete and redraw all rows and columns.

Table 7.1
The Table Toolbar

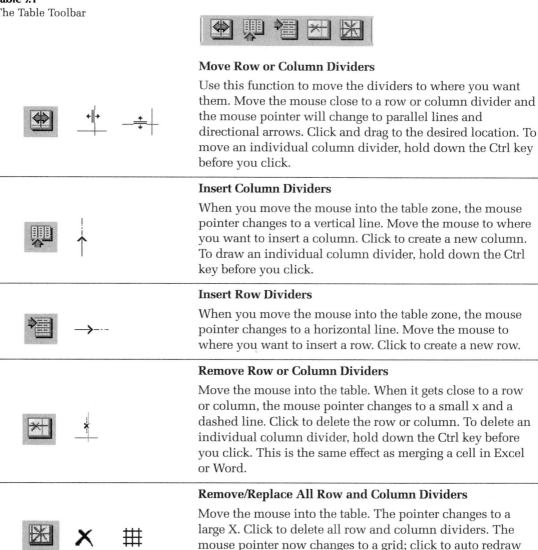

Move Row or Column Dividers

Use this function to move the dividers to where you want them. Move the mouse close to a row or column divider and the mouse pointer will change to parallel lines and directional arrows. Click and drag to the desired location. To move an individual column divider, hold down the Ctrl key before you click.

Insert Column Dividers

When you move the mouse into the table zone, the mouse pointer changes to a vertical line. Move the mouse to where you want to insert a column. Click to create a new column. To draw an individual column divider, hold down the Ctrl key before you click.

Insert Row Dividers

When you move the mouse into the table zone, the mouse pointer changes to a horizontal line. Move the mouse to where you want to insert a row. Click to create a new row.

Remove Row or Column Dividers

Move the mouse into the table. When it gets close to a row or column, the mouse pointer changes to a small x and a dashed line. Click to delete the row or column. To delete an individual column divider, hold down the Ctrl key before you click. This is the same effect as merging a cell in Excel or Word.

Remove/Replace All Row and Column Dividers

Move the mouse into the table. The pointer changes to a large X. Click to delete all row and column dividers. The mouse pointer now changes to a grid; click to auto redraw all rows and columns.

CHAPTER 7

Moving the Table Tools on the Image Toolbar

You can move the Table toolbar up to the standard toolbar area. This will give you more space in your Original Image view and it will make it easier to zoom in to edit the dividers.

1. To grab the toolbar, click the light gray horizontal line that divides the buttons.
2. Hold left mouse button and drag to the top of the Original Image view.
3. Horizontal viewing makes it easier to see the tool buttons.

Zoom in the Original Image View

1. Position the mouse pointer in the table.
2. Click with the right mouse button.
3. Select Zoom.
4. Click 50%.

Remove/Replace all Row and Column Dividers

Figure 7.12
Remove/Replace All Row and Column Dividers button

1. Click Remove/Replace All Row & Column Dividers (Figure 7.12).
2. Position the mouse in the table zone. The mouse pointer changes to a large X.
3. Click the left mouse button. All the dividers are removed. The mouse pointer changes to a grid box.
4. Click again and all the dividers are redrawn. Try a few times for practice.

For the next exercise, make sure row and column dividers are removed. This way, you have a blank table on which to draw the row dividers where you like.

Insert Row Dividers

Use Insert Row Dividers to divide your table into rows. You can have one row per line as in the phone bill, or you could just draw rows to keep the calls for each phone number together; that way, you can have multiple lines of text in a table cell.

Make sure there are no column or row dividers on the table.

Figure 7.13
Insert Row Dividers

1. Click Insert Row Dividers (Figure 7.13).
2. Move the mouse pointer into the table; it changes to a sideways V and a horizontal line to show where it will be drawn.
3. Position the mouse where you want the row divider and click to draw it.
4. Move the mouse to another row where you want another row divider, and click to draw it.
5. When finished splitting the table, select Draw Regular Zones to stop drawing. Otherwise, when you click you will accidentally draw another row.

Insert Column Dividers

Use Insert Column Divider to divide your table into columns. In this phone bill, we will keep all the columns separate. We could, however, have the date, time, and the text "mobile" in one column, and the phone numbers, cost, and duration in separate columns. You can place the columns where you want them to tabulate or format your table for the information you need.

Figure 7.14
Insert Column Dividers

1. Click Insert Column Dividers (Figure 7.14).
2. Move the mouse into the table; the pointer changes to an inverted V and a vertical line to show where the divider will be drawn.
3. Position the pointer where you want the new column divider and click to draw.
4. Position the pointer where you want the next column divider and click to draw.
5. When finished splitting the table, select Draw Regular Zones to stop drawing.

NOTE
To avoid a blank column on the left and right side of the table, do not draw a column on the left and right side of the table.

Insert an Individual Cell Column Divider

This is a really neat function—by using the Control key, you can insert or remove the column divider of just one cell. It is like splitting cells in Excel and Word. You can see how this works by placing the pointer between two rows, then holding down the Control key. Notice that now, instead of the mouse pointer having a line stretching from the top to the bottom of the table, it is just between the two row dividers where the mouse is located.

1. Click Insert Column Dividers (Figure 7.14).
2. Hold down the Control key.
3. Place the mouse pointer (the inverted V) where you want the cell divider; a small vertical line will show between the row dividers.
4. Click the left mouse button.
5. Try this between some other row dividers. Create more row dividers if needed.

Move Row or Column Dividers

Sometimes, the row and column dividers are just not quite in the right place. Rather than deleting and redrawing them, just move them to where you need them. This button allows you to move either row or column, depending on which one you have selected. Make sure you have completed the steps above, so you have some row and column dividers to move. Click Move Row or Column Dividers (Figure 7.15).

Figure 7.15
Move Row or Column
Dividers

Change the Row Height

1. Move the mouse over a row divider.
2. The mouse pointer changes to parallel lines and two arrows.
3. Click and hold the left mouse button.
4. Drag to new position and release the mouse button.

Change the Column Width

1. Move the mouse over a column divider.
2. The mouse pointer changes to parallel lines and two arrows.
3. Click and hold the left mouse button.
4. Drag to new position and release the mouse button.

Change the Column Width of an Individual Cell

This is done using the Control key, just as you did for drawing individual column dividers. Remember: It only works for columns.

1. Hold down the Control key.
2. Place the mouse pointer on the cell's column divider.
3. Click and hold the left mouse button and drag to new location.

Remove Row or Column Dividers

Use this button to delete row or column dividers and the Control key to remove the column divider from one cell.

Figure 7.16
Remove Row or
Column Dividers

1. Click the Remove Row or Column Dividers button (Figure 7.16).
2. The mouse pointer changes to a small *x* when close to a row or column divider.
3. Position the mouse on a divider and click to remove. This removes the entire row or column divider.

You can also remove a column divider for an individual cell. When you used the Control key to draw individual cell columns, you could see the drawing line change when you held the key down. The same happens here, although it is harder to see. The column line that is to be deleted dims slightly. When you hold the Control key down, you can just see the selected column divider dim.

This is like merging cells in Word or Excel.

1. Hold down the Control key.
2. Place the mouse pointer on the cell's column divider and click to delete.

That's enough practice for now on the Table tools. Next, let's fix up our telephone bill.

Fixing the Phone Bill Table

You have seen how easy it is to use the Table tools to divide up your table, and also how to fix it if OmniPage has miscalculated where it has drawn dividers.

First, we need to set back on all the row and column dividers that OmniPage automatically calculated so that the document is set for this exercise, as if it had just been scanned.

Set the Perform OCR option to Spreadsheet, and click the Additional button to reprocess the page; tell OmniPage to discard current zones and find new ones. You will have noticed that when you used Remove and Replace All Dividers, the additional column dividers between the date and time disappear. This is another quick way to improve the alignment of the row and column dividers. OmniPage sometimes does a better job when you remove and replace all dividers.

Remove Column Dividers from Date and Time Columns

Notice how the words "Telephone Service" and the date and time have been spread over several cells (Figure 7.17)?

Let's fix this up.

Figure 7.17
Cell dividers in wrong positions

05	Sep	03:17	pm	Mobile
05	Sep	04:34	pm	Mobile
Telephone Service				02-957 2674
10	Aug	12:08	pm	Mobile
23	Aug	10:23	am	Mobile
31	Aug	04:49	pm	Mobile
01	Sep	10:22	am	Mobile
05	Sep	03:06	pm	Mobile

1. Click Remove Row or Column Dividers.
2. Move the mouse pointer to the divider between the date and the month.
3. Left-click to remove the column divider.
4. Move the mouse pointer to the divider between the time and the a.m./p.m.
5. Left-click to remove the column divider.
6. Repeat to remove all remaining portions of dividers in the date and time columns.

NOTE

If the column dividers do not go the full height of the table, only the selected portion of the divider is removed.

Remove the Column Dividers in the Middle of the Text "Telephone Service"

1. Click Remove Row or Column Dividers.
2. Move the mouse pointer to the column cell divider between the "o" and the "n" of "Telephone Service."
3. Hold down the Control key.
4. Left-click to remove.
5. Repeat to remove the divider between "Service" and the phone number.
6. Do this again for the one below.

Now, reprocess the table with the new dividers and see what happens when you select different format views and how these affect the saved Word document.

Reprocess the Table with the New Dividers

When reprocessing the page this time, use the Zoning Instructions option Use only Current Zones, which contains all the new dividers you have drawn. If you choose one of the other options, you will lose the dividers you have drawn and will have to start again. Once you have reprocessed the page, change the format view settings in the Text Editor and save to see the difference each format makes in Word.

The Zoning Instructions prompt when reprocessing the page will appear when you have selected the option Find Zones in Addition to Template/Current in the Process panel of Tools > Options or the AB (Options) button on the toolbar.

1. Click the Additional button.
2. Click Reprocess All Pages.
3. Use only current zones.

Saving as Different Document Formats

Compare the results of saving our table as a Word document using two of the format views in the Text Editor. First, you will save it using Retain Flowing Columns. Remember that this will place the table in a frame; True Page will do the same. Then, you will save it using the Retain Font and Paragraph format. Compare the results when you have finished.

Saving Using Retain Flowing Columns

1. In the Text Editor view, click Retain Flowing Columns view button (bottom left-hand corner of the Text Editor view).
2. Click Additional button on toolbox. The Automatic Processing box pops up.

3. Click Export Document again.

4. The Save As dialog box pops us.

5. Make sure you are still in your "training" directory.

6. Type in the File name field: "phone2."

7. In the Save as Type field, click the down-pointing arrow and select Word 97.

Word launches and the table is in a frame at the top of the page, making editing extremely awkward (Figure 7.18).

Figure 7.18
The file "phone" with Text Editor view layout set to "Retain Flowing Columns"—it exports with a frame

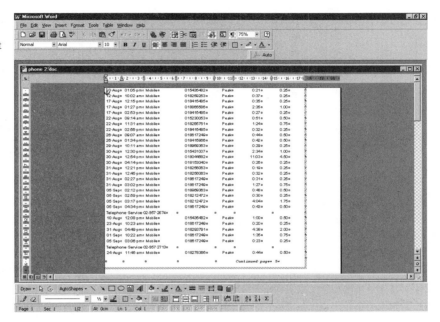

Next, we will go back to OmniPage and change the layout to Retain Font and Paragraph.

Saving Using Retain Font and Paragraph

1. On the task bar, click OmniPage to make it the active window.

2. In the Text Editor view, click the Retain Font and Paragraph layout button.

3. On the toolbox, click Additional.

4. The Automatic Processing box pops up.

5. Click Export Document Again.

6. The Save As dialog box pops up.

7. Type in the File name field: "phone3."

Word launches and the table is now in a format that you can easily work with.

Figure 7.19
The file"phone" with
Text Editor view layout
set to "Retain Font and
Paragraph"

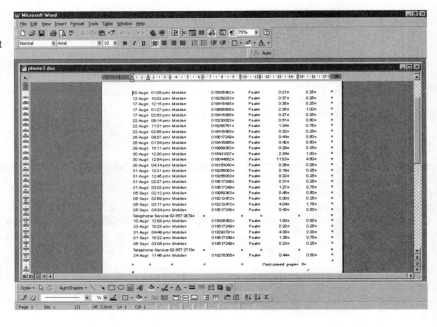

Table Borders and Gridlines

Now, let's go back to OmniPage and introduce a quick way to display table borders and gridlines. OmniPage saved the table in Word as a table, but you can't see the gridlines of the table. You have just drawn all the row and column dividers in OmniPage, so why not have OmniPage export the table with gridlines? If you want to display the gridlines you can, of course, format them in Word.

OmniPage refers to the line outside the table as the "border," while "gridlines" are inside the table.

1. On the task bar, click OmniPage to make it the active window.
2. In the Original Image view, right-click in the table.
3. The table grays out and is selected. The shortcut menu pops up (Figure 7.20).

Figure 7.20
Zone Border and Grid
settings

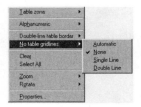

4.   Click Automatic Table Border. Click Double Line.

5.   Right-click again. Click Automatic Table Gridlines. Click Single Line.

6.   On the toolbox, click Additional.

7.   The Automatic Processing box pops up.

8.   Click Export Document Again.

9.   The Save As dialog box pops up.

10. Type in the File name field: "phone4."

Figure 7.21
Table Borders and
Gridlines

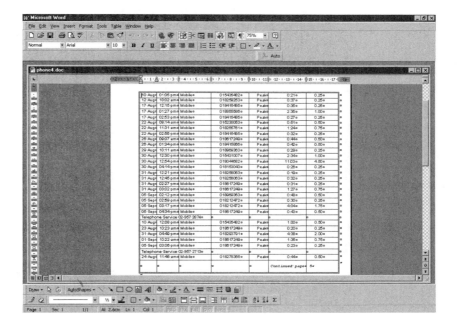

Word launches and the table now has a border and grid lines on the table (Figure 7.21).

Jazz Up Your Table

Now that you have the layout and format of your table as you want, let's take a quick look at how you can use the Text Editor to jazz up your table with font size, color, and cell alignment.

Any formatting you do in OmniPage may not automatically transfer to the application to which you are exporting it. This depends on that application's formatting capabilities, as we will see shortly by saving our document to both Word and Excel. On the task bar, click OmniPage to make it the active window. In the Text Editor view, you can do all the formatting available in OmniPage. In OmniPage, you can also select the cell alignments so the data is at the top, middle, or bottom of the cell.

In this exercise, we will select ten rows from the table and format them with a 1.5-point navy border, then save as an Excel spreadsheet and as a Word document, and look at how the border format has been applied.

NOTE
Sometimes, OmniPage does not get the alignment of the cells perfect. You may have to make some adjustments when you export the document. If you want the alignment of cells to be exported as in the Original Image, use No Formatting in the Text Editor view. Any formatting you do in the Text Editor view will not be saved in the output document. You will then need to format the document in the application you export to.

Selecting Cells in OmniPage

Let's select the cells to format with the navy border. You select cells just as you would in Excel or Word, by clicking and dragging.

1. Click in the Text Editor view to make it the active view, and zoom to 50%. You may want to slide the window divider bar to make the Text Editor window larger.

2. To highlight part of the spreadsheet or table, click in the cell at the top left of the cells to highlight. For this exercise, highlight ten rows.

3. Left-click, hold, and drag ten rows down and across to the last column, to the bottom right cell to be highlighted.

4. The selected cells become black (Figure 7.22).

Figure 7.22
The file "phone" with ten rows highlighted in the Text Editor view

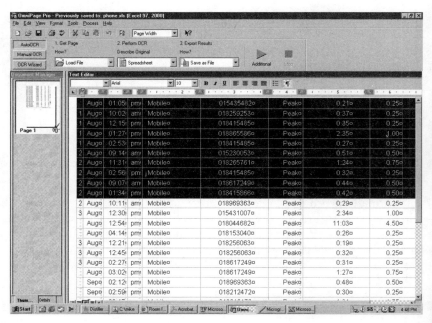

Set the Borders and Background Properties of the Cells

Here, you access the borders and background properties of the selected table cells. You can set the style, width, and color of the gridlines around the selected cell(s) and their background color. You can choose to apply the formatting to the selected cell(s) or to the entire table.

1. With the mouse pointer still in the selected cells, right-click for the shortcut menu.
2. Click Borders and Background.
3. The Borders and Background dialog box pops up (Figure 7.23). Now, you can select the style, width, and color of line, and which lines you want drawn, (i.e., top, side, or middle). You can choose whether to border the entire spreadsheet/table or selected cell(s).

Figure 7.23
Borders and
Background dialog box

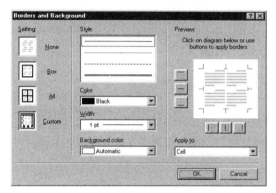

4. In Settings, click All.
5. In the Color box, select Navy.
6. In the Width box, select one and a half.
7. Leave Background Color as Automatic.
8. In the Apply To field, make sure Cell is selected.
9. Now, because you have selected a color after you selected Settings to Cell, you will have to click All again to set the color and width changes.
10. Click OK to accept the changes.

Because three views are displayed, it is hard to see any changes, so close the Original Image view. The Text Editor now shows the changes we have made to the cells (Figure 7.24), and when saved as a Word document, the table is displayed as in Figure 7.25.

CHAPTER 7

Figure 7.24
Changes to cells in
spreadsheet in the
Text Editor view

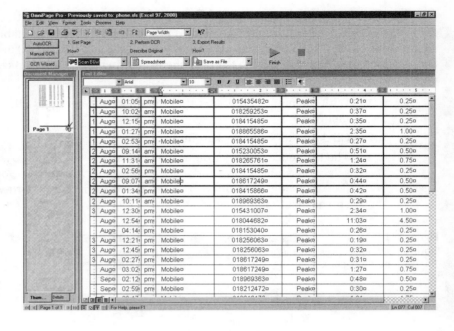

Figure 7.25
Font color, shading,
and backgrounds saved
and exported to Word

1	Aug¤	10:02¡	am	Mobile¤	018259253¤
1	Aug¤	12:15¡	pm	Mobile¤	018415485¤
1	Aug¤	01:27¡	pm	Mobile¤	018865586¤
1	Aug¤	02:53¡	pm	Mobile¤	018415485¤
2	Aug¤	09:14¡	am	Mobile¤	015230053¤
2	Aug¤	11:31¡	am	Mobile¤	018265761¤
2	Aug¤	02:56	pm	Mobile¤	018415485¤
2	Aug¤	09:07¡	am	Mobile¤	018617249¤
2	Aug¤	01:34¡	pm	Mobile¤	018415866¤
2	Aug¤	10:11¡	am	Mobile¤	018969363¤
3	Aug¤	12:30¡	pm	Mobile¤	015431007¤

CHAPTER 7

NOTE

The background color of a table can be retained only if the whole table has the same background color. Retaining the background color of different-colored cells within a table is not supported. To select the retain background color option: On the menu, click the AB options button, click the Process tab (Figure 7.26), then click Retain Text and Background Color to switch on or off.

Figure 7.26
Options setting to "Retain Text and Background Color"

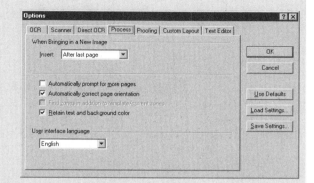

You can change the color of the text, the background, the cell, or the table background in the Text Editor view via the menu by selecting Format Font or Format Borders and Background.

Using Font and Background Color

Font Color

Use this to choose a color for the selected text. Use the Text Editor view to edit cells and fonts. Just highlight the text in the cell. On the menu, click Format, then Font. Click Font Color. The Automatic setting is the default; it means the color defined in your Windows Control Panel. By default, font color is black. Click the down-pointing arrow and select a color you want. Then, click OK. To shade the text and not the cell, you need to select Font Background Color.

Background Color

On the menu, click Format > Font > Background Color. You can also change or remove a background color. The setting Automatic is the default. By default, background color is white. Just click the down-pointing arrow and select the color of your choice. Click OK.

Borders and Background

Highlight the cell, cells, or table. To shade the entire table, you do not need to highlight. On the menu, click Format > Borders and Background. Click Background Color. Click the down-pointing arrow and choose the color you want. In the Apply To field, click the down-pointing arrow and select Cell or Table. Click OK.

Reprocess the Page and Save with New Formatting

Now that you have applied the formatting to your table, we will now resave the page with the new formatting as an Excel spreadsheet, then as a Word document.

1. On the AutoOCR toolbox, click the Finish button.
2. The Automatic Processing box appears (Figure 7.27).

Figure 7.27
Auto Processing box to finish processing

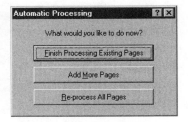

3. Click Finish Processing Existing Pages.
4. The Save As dialog box appears.
5. Click "phone.xls." We will copy over the last save.
6. Click Yes to replace the existing file.

Error in Format Exporting

Now, because you previously saved and launched Excel, the file "phone.xls" is already open in Excel. You will get an error message: "Error in format exporting." This will happen any time you try to save a document when a file of the same name and type is already open. To fix this, you must first close the existing open document or save your document with a different file name.

1. On the task bar, click Excel to make it the active window.
2. Close the file "phone.xls" without saving any changes.
3. On the task bar, click OmniPage to it make the active window.

Saving the Spreadsheet as an Excel Spreadsheet

1. Click Finish Processing Existing Pages.
2. In the Save As dialog box, click the file "phone.xls." This will overwrite the existing file of the same name.
3. Make sure Save as Type is still set on Excel 97.
4. Click OK.
5. Click Yes to replace existing file.

The spreadsheet is now in Excel with navy borders; however, the width of the borders has not changed. This is because OmniPage-to-Excel does not retain this formatting property. Line width is set in points in OmniPage and Word; however, in Excel you only have a choice of fixed line sizes. If you export the spreadsheet to Word, Word maintains the width of the borders. Let's now save the telephone bill as a Word table. We will come back to the Excel spreadsheet and fix the missing leading zeros later.

Saving the Spreadsheet as a Word Table

1. On the task bar, click OmniPage to it make the current window.
2. On the toolbox, click the Additional button to Export Document Again.
3. The Automatic Processing box pops up.
4. Click Export Again.
5. In the Save As field, click the down-pointing arrow and select Word 97.
6. In the File name field, type "phone."
7. Click OK.

Word launches, and the document appears in Word (Figure 7.28) with the correct formats.

▶ Navy 1.5 pt size borders

▶ Numbers are aligned

▶ Leading zeros are in cells

Figure 7.28
The file "phone" saved
in Word 97 format

	Aug¤	01:05	pm	Mobile¤	015435482¤	Peak¤	0:21¤	0.25¤	¤
1	Aug¤	10:02	am	Mobile¤	018259253¤	Peak¤	0:37¤	0.25¤	¤
1	Aug¤	12:15	pm	Mobile¤	018415485¤	Peak¤	0:35¤	0.25¤	¤
1	Aug¤	01:27	pm	Mobile¤	018865586¤	Peak¤	2:35¤	1.00¤	¤
1	Aug¤	02:53	pm	Mobile¤	018415485¤	Peak¤	0:27¤	0.25¤	¤
2	Aug¤	09:14	am	Mobile¤	015230053¤	Peak¤	0:51¤	0.50¤	¤
2	Aug¤	11:31	am	Mobile¤	018265761¤	Peak¤	1:24¤	0.75¤	¤
2	Aug¤	02:56	pm	Mobile¤	018415485¤	Peak¤	0:32¤	0.25¤	¤
2	Aug¤	09:07	am	Mobile¤	018617249¤	Peak¤	0:44¤	0.50¤	¤
2	Aug¤	01:34	pm	Mobile¤	018415866¤	Peak¤	0:42¤	0.50¤	¤

Replacing Leading Zeros in an Excel Spreadsheet

Now, let's go back to the saved Excel spreadsheet. Remember the "Phone Number" column, where the leading zeros were dropped off? This is because the data comes across to Excel as a number and Excel does not display leading zeros on numbers. But Excel can display leading zeros if the cell is formatted as text. An easy way to fix this is with a simple Excel formula.

When saving a document that contains numbers with a leading zero such as telephone numbers, i.e., 0800 or 0011, the zeros are dropped off when saved to a spreadsheet. We'll use an Excel formula to replace the missing zeros in the data column. You can use this same process and Excel function to append or prepend any text or number to existing data.

Add Leading Zeros to Columns of Data

We will insert a blank column in Excel to hold the new phone number with the zero in front. We'll create our formula to add a text zero by enclosing the zero in quotes. This will make the zero and the rest of the cell a text format. The formula then joins the phone number to the zero with the join ("&") function. You can't use the plus ("+") function because you can't add text to a number; they are two different types.

Once the formula has reconstructed our phone number, we can delete the original. But because the formula is based on the original number, when we delete it we get an error. Therefore, you must first copy the new phone number and paste over the top of the formula.

Let's do it.

1. On the task bar, click OmniPage to make it the active window.
2. In the Text Editor view, click the No Formatting layout view button.
3. Now, save "phone" to an Excel file format.
4. On the AutoOCR toolbox, click Additional.
5. The Automatic Processing box pops up.
6. Click Export Document Again.
7. The Save As dialog box pops us.
8. Type in the File name field: "phone4."

Excel launches, and the spreadsheet displays with the new dividers you set in the exercises above. The leading zeros on the telephone numbers are missing (Figure 7.29).

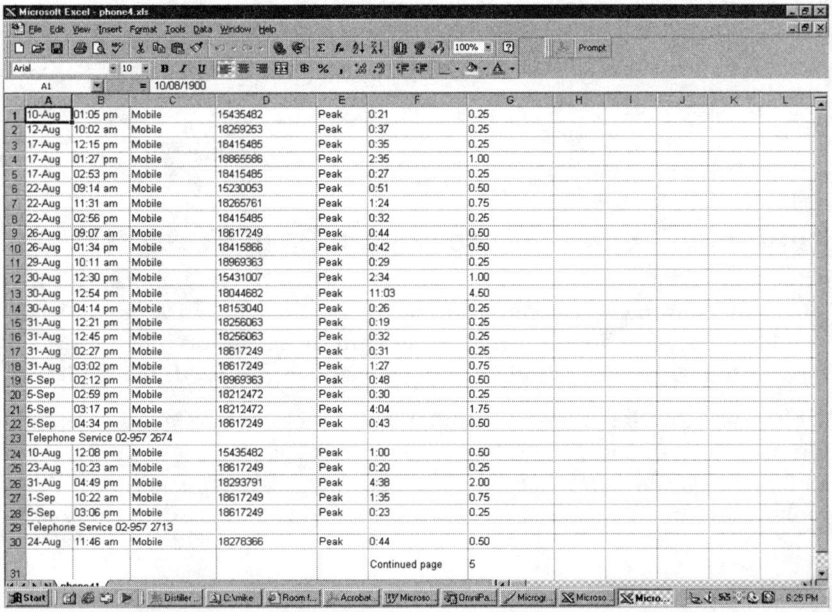

	A	B	C	D	E	F	G
1	10-Aug	01:05 pm	Mobile	15435482	Peak	0:21	0.25
2	12-Aug	10:02 am	Mobile	18259253	Peak	0:37	0.25
3	17-Aug	12:15 pm	Mobile	18415485	Peak	0:35	0.25
4	17-Aug	01:27 pm	Mobile	18865586	Peak	2:35	1.00
5	17-Aug	02:53 pm	Mobile	18415485	Peak	0:27	0.25
6	22-Aug	09:14 am	Mobile	15230053	Peak	0:51	0.50
7	22-Aug	11:31 am	Mobile	18265761	Peak	1:24	0.75
8	22-Aug	02:56 pm	Mobile	18415485	Peak	0:32	0.25
9	26-Aug	09:07 am	Mobile	18617249	Peak	0:44	0.50
10	26-Aug	01:34 pm	Mobile	18415866	Peak	0:42	0.50
11	29-Aug	10:11 am	Mobile	18969363	Peak	0:29	0.25
12	30-Aug	12:30 pm	Mobile	15431007	Peak	2:34	1.00
13	30-Aug	12:54 pm	Mobile	18044682	Peak	11:03	4.50
14	30-Aug	04:14 pm	Mobile	18153040	Peak	0:26	0.25
15	31-Aug	12:21 pm	Mobile	18256063	Peak	0:19	0.25
16	31-Aug	12:45 pm	Mobile	18256063	Peak	0:32	0.25
17	31-Aug	02:27 pm	Mobile	18617249	Peak	0:31	0.25
18	31-Aug	03:02 pm	Mobile	18617249	Peak	1:27	0.75
19	5-Sep	02:12 pm	Mobile	18969363	Peak	0:48	0.50
20	5-Sep	02:59 pm	Mobile	18212472	Peak	0:30	0.25
21	5-Sep	03:17 pm	Mobile	18212472	Peak	4:04	1.75
22	5-Sep	04:34 pm	Mobile	18617249	Peak	0:43	0.50
23	Telephone Service 02-957 2674						
24	10-Aug	12:08 pm	Mobile	15435482	Peak	1:00	0.50
25	23-Aug	10:23 am	Mobile	18617249	Peak	0:20	0.25
26	31-Aug	04:49 pm	Mobile	18293791	Peak	4:38	2.00
27	1-Sep	10:22 am	Mobile	18617249	Peak	1:35	0.75
28	5-Sep	03:06 pm	Mobile	18617249	Peak	0:23	0.25
29	Telephone Service 02-957 2713						
30	24-Aug	11:46 am	Mobile	18278366	Peak	0:44	0.50
31						Continued page	5

Figure 7.29
The file "phone" with Text Editor layout set to "No Formatting"

Let's fix that now.

1. Right-click the Column E label at the top of the spreadsheet. The entire column is highlighted.
2. Click Insert. A blank column is inserted.
3. Click in Cell E1.

Now enter the formula:

1. Press the Equals key (=) to start the formula.
2. Type open double quotes (") then a zero, then close double quotes ("). This is the text zero you want added to the front of the number.
3. Type an ampersand (&). This is used to join text.
4. Click in D1, the cell containing the phone number. The formula should read ="0"&D1.
5. Press Enter to finish the formula and enter the result in the cell.

The phone number now has the leading zero displayed (Figure 7.30).

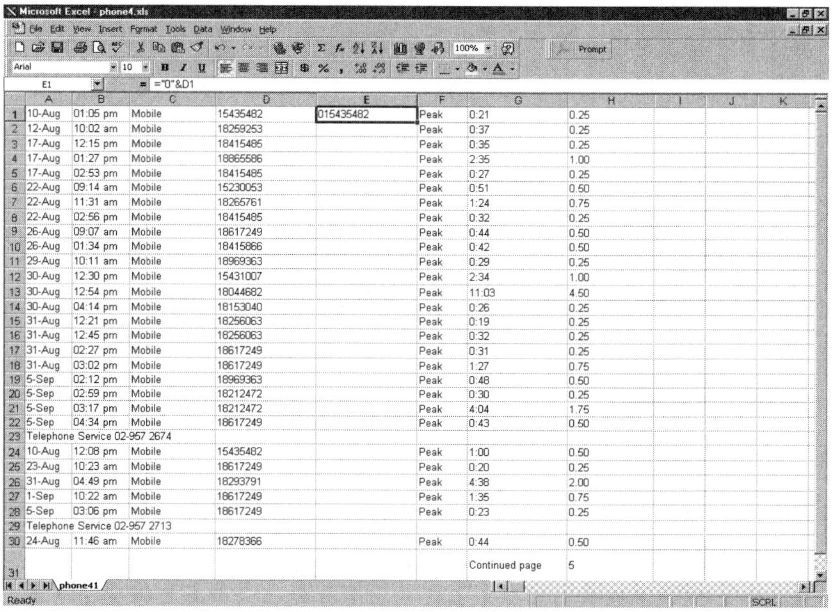

Microsoft Excel - phone4.xls

E1 = ="0"&D1

	A	B	C	D	E	F	G	H
1	10-Aug	01:05 pm	Mobile	15435482	015435482	Peak	0:21	0.25
2	12-Aug	10:02 am	Mobile	18259253		Peak	0:37	0.25
3	17-Aug	12:15 pm	Mobile	18415485		Peak	0:35	0.25
4	17-Aug	01:27 pm	Mobile	18865586		Peak	2:35	1.00
5	17-Aug	02:53 pm	Mobile	18415485		Peak	0:27	0.25
6	22-Aug	09:14 am	Mobile	15230053		Peak	0:51	0.50
7	22-Aug	11:31 am	Mobile	18265761		Peak	1:24	0.75
8	22-Aug	02:56 pm	Mobile	18415485		Peak	0:32	0.25
9	26-Aug	09:07 am	Mobile	18617249		Peak	0:44	0.50
10	26-Aug	01:34 pm	Mobile	18415866		Peak	0:42	0.50
11	29-Aug	10:11 am	Mobile	18969363		Peak	0:29	0.25
12	30-Aug	12:30 pm	Mobile	15431007		Peak	2:34	1.00
13	30-Aug	12:54 pm	Mobile	18044682		Peak	11:03	4.50
14	30-Aug	04:14 pm	Mobile	18153040		Peak	0:26	0.25
15	31-Aug	12:21 pm	Mobile	18256063		Peak	0:19	0.25
16	31-Aug	12:45 pm	Mobile	18256063		Peak	0:32	0.25
17	31-Aug	02:27 pm	Mobile	18617249		Peak	0:31	0.25
18	31-Aug	03:02 pm	Mobile	18617249		Peak	1:27	0.75
19	5-Sep	02:12 pm	Mobile	18969363		Peak	0:48	0.50
20	5-Sep	02:59 pm	Mobile	18212472		Peak	0:30	0.25
21	5-Sep	03:17 pm	Mobile	18212472		Peak	4:04	1.75
22	5-Sep	04:34 pm	Mobile	18617249		Peak	0:43	0.50
23	Telephone Service 02-957 2674							
24	10-Aug	12:08 pm	Mobile	15435482		Peak	1:00	0.50
25	23-Aug	10:23 am	Mobile	18617249		Peak	0:20	0.25
26	31-Aug	04:49 pm	Mobile	18293791		Peak	4:38	2.00
27	1-Sep	10:22 am	Mobile	18617249		Peak	1:35	0.75
28	5-Sep	03:06 pm	Mobile	18617249		Peak	0:23	0.25
29	Telephone Service 02-957 2713							
30	24-Aug	11:46 am	Mobile	18278366		Peak	0:44	0.50
31							Continued page	5

Figure 7.30
The file "phone" in Excel with the results of the formula in column E1.

Applying the Formula to All Remaining Cells

Copy the formula you have just created to the rest of the cells in column E. Excel will automatically update the formula with the corresponding cells: D2, D3, D4, etc.

1. Click in E1.
2. Position the mouse on the bottom right-hand corner of E1, the little black square. The mouse pointer changes to a fine cross.
3. Hold down the left mouse button and drag down to the bottom of column E to fill all cells.
4. The formula is now copied to every cell that needs the leading 0.

You could save the file now, but the new phone number is only a formula based on the original number. We must change it from a formula to a value.

Pasting the New Phone Number

To keep the new phone number as a number, we must copy column E and paste the "value" (the displayed number) of the cell back on top of itself, overwriting the formula.

1. Highlight the entire column E. Right-click the column E label at the top of the spreadsheet. The entire column is highlighted.
2. Select Copy.
3. Right-click again on the column E label.
4. Choose Paste Special.
5. In the Paste options at the top, select Values (Figure 7.31).
6. Click OK.
7. Save the file.

Figure 7.31
Excel Paste Special value

Now, the new phone number is a text cell in Excel with the leading zero. You can use the join function ("&") to join together any number of text and numeric items.

Extra Table Practice Exercise

For extra practice, you can experiment using the file "Tptable" (Figure 7.32). It can be downloaded from the Web site (see Introduction), or you can find it in the appendix.

This document has columns and a table.

Figure 7.32
The file "tptable"

True Page Sample

OmniPage Professional allows you to recognize, edit, and save documents in their original, full page formats when you use True Page recognition. With True Page, you can even edit any images on the page by simply clicking on the image. This opens a complete set of editing tools in our Image Assistant editing package. Image Assistant features are highlighted

Image Editing for Every Business

Image Assistant has automatic, intelligent tools that anyone in your office can use. And, for the professional graphic artist, it has the most complete set of professional features available in our image editing software. Whether your business consists of you and your computer or you and a cast of thousands,

Image Assistant is your image editing tool. Image Assistant is a 24 bit color image editor that lets just about anyone, even beginners, produce professional color output: from a color slide to a four color separation.

Assist Mode

You may not be a graphic artist; but you know how your image should look. In Assist Mode, you choose just the right effect for your image by looking at sample thumbnails onscreen. For example, if you're setting contrast, you'll see 15 samples of how your image will look with 15 different contrast settings. You just click on the sample that looks right to you, and your image is transformed. And, multiple levels of Undo and Redo let you experiment to your heart's content.

Imaging for Pros

Image Assistant's true power and versatility are clear to the professional graphic artist. You can edit in bilevel, grayscale, RGB, or CYMK and access complete PANTONE color support. Image Assistant has all the tools and features you expect from a high end image processing product.

Automatic Scanning Controls

Image Assistant completely automates the task of capturing images. For example, it can separate a scanned photo from unwanted text, crop it and rotate it. It determines whether you're working with a line art, grayscale, or color image and opens it in the appropriate environment. You also have complete manual control for all settings if you need it.

Editing Tools

Image Assistant provides all the features you need to edit color, grayscale and black and white images. It can even convert images to a different type; for example, you can convert grayscale images into line art and vice versa. Grayscale images are made of various shades and tones. Consequently, the editing tools in Image Assistant let you paint and edit in shades and tones of grays. You can smudge grays together, paint with any gray from within an image, and even create custom brushes from different patterns and textures in the image. Electronic tools such as the pencil, eraser, paintbrush and airbrush are also available.

10 Aug	01:05 pm	15435482	0:21	0.25
12 Aug	10:02 am	18259253	0:37	0.25
17 Aug	12:15 pm	18415485	0:35	0.25
17 Aug	01:27 pm	18865586	2:35	1.00
17 Aug	02:53 pm	18415485	0:27	0.25
22 Aug	09:14 am	15230053	0:51	0.50
22 Aug	11:31 am	18265761	1:24	0.75
22 Aug	02:56 pm	18415485	0:32	0.25

This file is a multi-layout document. You may need to draw manual zones or set up a custom layout, depending on the Perform OCR option you choose. We will use the Manual OCR toolbox this time. So that we don't repeat instructions on how to do this exercise, and since you have already learned how to draw zones, you can refer to this chapter and the chapter on zones (Chapter 4). By using Manual OCR, you can scan the page or load the file. Then, before clicking the Perform OCR button, you can draw the table and text zones. If you choose not to draw any zones, clicking the Perform OCR button will automatically draw zones based on the Perform OCR option set. Listed below are the exercises to do.

1. Click the Manual OCR button.
2. Set Get Page to Load File or Scan B&W.
3. Set Perform OCR to Automatic.
4. Click the Get Page button to scan the page or load the file.
5. Use the Draw Rectangular button on the zone toolbar to draw a table zone around the table (Figure 7.33).

Figure 7.33

The file "tptable" with a manually drawn table zone

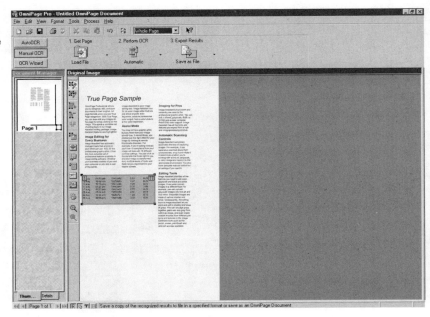

6. Right-click in the table and set the Properties to a table zone.

7. Practice drawing zones around the columns of text and heading.

8. Change the properties for each column. The long column to the right of the table should be set to single column. The heading should be set to single column. Draw one zone around the columns of text above the table and set the properties to Multiple Columns.

NOTE

Remember, when you draw a zone around two or more columns and set the properties to a multiple column zone, OmniPage will break that zone up into the single columns of text that make up that multiple-column zone.

9. Process the document by clicking Perform OCR on the toolbox.

10. Practice proofreading.

11. In the Original Image view, make changes to the table with the Table toolbar buttons.

12. In the Original Image view, click in the table and switch on Borders and Gridlines.

13. In the Text Editor view, format cells and table.

14. To see the effect of different layout views, change the layout views in the Text Editor view and save to Word 97.

15. Save to Excel 97.

8

Logos, Signatures, Line Art, and Color Photos

Graphics and logos can cause issues with OmniPage users. Users often call us, saying they can't get their letterheads or logos to scan properly, their line art comes out fuzzy, signatures are missing, or the logo is in bits and pieces all over the place. In this chapter, you will learn why those things happen and how to get great results when scanning any document that contains a graphic. You will also learn how to save scanned graphics, logos, signatures, and photos as separate files to use in other applications. We will show you some neat tricks to use to edit the graphic, including cropping and making an image e-mail ready. Finally, we will walk through scanning a complex page with columns, a table, and a color photograph.

One important thing to remember when using graphic zones is to use the Text Editor views True Page or Retain Flowing Columns—this will ensure the graphic is reproduced in the same location—or as near as possible to the same location—as the original. With the other two Text Editor views—Retain Font and Paragraph Formatting and No Formatting—the graphic will not be in the original location. Select the Text Editor view before saving your document.

Working with Graphics

As far as OmniPage is concerned, anything other than text is a graphic, except straight lines, which OmniPage does not recognize as either text or a graphic.

Remember, OmniPage's primary purpose in life is to detect and recognize text, and it does a very good job of it. It will detect the text within logos, and sometimes recognize parts of a photo as text. This is because the pattern of dots in a photograph sometimes resembles tiny characters. You will experience this in the exercise "Scanning a Document Containing a Color Photo."

You need to tell OmniPage to accept a photo, drawing, sketch, handwritten recipe, logo, or signature as a graphic. To identify an area of a page as a graphic, it must be enclosed in a graphic zone. Most of the time, OmniPage will correctly identify a graphic within a document. Graphic zones tell OmniPage to treat everything inside the zone as a graphic, even if it contains text—for example, the text within a logo you want to preserve.

How often have you scanned a document that contains a graphic, only to find that when you open the results (in Word, for example) the graphic is displayed at the bottom of the page? This is usually because the Text Editor view was set for Retain Font and Paragraph Formatting or No Formatting. Use the OmniPage Text Editor view Retain Flowing Columns or True Page to place the graphics in their original location. The other reason could be that Page Layout View in Word is not selected.

If you are using OmniPage Limited Edition, which comes free with many scanners, know that, while it is OK for basic scanning, it does not support graphics or multi-column documents. If you have a multi-column document, you should use OmniPage Pro, not the Limited Edition.

TIP

If you find the graphic does not appear in, for example, Word, after exporting the results, check the following: After clicking on Export Results, in the Save As dialog box, click Advanced, and make sure Retain Graphics is switched on. A check means it is selected.

By default, it is On. If it has been switched Off, it will remain off until you change it again. See Figure 8.1.

Figure 8.1
Switch on Retain Graphics to ensure graphics show in WP Applications

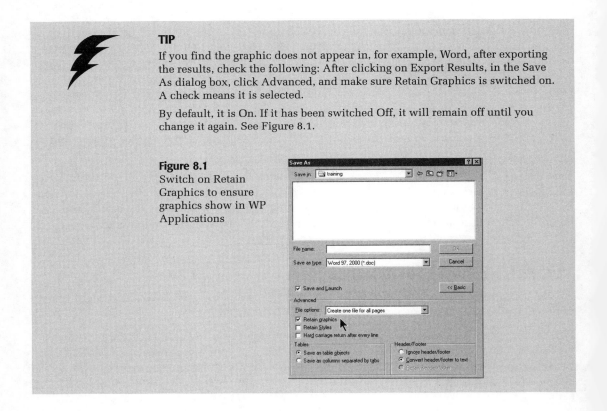

Capturing Logos

Logos often contain a graphic mixed in with text. Sometimes, the text is curved or flows around the graphic. OmniPage will identify the text where it can, as well as parts of the graphic that may look like a character. Often, the logo is not reproduced with the logo and text combined, and they become two separate zones. When scanning a document with a logo, you draw a graphic zone around the entire logo. Include the graphic, address, and telephone details, so all the details will be preserved in one zone. You may need to test scanning in black and white, color, or grayscale for the best result.

If the graphic is line art or a single color graphic, scanning in black and white mode will give the best result. However, if you're scanning a color graphic and it is to be printed on a black and white laser printer, scan in either grayscale or black and white. And if the graphic contains many colors, scanning in grayscale may give the better result. Finally, scan your color logo in color if you are going to print in color.

Scanning a Logo

In this exercise, you will scan a letterhead logo. The file name is "logo.tif" (Figure 8.2). You will locate this file in the appendix, or it can be downloaded from the Web site (see Introduction). We will save the logo to a Word document. Later in this chapter, you will see how to save the logo for use in other software applications.

Figure 8.2
Example of letterhead
exercise to capture the
logo

Omnipage Training

1. **Set up the OCR Options and Process settings**. Place the letterhead face down in the scanner. Click the Manual OCR toolbox. On the right of the Get Page button, click the down pointing arrow and select Scan B&W. The example you are using is B&W. If you are scanning a color logo and have a color printer, select Scan Color. Leave the Perform OCR button as Automatic. You will be drawing a manual zone around the logo and changing it, so this setting doesn't really matter. Leave Export Results as Save as File.

2. **Scan and OCR process the logo**. In the Manual OCR toolbox, click the Get Page icon. The logo is scanned and appears in the Thumbnail and Original Image view. Then, click the Perform OCR icon to process the page. In the Original Image view, notice how OmniPage has drawn a graphic zone around the large O and a text zone around the text. In the Text Editor view, the logo doesn't look like the original at all!

Next, let's delete the automatic zones and draw a manual zone around the whole logo so we can capture it in its entirety, with the graphic and the text maintained in their same relationship.

1. **Zoom the Original Image View**. In the Original Image view, right-click, select Zoom, then click 50%. Use the Scroll arrows, so that the logo is in the middle of the screen. Zooming in makes drawing zones easier.

2. **Delete the Existing Zones**. Right-click in one of the zones and select "Select All." On the keyboard, press Delete or right-click and select "Clear."

3. **Drawing the Correct Zone**. On the Image toolbar, click the Draw Rectangular Zone button. It is the default. Move the mouse to the top left-hand corner of the logo. Click and hold down the mouse button; drag to the lower right corner to draw a zone around the logo. Be sure to include the text "OmniPage Training." Finish drawing the zone just below the text, as shown in Figure 8.3. Release the mouse button when you have drawn the zone.

Figure 8.3
Logo selected with a
graphic zone to extract
from the letterhead

4. **Set the Zone Property**. Position the mouse in the logo, right-click to display the shortcut menu, then move the mouse to the top entry. In the submenu, click Graphic Zone.

Now, you will need to OCR the graphic. Although the graphic is not text, you still have to perform the OCR process for the logo to be recognized as a graphic. You need to reprocess the page with the new zone and zone information. OmniPage will then overwrite the previous recognized text and graphic with the single graphic of the logo.

1. **Perform OCR**. Click the Perform OCR button to start the OCR process. Click OK on the prompt to replace existing text. The logo appears in the Text Editor view. Click the Text Editor view "True Page" so the logo will be saved in exactly the same place on the page. You may need to scroll to the right and down a little to see the graphic. The graphic shown in the Text Editor view will not appear as sharp and clear as when it is printed. This is because the screen can only display a resolution of about 75 to –90 dpi, and the image is 300 dpi. The laser printer will print a clear, sharp image, as the printer's resolution is 300 dpi or better.

2. **Export Results**. Click the Export Results button, which should be set to the Save as File option (we set this up in step 1). In the Save In field, select the folder, C:\Training. In the file name field, type in "logo," and in the "Save as Type" field, select Word (or your word processing application). Finally, click in the Save and Launch checkbox to launch the program.

When Word opens, the logo will be displayed in its original location and as one object. Print it out to see how clear it is. You may want to experiment saving using other Text Editor views.

That's how easy it is to scan a letterhead and logo. If you wanted to include the company details, you would simply draw the graphic zone around the logo *and* the company details.

Later, we will see how to save the logo as a tif image file. Remember, you cannot save the logo in the Text Editor view as a tif file, so we will show you a great way to instantly access your image-editing software program to save it.

To save the graphic zone as a separate image file, see the instructions on manipulating scanned graphics a little later in this chapter. To save as an image file, follow these steps.

1. To open the logo in your image-editing software, simply double-click the logo when the graphic appears in the Text Editor view.
2. Your image editing program launches and opens with the vertical logo.
3. On the menu bar, select File > Save, and save the logo as a tif file.

Scanning a Vertical Logo

In this exercise, you will scan a vertical letterhead. The file name is "letter.tif." You will locate this file in the appendix, or it can be downloaded from the Web site (see Introduction). We scanned the logo in Figure 8.4 from a faxed copy of a letter. It gives you a good idea of how a faxed logo reproduces.

Figure 8.4
The results from scanning a vertical logo

SIMPLE ● TECHNOLOGY

1. Use the Manual OCR toolbox.
2. Scan the letterhead you have with the vertical logo.
3. Clear all zones.
4. Draw a rectangular zone around the vertical logo only.
5. Change the Properties to Graphic Zone.
6. On the Manual OCR toolbox, click the Perform OCR icon.
7. In the Text Editor view, select "True Page."
8. Click the Export Results button to save as document file.

To save the graphic zone as a separate image file, see the instructions on manipulating scanned graphics later in this chapter.

It's that simple. Now that you know how easy it is to extract a logo from a letterhead, let's look at creating an electronic signature. The process follows the same steps, except you have to either write the signature first or extract it from a hard copy.

Capturing Signatures

OmniPage may attempt to recognize parts of a signature as text. This is because the image of the signature appears as solid lines and may form the shape of a character. It may not even detect the signature. When scanning a document with a signature, draw a graphic zone around the entire signature. Scanning in black and white will give the best results.

You can scan signatures within a document and save the signature as an image file to create an electronic signature for use in other software applications.

When creating a signature for scanning, use a fine point, black felt tip pen: 0.5 mm is a good size. It gives a much clearer and more defined line than a ballpoint pen. If you use a ballpoint pen, the line, when magnified, can be just a mass of broken dots, not one smooth continuous

CHAPTER 8

line, and it does not give a clear image. Different colored pens may not give as dark an image as a black felt pen when scanned.

In this exercise, you will scan a signature (Figure 8.5). The file name is "signature.tif." You can find the file in the appendix at the back of the book, or it can be downloaded from the Web site (see Introduction). Why not practice using your own signature?

Figure 8.5
Signature

The process and steps for capturing a signature are exactly the same as for capturing a logo. Repeat the steps as given above. Draw a single graphic zone around the signature—in some cases, you may need to draw an irregular zone shape—then reprocess the page.

Capturing Line Art

Line art is made up of black and white lines, like a sketch made with a black pen (Figure 8.6). You have probably guessed by now that the way to capture line art graphics is to delete all the automatically drawn zones and redraw new graphic zones. If you don't do this, the example will come out an absolute mess, because all the text will be recognized and will be separated from the symbols.

Figure 8.6
Example of a line art drawing scanned in black and white, lineart.tif

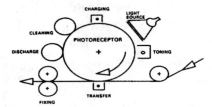

In this example, we will be using the line art drawing "lineart.tif." You can find this file in the appendix at the back of the book, or it can be downloaded from the Web site (see Introduction).

Always scan line art in black and white. It will give a much sharper and clearer image. If you use grayscale or color, you can end up with a not so sharp image. Sometimes, the image may be quite "fuzzy." This could be because the scanner has the "Unsharp Mask" option turned off. The Unsharp Mask is a standard tool on most native scanner interfaces. When scanning in black and white, the lines will have jagged edges. Jagged edges are known as "jaggies." They are hard to see unless magnified. When scanning the same object in grayscale, these jaggies (as shown in Figure 8.7) are smoothed with shades of gray, giving them fuzzy edges. The Unsharp Mask turns on and off this smoothing.

This "fuzziness" depends on your native scanner interface setting options. These native scanner options are not accessible through OmniPage's Option Scanner Settings panel. You have to switch the "Native Twain Interface" option on; this will display your native scanner interface before you scan a document. You can then choose the option Unsharp Mask to stop the fuzziness.

Figure 8.7
Enlarged view of a portion of Figure 8.6—on the left is the line art graphic scanned in black and white, and on the right, it's scanned as grayscale with Unsharp turned off

To access your scanner's native scanner interface before the scanning starts, do the following:

1. On the standard toolbar, click the AB Button.
2. Click the Scanner tab.
3. Click the Advanced button to access the Scanner Setup Wizard (see Chapter 13).
4. In the Scanner Setup Wizard, select the option Test and Configure Current Scanning Source.
5. Click Next.
6. Click Advanced.
7. Click Show Native Scanner Interface.
8. Click Next.
9. Click the checkbox Skip this Test. The scanner is already working and you only want to turn on the Show Native Scanner Interface at this next scan time.
10. Click Next again.
11. Keep clicking Next and Skip this Test until the Options Setting panel comes back into view.
12. Click OK to close OmniPage's Option Settings panel.

Next time you click Get Page or the Start button to scan a page, the native scanner interface will display. You can then change the settings to suit what you are scanning.

NOTE

The Twain Scanner Interface is used by every program you use to scan. The Twain Scanner Driver settings will remain as you *last* set them, until you change them again. What can happen is that a setting may be switched ON when using a program other than OmniPage to scan. These retained settings may interfere with getting a good scan when next using OmniPage.

You may get only one-quarter or one-half page scanned. This can be because the "select" scan area has been left on, or an auto-detect scan area is selected. Nearly every scanner will have some setting that is not available via the OmniPage scanner settings. When this happens, reset the Twain Scanner Driver settings; most of the Twain interfaces will have a reset button.

CHAPTER 8

In Figure 8.8, you can see what happens when you choose to scan a line art graphic in black and white to stop the fuzziness. Compare this to the grayscale scan with the Unsharp Mask on and off. Both grayscale scans are fuzzier than the black and white, and the scan with Unsharp Mask off is the fuzziest.

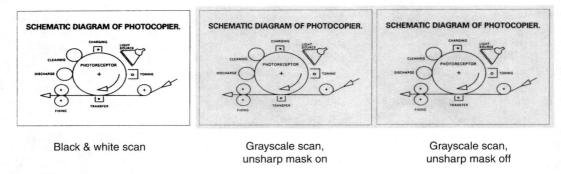

Black & white scan   Grayscale scan,   Grayscale scan,
                          unsharp mask on   unsharp mask off

Figure 8.8
The difference of scanning in black and white and grayscale with Unsharp Mask on and off

Capturing Color and Black and White Photos

When scanning documents that contain color photos (Figure 8.9 shows one of OmniPage's installed sample files, "Sample_single2.tif"), OmniPage can recognize and retain the colored text as well as the color photo. The color photo will be saved in your document, and the colored text will be reproduced in one of 256 colors (see Chapter 13 for more on saving colored text).

Figure 8.9
Example of a document containing a color photo (in black and white here)

If you want colored text and backgrounds reproduced in your document, make sure that Retain Text and Background Color is selected in the Options Process panel, as seen in Figure 8.10. The Text Editor also allows you to change the color of text and backgrounds. The default for this option is switched off.

Figure 8.10
File Save Advanced Option settings showing Retain Text and Background Color switched on

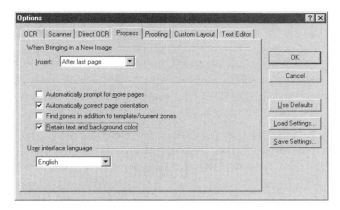

For the best OCR recognition, OmniPage scans documents at 300 dots per inch. When scanning in color, the process will take longer, as over 30 times more information is sent from the scanner to the PC. The photo will be saved in your document at 150 dpi. This is the tradeoff between image quality and file size. A resolution of 150 dpi gives the best picture quality and a small file size. The graphic/photo is saved as a BMP file format in applications that can accept embedded images—except for HTML, where it is saved as a separate JPG file. You can save the results as a PDF file, as PDF files have their own image file type.

In this exercise, you will scan a color photo only. The file name is "beautifulday.tif." The photo can be downloaded from the Web site (see Introduction). Alternatively, scan your own photo. This photo is a picture of Sydney Harbor Bridge, in Sydney, Australia.

We will use the Manual OCR toolbox for this job, using all the same steps as for the previous exercises. Draw a zone around the entire picture (or the part of the picture you want), perform OCR, and save. As all the steps are the same as for previous exercises—let's scan and use this photo for the next section, "Manipulating Scanned Graphics."

1. Click the Manual OCR toolbox.
2. Click the down pointing arrow of Get Page; select Scan Color.
3. Leave Perform OCR to Automatic.
4. Leave Export Results as Save as File.
5. Place the photo in the scanner.
6. Click the Get Page button. The scanner starts.
7. The photo displays in the Thumbnail and in the Original Image view.

CHAPTER 8

Manipulating Scanned Graphics

Sometimes you will want to fix up the graphic that has been scanned. It may be that the graphic is slightly skewed and you would like to crop or straighten it. The graphic may be too dark or too light, or the people in the photo may have "red eye" that you would like to fix before saving. You may just want to save the graphic as an image file so you can use it later in other applications. For example, you may want to capture your signature so when you do a mail merge, you do not have to sign all the letters. You simply insert your signature image file into your mail-merged document. That way, when you print the mail out, all the letters are already signed. It really saves on the hands and you can still read your last signature. We will show you how to rotate and crop the graphic you have scanned, and you'll see how easy it is to open a graphic in your image-editing program and save it as several different file types. We'll also show you how to insert and work with graphics in Word.

OmniPage saves results of scanned pages as document files, not image files. This is why you need to use an image editing program to save individual images. You can use File > Save Image from the menu bar, but it only saves entire pages as an image file.

To open a graphic in your image program, double-click the graphic in the Text Editor view. That's all there is to it. By double-clicking on the photo, you launch your image editing program and the photo automatically displays in the window, ready for you to edit if required. OmniPage images are in BMP format in the Text Editor view. By default, many Windows installations default to MS Paint as the image application for BMP files. MS Paint is a limited application. If you have a different image-editing application, you should change the file association (see the caution below).

In this section, we will use OmniPage to rotate and crop an image, recognize the graphic zone, then open the graphic in an image-editing program. We'll save the result in several different image file formats. We will look at the differences between PCX, TIF, and JPG file types.

CAUTION

If you get the error message as shown in Figure 8.11, you may already have the program open, so close the image-editing program. It may also mean that you have not associated BMP files with one of your image-editing programs. If you are not sure how to do this, refer to Windows Help for details on associating files.

Figure 8.11
This error message displays if the image editing program is already open or there is no program associated with BMP files

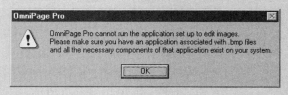

Rotating the Image

Use the Rotate button on the Image toolbar in the Original Image view. This will rotate the entire page. Of course, if the page contains text, this rotation will be inappropriate. In that case, open the graphic in the image editing program and use the Rotate tools in that application. The Rotate tools will allow degrees of rotation, where OmniPage only rotates in increments of 90 degrees.

1. In the Original Image view, place the mouse in the photo.
2. Right-click and choose Rotate.
3. Click 270, or any other appropriate setting to adjust the photo.
4. Rotate until the photo displays upright in the Original Image view.

Cropping a Photo

What would you do if you wanted to use only a portion of the photo? In photo-editing software programs, this is called "cropping." You can "crop" a photo in OmniPage by drawing a graphic zone around the portion you want.

Drawing the Graphic Zone

If you've downloaded the file "beautifulday.tif" from the Web site, draw a zone around the Sydney Harbor Bridge and the skyline, as shown in Figure 8.12.

Change the properties of the zone to a graphic, as shown in Figure 8.13.

Figure 8.12
The position of the
graphic zone

Figure 8.13
The zone properties
drop-down box and
selection required

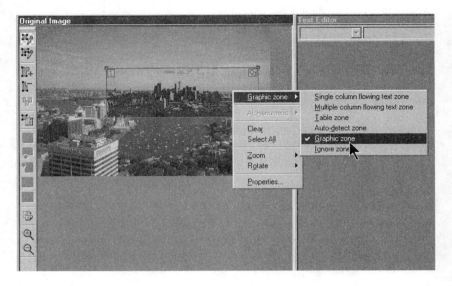

This is how we can crop in OmniPage. Now, we need to recognize the cropped photo.

Recognizing the Cropped Portion of the Photo

Recognizing the cropped portion is easy, provided you have left Perform OCR set to Automatic.

1. On the Manual OCR toolbox, click the Perform OCR button.
2. The cropped portion of the photo displays in the Text Editor view, as shown in Figure 8.14.

Figure 8.14
The cropped portion of
the photo in the Text
Editor view

If it does not turn out the way you would like, or if you need to change the cropped area, simply resize or delete the zone in the Original Image view, redraw the zone, and rerecognize it. Of course, you can also crop the photo from within your image editing software.

Launching Your Image Editing Software

To save the cropped photo as an image file, we need to open it in an image editing software program. Simply double-click the photo in the Text Editor view. The photo automatically displays in the window, ready for you to edit if required.

Once you have the photo displayed in the image editing software program, you can save it and print it.

Saving the Image

In its File menu, OmniPage has a "Save Image" option, which saves each entire scanned page as an image file, unlike the Save, Save As, and Export Results, which save the recognized text and graphics in a text document format. You can use File > Save Image to save the entire photo displayed in the Original Image view as a JPG, PNG, PCX, BMP, GIF, DCX, or TIF (seven different formats). DCX and TIF are file types that support multi-pages. You cannot save the individual graphic as a PCX, TIF, BMP, or JPG.

To save graphic zones that are in the Text Editor view as images, double click them to open them in your image editing program and save them from there.

For archiving photos or images, it is best to save as a PCX or TIF file; these file types save all of the color and pixel information. The JPG format is a smaller file type, and it's quick to e-mail; however, a JPG file—since it discards some of the pixels and colors—loses some of the definition in the image. Every time you save and resave a JPG file, it loses more of this information.

The JPG File Save settings determine how many pixels and colors to discard. If you enlarge a JPG image, you will see the JPG artifacts. These artifacts are the conglomerations of pixels of similar colors from the original photograph. They are combined into one color and one shape approximately the same as where the original pixels were. See Figure 8.15.

Figure 8.15
Shows JPG artifacts and the "lost" image information

Individual Pixels   JPG Artifacts

If you save a photo as a JPG and then decide you want to crop or enlarge the image, it will become very pixilated. If you think you may want to enlarge or crop portions from a photo later on, save them as PCX or TIF files.

Saving the Cropped Photo as a JPG

As mentioned above, JPG is a good format for e-mailing and Internet use. Here's how to save images in JPG format:

1. In the image editing software, on the menu, click File.
2. Click Save As.
3. Make sure you are still in your training directory, in the Save In field.
4. In the File name field, type "beautifulday2."
5. In the Save as Type field, click the down pointing arrow and select JPEG File Interchange (*.jpg).
6. Click OK.
7. The JPEG Options Box displays (Figure 8.16).

Figure 8.16
The JPG Options Box in Micrografx Photo Magic

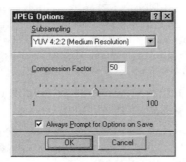

This dialog box will differ, depending on your color scanning software. This is where you choose how much information you want removed from your picture. Do you really need millions of different colors, or can you get along with a couple thousand instead?

Sampling Method

This is how the program works out how to conglomerate the pixels into artifacts. Artifacts are shapes of the same color. The program looks at the color around each pixel and determines whether the color is similar to and should be included in the new artifact of that color, or whether it's different enough to exclude and put into another artifact.

Compression Factor

The compression factor determines how much should be left out when the image is compressed. Some programs call this picture quality. The two scales are the inverse of each other: A compression factor of 10 is the same as a picture quality of 90. Select a compression factor of 10. It is best to have the option Always Prompt for Options on Save selected. Compression above 30 or picture quality below 70 will generally result in poorer picture quality.

To finish saving the image in JPG format, select compression of 10 or picture quality 90. Click OK and close your color scanning program.

Saving the File in a PCX Format

If you want to archive and at a later stage crop a portion of this photo, you need to save the whole image as a PCX file to maintain the sharpness. Here's how to save as a PCX file:

1. In the Original Image view, on the menu click File Save Image (Figure 8.17).

Figure 8.17
The File menu with
Save Image Option

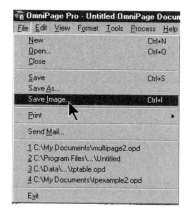

2. In the Save as Type field, click the down-pointing arrow.
3. Click PCX Files (*.pcx).
4. In the File Name field, type "beautifulday2."
5. Click OK.

That's it. The entire photo is now saved as a PCX file.

Bringing a Photo into a Word Document

An important part of working with scanned images is getting them into Word or another word-processing application. As some of you may already have discovered, inserting images can at times be frustrating. Sometimes they are too big, or do not go where you want them, or they seem to move around by themselves.

When bringing photos or graphics into Word, it's a good idea to insert them into a text box. It gives you greater control over the photo size and its placement. If you are writing a newsletter, you should always use text boxes. You can link the text boxes together to control the text flow. If you don't use text boxes, the photo can insert in its original size, throwing everything out.

Creating a Text Box to Insert the Photo

Figure 8.18
The cursor shape for inserting a text box into Microsoft Word

1. Launch your word processor, in this case Word.
2. On the menu bar, click Insert.
3. Click Text Box.
4. The cursor changes to cross hairs (Figure 8.18).
5. Position the mouse in the top left-hand corner of where you want to start drawing the text box.
6. Click and hold down the left mouse button and drag to the bottom right-hand corner of where you want the text box to finish.
7. Release the mouse button to anchor the finish point. A frame appears (Figure 8.19).

Figure 8.19
Text box frame for inserting a photo in Microsoft Word

Now that we have a picture placeholder for our photo, let's insert the photo into the frame.

Inserting a Photo into the Text Box

1. Click in the frame; the frame handles appear.
2. On the Word menu, click File.
3. Turn on Thumbnails, so you can ensure that you have the right photo.
4. Click the Thumbnail button on the top right-hand side of the dialog box (Figure 8.20).

Figure 8.20
Switching Thumbnails in Microsoft Word Insert Picture

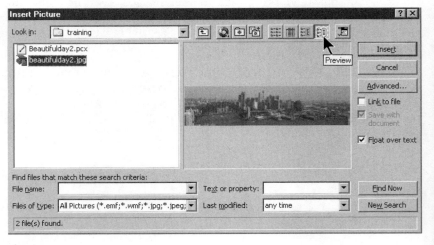

5. Make sure you are in your training directory.

6. Make sure you have All Pictures selected in the Files of type field (Figure 8.21).

Figure 8.21
Files of type to select in Microsoft Word's Insert Picture

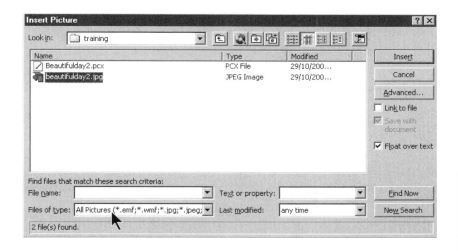

7. Double-click the file beautifulday2.jpg.

The photo displays in the text box with a border around the text box (Figure 8.22).

Figure 8.22
Cropped JPG photo in text box in Microsoft Word

TIP
You can also use the Insert Picture function to replace photos in documents. To select the photo, click inside the text box, not on the outside border of the text box frame. Then, delete the original image in the text box and insert the new image.

CHAPTER 8

Removing the Border from the Text Box Frame

In the figure below, you will see a border line around the outside of the text box frame. You can remove the border line from the text box frame. Here's how:

1. To select the frame, click the border of the text box frame; the handles appear.
2. Right-click the outside frame.
3. Click Format Text Box.
4. Click Colors and Lines.
5. In the Line Color field, click the down pointing arrow.
6. Click No Line.
7. Click OK.

The border is switched off.

Once the photo is in your document, you can move it easily, because it is in a text box. You can also format the text box—its borders, position, and wrapping requirements.

TIP
It is a good idea to leave the border switched on until you move the photo to the new location. It makes it a little easier to see the frame and handles.

Moving the Photo with the Text Box

To move a photo and its text box:

1. Click the outside of the text box frame; the handles appear.
2. Move the mouse on to the frame. It turns to a cross with arrowheads. Click and hold down the left mouse button.
3. Drag to where you want the photo.
4. Release the mouse button.

If you grab one of the frame handles, the mouse changes to a diagonal line with arrowheads. This will change the size of the text frame. Grabbing a corner handle will proportionally resize the frame. If you grab a side handle, the frame will be become elongated, as may the image.

If you don't use a Word text box for a photo:

▶ You can't move the photo easily.
▶ It can display in Word in its original size and you may have to manually resize it.

How do you move the photo without a text box frame?

> ▶   You have to enter hard paragraph marks by pressing the Enter key to position
> the photo (Figure 8.23).

Figure 8.23
The top photo is in a
text box; the bottom
photo is not

Notice the returns in Figure 8.23 required to bring the photo down the page. You can format
its placement by clicking on Format the Picture, selecting Wrapping > Float Over Text, and
setting its position on the page. This is like desktop publishing and it takes time to work out.
It can get quite messy, so that's why text boxes are "no fuss."

Word's Float Over Text Option for Photos

You can insert the photo to float over the text. Floating pictures are inserted in the document
so you can position them precisely on the page or in front of or behind text or other objects.
The image displays automatically with handles, so you can move it easily. The Word option,
"Float over Text," brings in the photo much larger than the original, and you will have to
manually resize the image in the document and play around with the picture formats.

In the next section, we will look at a complex page layout and bring together all the tools
covered. It will show what happens with a real life document and how parts of the page may
not be zoned correctly. We will see how to fix the page and resave as a Word document.

A Complex Layout with a Color Photo

Now that you know how to capture a logo and scan a signature and color photo, let's take a
look at a more complex document. This section will give you detailed instructions on what
to do when you have a color photo in a document surrounded by text, columns, tables, and
graphics. We included this because we know so many of you have a need for this type of
scanning.

CHAPTER 8

In this section, you will discover:

▶ Fixing lost components

▶ Changing zone properties, expanding and resizing zone frames

▶ Tips and notes on when to use JPG file format

▶ How to retain graphics and headers and footers

▶ An explanation of resolution and a table detailing supported image file types

▶ Working with frames in Word

▶ How to reduce Microsoft Word document file sizes

In this exercise, you will be using the example below (Figure 8.24). The file name is "Doc containing colored photo." You can download this file from the Web site (see Introduction). We have selected a document with many elements on the page; it requires a good deal of practice at editing zones. You may get different results, so make the adjustments as necessary. Follow the instructions below.

Figure 8.24
Exercise for this
section

<u>Pixel Colour</u>

Colour depth is the information required to define the colour of each pixel or dot. Windows uses numbers to represent colours. For example, for Black and White, Windows uses 0 for white and 1 for black. For gray scale, 0 for white and 255 for black and the numbers in between will define 254 different shades of gray.

Change in Size

<u>Black and White, Line Art</u>	○ ●	1 bit (0 or 1)	1X
<u>Gray Scale</u> 256 shades from white to black	○ ◐◑●● ●	8 Bits (1 Byte)	8X
<u>256 Colour</u> Windows basic 256 colours from white to black	○ ● ○ ● ●	8 Bits (1 Byte)	8X
<u>24 Bit colour</u> 16 Million colours from white to black	■○ ○ ◐ ● ●	24 bits (3 Bytes)	24X
<u>30 Bit colour</u> 1 Billion colours from white to black	■○ ○ ◐ ● ●	32 bits (4 bytes)	32X

FILE SIZE

RELATIVE CHANGE IN FILE SIZE REQUIREMENTS				
	RESOLUTION			
COLOUR DEPTH	200 DPI	300 DPI	600 DPI	1200 DPI
Black and white line Art	1X	2.25X	9X	36X
256 Grey Scale	8X	20X	72X	288X
256 Colours	8X	20X	72X	288X
24 Bit Colour (16 million Colours)	24X	54X	216X	864X
30 Bit Colour (1 billion Colours)	32X	72X	288X	1152X

This is an example of a digital image at a resolution 1024 x 768 pixels. This is the same as scanning the photograph at <u>150DPI</u>. The quality of the printed image depends on the quality of the paper used, the features and resolution of the colour printer. See your local computer store for examples. You will be amazed at what is possible these days. File sizes:- BMP = 6.2Mb. JPG(10%) =76Kb

Explanation of File Sizes
On the Multimedia Scanning Training CDROM, this same photo is scanned at 100DPI. It's saved in JPG format with 30% compression. The File size is 72Kb. The same photograph scanned at 300DPI and saved in BMP format is 6.2Mb. At 600DPI it would be about 24Mb. As the resolution of Computer Screens is between 75-85DPI, there is no difference in viewing an image scanned at 100DPI or 600DPI. When you Zoom into the image, then you will notice the difference.

Scan the Document and Review Missing Areas

We will scan the document using the Manual OCR toolbox and have OmniPage automatically draw the zones by setting Perform OCR to Automatic. Once the page is scanned, we will review the drawn zones and the recognition results. After identifying the zones that need "repairing," we will make the changes and reprocess the page.

1. Click the Manual OCR toolbox.
2. Click the down pointing arrow of the Get Page and select Scan Color.
3. Leave Perform OCR as Automatic so it will detect all the columns and photos.
4. Leave Export Results as Save As.
5. Place the document in the scanner.
6. Click the Get Page button.

The document appears in the Original Image and Thumbnail view. Now, we need to OCR the document and let OmniPage automatically draw the zones.

1. Click the Perform OCR button.
2. The zones are drawn automatically, the OCR process runs, and the image appears in the Text Editor view.
3. The OCR Proofreading dialog box displays; close it for now. We do not need to do any proofing yet.

We want to see the results of the recognized text. The best way to see this is to expand the Text Editor view. To see more of the recognized document in the Text Editor view, enlarge the Text Editor view. There are several ways to do this:

1. Click the vertical view divider bar between the Original Image view and the Text Editor view.
2. Hold the mouse button down and drag to the left to make the Text Editor view larger.
3. Zoom in the Text Editor view. Click the right mouse button, click Zoom, click 100%.

Or . . .

1. On the menu, click View.
2. Click the Original Image view to switch off.
3. Zoom in the Text Editor view. Click the right mouse button, click Zoom, and click 100%.

Scroll around the Text Editor view and compare with your original. You will notice that not all components of the page have been recognized correctly (Figure 8.25). We will refer to them as miss-recognized components. Let's see what's happened.

Figure 8.25
Results using AutoOCR
showing zones,
recognized text, and
graphics with missing
areas and text

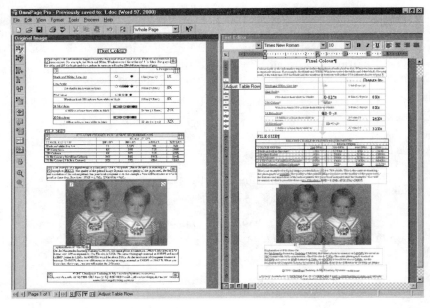

OmniPage has recognized what it can from the zones it has drawn. However, some areas of text and corners of the photo are missing. These areas are:

▶ **Zone 3—The Table** (Figure 8.26). Because OmniPage has zoned and recognized this area as a table, which is correct, the graphics in the table have been interpreted as text. However, in this case, we want the graphics maintained in the table, so we will have to change the properties of the table to a graphic zone. This way, the integrity of the table, including the graphics, is retained. Remember that saving this as a graphic means you will not be able to edit the table's contents in Word. If you needed to modify the contents in Word, first save the document as it is now with the text zone and the hieroglyphics in place of the small graphics. Then, redraw a graphic zone only around the graphics in the table, and resave the document. You can then recombine the two results in Word.

Figure 8.26
Zone 3 shows graphics
in the table not
recognized

Black and White, Line Art¤	O¤	1 bit (0 or 1)¤	
Gray Scale¤			
256 shades from white to black¤	O·03"□	8 Bits (1 Byte)¤	8X□
256 Colour¤	0000¤		
Windows basic 256 colours from white to black¤		8 Bits (1 Byte)¤	8X□
24 Bit colour¤	℗0·O·–¤		
16 Million colours from white to black¤		24 bits (3 Bytes)¤	24X□
30 Bit colour¤	ED◆O·¸¤		
1 Billion colours from white to black¤		32 bits (4 bytes)¤	32X□

▶ **Zone 7—Top left-hand corner of the photo** (Figure 8.27). The top left-hand corner of the photo has a chunk missing. This is because the bottom of the paragraph just above the photo (Zone 6) and the photo are too close together. The descending part of the letter "y" is directly above the missing corner of the photo. This is because OmniPage is looking for text, so it has "used" part of the area of the photo to make sure it can "see" all of the letter "y." Although the text zone does not include that area, it is not "available" for OmniPage to automatically draw the graphic zone.

Figure 8.27
Zone 7 shows the missing corner of the photo

▶ **Zone 6—Bottom of the paragraph above the photo** (Figure 8.28). This paragraph appears OK; however, when we fix the top left-hand corner of the photo below, we will need to adjust the paragraph. This is what it will look like when we start making adjustments. The last line is not included in the zone.

Figure 8.28
Zone 6 shows last line of paragraph not included in zone

This is an example of a digital image at a resolution 1024 x 768 pixels. This is the same photograph at 150DPI. The quality of the printed image depends on the quality of the and resolution of the colour printer. See your local computer store for examples. You possible these days. File sizes:- BMP = 6.2Mb. JPG(10%) =76Kb

▶ **Zone 7—The bottom of the photo**. The bottom of the photo is missing because the text of the paragraph of Zone 8 is very close to the photo. OmniPage has used some of the area of the photo to ensure the recognition of the text.

▶ **Zone 8—The explanation of pixels paragraph.** The paragraph Zone 8 extends into the photo Zone 7 (Figure 8.29), and the last line of the paragraph is cut off. Also, part of the bottom left-hand corner of the photo has been recognized as text, hence the character "h." This is because the two zones are very close to one another. To see where in the Original Image view OmniPage recognized the "h," go to the Text Editor view and double-click the letter "h" to open the Verify Text window (Figures 8.29 and 8.30).

Figure 8.29
Zone 7 and Zone 8 show how the paragraph and photo merge with part of the photo recognized as text

Explanation·of·File·Sizes·On·the·
Multimedia·Scanning·Training·CDROM, ·this·same·photo·is·scanned·at·100DPI.·It's·saved·in·JPG·format·with·30%·
compression.·The·File·size·is·72Kb.·The·same·photograph·scanned·at·300DPI·and·saved·in·BMP·format·is·6.2Mb.
At·600DPI·it·would·be·about·24Mb.·As·the·resolution·of·Computer·Screens·is·between·75-85DPI, ·there·is·no·
difference·in·viewing·an·image·scanned·at·100DPI·or·600DPI.·When·you·Zoom·into·the·image, ·then·you·will·

CHAPTER 8

Figure 8.30
The Verify Text window showing the area of the original image where OmniPage "detected" the letter "h"

▶ **Zone 9—The footer** (Figure 8.31). Some of the characters have not been recognized. This is because they are too small; they are less than 6 points. And because the document has been scanned in color, the characters are not quite as sharp as they would be if they had been scanned in black and white. If you rescanned the page in black and white, the characters would be recognized. Also, notice that the last line of the paragraph has been cut off. Hence, the gray down-pointing arrows; when you see these arrows, the easiest way to fix the problem is to make the zone bigger if possible.

Figure 8.31
Zone 9 shows the fonts are too small and therefore not crisp and sharp enough to be recognized correctly

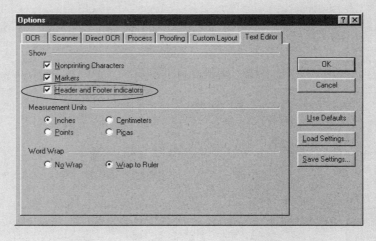

NOTE
OmniPage will not include a footer in a footer position on the first page of a document unless it is repeated on the following pages. This is a one-page document. It's not a multi-page document.

Even if you have switched on the option Header and Footer Indicators in the Options Panel under Text Editor, it still won't maintain the footer position on a single page document (Figure 8.32 below).

Figure 8.32
Option to recognize header and footer

Modify Zones and Properties

To achieve the results you want, you may need to make changes to the zones and properties. You will need to:

1. Change the properties of the zones.
2. Fix up, resize, and extend the zone to include the missing areas of the photo and paragraph.
3. Extend the zones so that all text appears in the Text Editor view.

We need to change some of the zone properties that have been automatically identified as single column. This is the footer at the bottom of the page and the table zone in the center of the page. We will change these to graphic zones. We are going to change the table to a graphic zone, as we want to maintain the graphics within the table and we do not want to make any changes to the table. When you have parts of a page where the text is too small for accurate recognition, and you do not want to modify the saved text, you can save it as a graphic. We are changing the footer to a graphic zone because the fonts are too small to be recognized, and we do not want to make any changes to it. We only have one page, so the content of the footer is not really considered a footer.

As we are going to be working in the Original Image view, maximize the Original Image view. On the menu, click View and select Original Image view, or use the icon on the navigation bar. Alternatively, you can drag the vertical view divider bar.

Change the Properties of Zone 3, the Table Zone

1. Position your pointer in the table zone, Zone 3.
2. Right-click.
3. Click the top option.
4. Click Graphic Zone.

The zone identifier has changed to indicate a graphic zone, as shown in Figure 8.33.

Figure 8.33
The table is identified
as a graphic zone

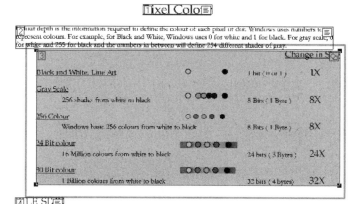

CHAPTER 8

Change the Properties of Zone 9, the Footer Zone

Repeat the steps above to change the Footer to a graphic zone (Figure 8.34).

Figure 8.34
The footer is identified as a graphic

Now that we have changed the properties of the table and footer zones, let's fix up the photo.

Resizing and Extending a Graphic Zone

If you need to, in the Original Image view, right-click and select Zoom. Then click in the graphic zone to select it. Scroll to the left so you can see the top left-hand corner of the photo. You may need to zoom in further to see the handles.

1. At the top left-hand side of the photo, position the mouse pointer on the lower right-hand handle of the missing corner. The cursor will change to a diagonal double arrow.
2. Click and hold the left mouse button.
3. Drag up and to the left to include the missing corner, as shown in Figure 8.35.
4. Release mouse button.

Figure 8.35
The top left-hand corner of the graphic zone extended to include the entire photo

That's all we have to do to fix the top left-hand corner of the photo. However, you will notice that the paragraph above the photo, Zone 6, merges into the top of the graphic zone of the photo (Figure 8.36).

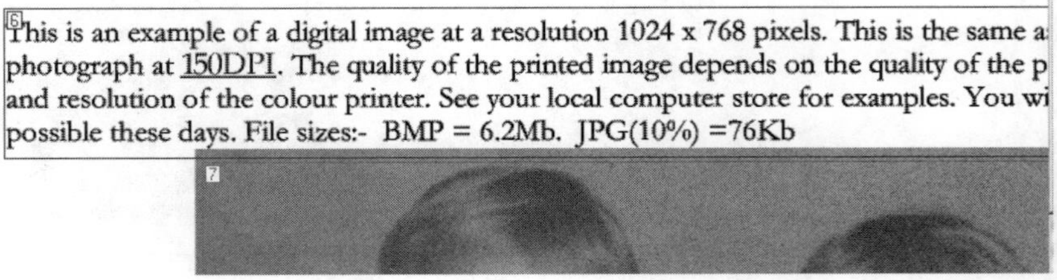

Figure 8.36
Paragraph zone frame merging into photo

This is an example of a digital image at a resolution 1024 x 768 pixels. This is the same a photograph at 150DPI. The quality of the printed image depends on the quality of the p and resolution of the colour printer. See your local computer store for examples. You wi possible these days. File sizes:- BMP = 6.2Mb. JPG(10%) =76Kb

To fix Zone 6, the paragraph above the photo:

1. While still in the Original Image view, click in Zone 6, the paragraph, to select it; the zone turns gray.

2. Now, move the paragraph. Click, hold down the left mouse button, and drag the paragraph upwards a little. As you do this, you will notice the last line of the paragraph will drop out of the zone frame. You want to be able to move the paragraph away from the photo's top border.

3. Now, extend the paragraph frame down to include the last line. Point the mouse pointer on the left-hand corner handle.

4. Move the mouse around until it changes to a double headed arrow (Figure 8.37).

Figure 8.37
Zone 6 shows which handle and cursor shape is required to extend the zone border to include the last line of the paragraph

This is an example of a digital image at a resolution 1024 x 768 pixels. This is the same photograph at 150DPI. The quality of the printed image depends on the quality of the and resolution of the colour printer. See your local computer store for examples. You w possible these days. File sizes:- BMP = 6.2Mb. JPG(10%) =76Kb

5. Click with the left mouse button and drag the zone frame down to include the last line of the paragraph.

6. Check the right side of the paragraph. You may need to expand the right side of the frame. When resizing the frame, it can move a little and characters may be excluded.

7. Release the mouse button.

8. Now, we need to click in Zone 7, the photo.

9. Grab the top left-hand handle, hold down the left mouse button, and drag up to include the top of the photo (Figure 8.38).

CHAPTER 8

Figure 8.38
Zone 6 is now in correct position; the top left corner of the photo, Zone 7, has also been reclaimed

COLOUR DEPTH	200 DPI	300 DPI	600 DPI	1200 DPI
Black and white line Art	1X	2.25X	9X	36X
256 Grey Scale	8X	20X	72X	288X
256 Colours	8X	20X	72X	288X
24 Bit Colour (16 million Colours)	24X	54X	216X	864X
30 Bit Colour (1 billion Colours)	32X	72X	288X	1152X

Fixing the Photo Zone and the Last Paragraph

Zones 7 and 8 had the same problem as Zone 6. Now, we have to fix up the paragraph below the photo. The last paragraph has grabbed the bottom left of the graphic zone from the photo (Figure 8.39), mistaking it for an "h" (Figure 8.40). Let's fix up the paragraph (Zone 8) and the bottom of the photo (Zone 7).

Figure 8.39
Shows Zone 8—the last paragraph—and Zone 7—the bottom of the photo—in the Text Editor view

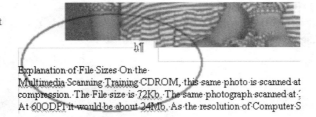

Figure 8.40
Zone 8 and Zone 7 in the Original Image view

1. Click in Zone 8 to select it.

2. Position the mouse pointer on the top right-hand handle of the area extending into the Photo, Zone 7. The cursor changes to a diagonal double headed arrow.

3. Hold down the left mouse button.

4. Drag down to below the bottom of the photo (Figure 8.41).

5. Release mouse button.

Figure 8.41
The position of the top left of Zone 8 when finished resizing the zone

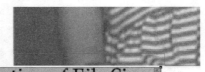

Next, let's fix the bottom of the photo.

1. To select the photo, click in graphic Zone 7.

2. At the bottom left of the photo, position the mouse pointer on the top right-hand handle of the zone (Figure 8.42). The cursor will change to a diagonal double-headed arrow.

Figure 8.42
Shows the top right-hand handle of the bottom of the photo, Zone 7, for resizing the frame to include the bottom of the photo

3. Hold down the left mouse button.

4. Drag down to below the bottom of the photo (Figure 8.43).

5. Release the mouse button.

Figure 8.43
The photo frame extended to the bottom of the photo

That's fixed the bottom of the photo, and now we're finished with editing zones. Before we rerecognize the document, make sure the Original and Text Editor views are sharing the screen so we can see what happens during the processing.

Remember how to do this?

1. Grab the window divider. Position the mouse on the window divider between the Original and Text Editor views.

2. Hold down the left mouse button.

3. Drag to the right to see more of the Original Image view.

Now, let's rerecognize the document with the edited zones and change the document layout. Then we will save the results.

Rerecognizing the Edited Zones

As you are using the Manual OCR toolbox, you need to click the Perform OCR Process button to have OmniPage reprocess the page with the new zones you have drawn.

1. Click the Perform OCR button.
2. Click Yes to rerecognize the zones.
3. The document is rerecognized and the Text Editor view displays the changes you have just made.
4. Close the OCR Proofreader box. No need to do any proofreading yet.
5. Scroll in the Text Editor view and review your document.

NOTE

You will notice that some of the zones OmniPage has recognized are not big enough, and the text flows below the zone. OmniPage tells you this has happened by placing small, light gray arrows on the bottom or the side of the text in the Text Editor view. When you export the page to Word, you may not notice the missing text. The text frame in Word will be too small and the bottom lines of text will not be displayed or printed. Therefore, it is a good idea to make the zones bigger in OmniPage before you export to an application.

Reviewing the Results in the Text Editor View

All the zones you fixed should be looking good now. The graphics in the table are now recognized. The photo has no missing chunks, the last paragraph fits nicely, and the footer text is all there.

If you scroll in the Text Editor view, you may find the heading at the top of the document—"Pixel Color," Zone 1—has wrapped the word "Color" out of sight or cut the bottom of the characters off. You may also find the heading "File Sizes," Zone 4, just above the table "Relative Change in File Size Requirements," is not big enough. It does not always happen, and each time you scan the document it may change. Even if we switch off Word Wrap in the Process settings, the characters at the bottom of the text may still be cut off. This is due to the tight zoning parameters that OmniPage's auto-zoning uses. Therefore, we will have to resize the zones. If a zone is not big enough for the text, OmniPage displays light gray down pointing arrows in the zone frame in the Text Editor view (Figure 8.44).

Figure 8.44
A zone frame with gray down-pointing arrows—this means the frame is not big enough for the contents

FILE:

Resize Zone Frames

We will need to resize the zones in the Original Image view. Here's how:

Figure 8.45

The handle and mouse shape required to resize a zone frame

1. Scroll in the Original Image view and locate Zone 1, Pixel Color.

2. Click in the zone to select it. The zones display in gray. The handles appear.

3. Position you pointer on the bottom left-hand corner (Figure 8.45); click and hold the left mouse button.

4. Drag up or down and out so there is a good amount of clear space around the text (Figure 8.46).

5. Release the mouse button.

6. Repeat for Zone 4.

Figure 8.46

Zone 1 Pixel Color resized to incorporate the contents of the zone

After resizing the zones, rerecognize the document by clicking on the Perform OCR button. A couple of paragraphs may need adjusting slightly; that is easy to do in Word.

Select Document Layout

Before we export the document to Word, you need to select the document layout in the Text Editor view for the Word document. Since we need it as close as possible to the original and we want to edit it, choose Flowing Columns—at the bottom of the Text Editor view, click the Flowing Columns icon. If you look at the results, you will see large, light gray arrows. These display the flow of the paragraphs, in the order they will be exported (not to be confused with the small gray arrows).

Saving the Results as a Word Document

We will now save the page as a Word document, and leave the Save and Launch selected. This will automatically save the document, then open it in Word.

1. On the Manual OCR toolbox, click the icon in the Export Results field.

2. Make sure you have your training directory selected.

3. Select Word 97 format in Save as Type.

4. In the file name field, type "Document Containing Photo."

5. Click OK.

The document then appears in Word, where you can easily make changes. Although we selected Flowing Columns in OmniPage, it often exports complex layout documents in frames, especially when manual zones have been drawn.

NOTE

If Retain Graphics is deselected at the time of exporting, your document will be saved without the graphics. In the default setting, Retain Graphics is selected.

You will notice in the first paragraph that the last word, "gray," has some problems. The bottoms of the "g" and "y" have been cut off (Figure 8.47).

Colour depth is the information required to define the colour of each pixel or dot. Windows uses numbers to represent colours. For example, for Black and White, Windows uses 0 for white and 1 **for** black. For gray scale, 0 for white and 255 for black and the numbers in between will define 254 different shades of gray. ¶

<u>Change in Size</u>

Figure 8.47
Scanned results in Microsoft Word with the bottom of the characters in the word "gray" cut off

This is what can happen when the zones in the Original Image view are not large enough to accommodate the text. Sometimes, the text frame in Word is the correct size and location, but the font size calculation may have resulted in a slightly larger font, so all the text won't quite fit. Let's fix this.

Working with Frames in Word

Working with frames in Word is a little like working with zones in OmniPage. They define the area in which text or a graphic will be displayed, and they have a defined location on the page and various properties associated with them. OmniPage uses frames to position the recognized text in the saved documents. The text within the frames of Word does not flow from one frame to another. Text boxes, on the other hand, can be linked to make the text flow. While they look the same, frames and text boxes differ slightly. For further explanation of frames and text boxes, reference the Microsoft Word Help entry, "The difference between a text box and a frame." To resize a frame to display all the text or picture within, first select the frame, then grab one of the handles and drag to resize.

1. Click in the paragraph to select the frame.
2. Click the border of the frame to switch on the handles.
3. You will need to expand the frame to expose the characters.
4. Point the mouse on the top right-hand handle and move it around until it changes to a double arrow.
5. Hold down the left mouse button and drag just a little downward to fully expose the word "gray."

The frame of the next paragraph hides the bottom border of the table (Figure 8.48).

FILE·SIZE¶

RELATIVE·CHANGE·IN·FILE·SIZE·REQUIREMENTS¤				
¤	RESOLUTION¤			
COLOUR·DEPTH¤	200·DPI¤	300·DPI¤	600·DPI¤	1200·DPI¤
Black·and·white·line·Art¤	1X¤	2.25X¤	9X¤	36X¤
256·Grey·Scale¤	8X¤	20X¤	72X¤	288X¤
256·Colours¤	8X¤	20X¤	72X¤	288X¤
24·Bit·Colour·(16·million·Colours)¤	24X¤	54X¤	216X¤	864X¤
30·Bit·Colour·(1·billion·Colours)¤	32X¤	72X¤	288X¤	1152X¤

Figure 8.48
The bottom line of the table border is hidden beneath the paragraph below

To fix it, follow these steps:

1. Click in the table.
2. Click the border of the frame to switch on the handles.
3. You will need to expand the frame to expose the border line.
4. Position the mouse on the bottom middle handle and move it around until it changes to a double arrow.
5. Hold down the left mouse button and drag down a little to fully expose the border line.

The heading "Explanation of File Sizes" (Figure 8.49) is cut off at the bottom.

Explanation·of·File·Sizes·¶
On·the·Multimedia·Scanning·Training·CDROM,·this·same·photo·is·scanned·at·100DPI.·It's·saved·in·JPG·format·with·30%·compression.·The·File·size·is·72Kb.·The·same·photograph·scanned·at·300DPI·and·saved·in·BMP·format·is·6.2Mb.·At·600DPI·it·would·be·about·24Mb.·As·the·resolution·of·Computer·Screens·is·between·75-85DPI,·there·is·no·difference·in·viewing·an·image·scanned·at·100DPI·or·600DPI.·When·you·Zoom·into·the·image,·then·you·will·notice·the·difference.¶

Figure 8.49
The bottom characters in the heading "Explanation of File Sizes" is cut off

To fix this, you need to move and expand the last paragraph frame. The bottom of the heading is under the paragraph's frame. Do the following:

1. Click in the paragraph below the heading.
2. Click the border of the frame to switch on the handles.
3. You will need to move the frame. Position the cursor in the middle of the paragraph, hold the left mouse button, and drag down a little to make room to expand the heading frame.

4. Click in the heading frame.

5. Click the frame border to switch on the handles.

6. Grab the middle handle by pointing to it, hold down the left mouse button, and drag down just a little to expose the bottom of the characters of the heading "Explanation of File Sizes."

In the last paragraph, the words DPI need fixing. In addition, in the last line of the paragraph, the bottoms of the characters are cut off (Figure 8.50).

On the Multimedia Scanning Training CDROM, this same photo is scanned at 100DPI. It's saved in JPG format with 30% compression. The File size is 72Kb. The same photograph scanned at 30ODPI and saved in BMP format is 6.2Mb. At 60ODPI it would be about 24Mb. As the resolution of Computer Screens is between 75-85 DPI, there is no difference in viewing an image scanned at 1OODPI or 600DPI. When you Zoom into the image, then you will notice the difference.¶

Figure 8.50
The text to be edited

Notice that the zeros have been recognized as 0's. The text should read 300DPI, 600DPI, and 100DPI. This can also be edited in OmniPage's Text Editor view before exporting. To fix these, simply delete the incorrect "O's" and type in zeros. This would have been picked up in the Proofreader. Try running the Proofreader in OmniPage; on the standard toolbar, click the button with ABC and a check in it.

To expand the frame to expose the bottom of the last line of characters in the paragraph, do the following:

1. Click in the paragraph below the heading "Explanation of Pixels."

2. Click the border of the frame to switch on the handles.

3. You will need to expand the frame downward to expose the bottom of the characters. Point the mouse on the bottom middle handle and move it around until it changes to a double arrow.

4. Hold down the left mouse button and drag down a little to expose the bottom of the characters.

There are a lot of steps involved in scanning and editing in this exercise. If you've followed us through every step, you should be feeling a little bit more in control when scanning complex documents. The steps we have gone through here can apply to any document. You have seen how the size of zones can affect the saved result in Word. Most importantly, you now know how to recognize what has happened and what to do to remedy it.

OmniPage saved the photo in this exercise in BMP format at 150 dpi with no compression, so it can be read by most word processors. The document is 1.743MB in size, and the large photo file takes up nearly all of the size. You can reduce the file size by rescanning the document and extracting the photo during the scanning process with a graphic zone. Change the image to a JPG format and replace the photo in the Word document with the JPG image. Alternatively, you can use OmniPage and save the document in HTML format. This automatically creates separate JPG files for each graphic. We will cover this in Chapter 10.

OmniPage saves a graphic at 150 dpi. If you need a higher resolution, scan the graphic or photo separately using your color imaging scanning software—for instance, Adobe Photoshop or Photo Deluxe. You might require higher resolution if, for instance, you want to enlarge the photo to twice its original size. In this case, you would need to scan at 300 dpi.

Supported File Types

We have spoken quite a lot throughout this chapter about image file types that you can save and open in OmniPage. The table below lists the types of image files you can open and the file types for saving the scanned images. Saving scanned images is not the same as saving a graphic zone. A graphic zone from the Text Editor view is saved in a BMP file format in applications that support embedded graphics, or as separate JPG files when saving the document as HTML.

Table 8.1
OmniPage Pro 11 can Open and Save these Image File Types

File Type	Multi-page	Open/Save	B/W, Gray, Color
Bitmap (*.bmp)	No	Open and Save	All
DCX (*.dcx)	Yes	Open and Save	All
GIF (*.gif)	No	Open and Save	All
JPEG (*.jpg)	No	Open and Save	Gray, Color
PCX (*.pcx)	No	Open and Save	All
PDF (*.pdf)	Yes	Open (see NOTE)	All
PNG (*.png)	No	Open and Save	All
TIF compressed G3/G4 (*.tif)	Yes	Open and Save	Black and white
TIF compressed LZW (*.tif)	Yes	Open and Save	All
TIF FX (*.xif)	Yes	Open	All
TIF PackBits (*.tif)	Yes	Open and Save	All
TIF uncompressed (*.tif)	Yes	Open and Save	All

CHAPTER 8

NOTE

Image files can have a resolution up to 600 dpi, but 300 dpi is recommended for best OCR results. OmniPage Pro stores black and white images at their original resolution, and grayscale and color images at not more than 150 dpi.

You cannot save original images to PDF format, but you can save recognition results to four variants of PDF; all of these save the recognition results as viewable pages. See Chapter 10, "Saving, Publishing, and Sending Documents."

Images are saved as displayed whenever possible. For example, if you have a black and white image and want to save as a JPEG, you will be prompted to convert it to grayscale. This is because JPG does not support black and white. It only supports grayscale and color. If you try to save a grayscale or color image to TIF G3 or G4, conversion to black and white will be offered. TIF G3 and G4 only support black and white, like a fax.

9

Multiple-Page and Long Documents

Now that you are an expert at scanning single- and multi-column documents and you know how to use automatic and manual zones, let's look at how to scan multiple-page and long documents. In this chapter, we will cover scanners and ADFs (Automatic Document Feeder), scanning in 3D, and scanning books. We'll also look at how to easily divide long documents into smaller ones in a single process, how to scan double-sided pages, and even how to set up your scanner to work unattended.

Most of your scanning may be documents of more than one page. Everything we have covered so far applies to multi-page documents as well as single pages. By far the quickest and easiest way to scan documents is to use the setting Automatic in Perform OCR, unless your documents are better scanned with one of the other OCR settings or templates. Examples of multi-page document scanning are books, reports, manuals, and transcripts. Remember, it is the Text Editor view that determines the layout of your saved document.

Scanners and Multi-Page Documents

Does your scanner have an Automatic Document Feeder (ADF)—for example, on a photocopier, a place to stack a bunch of pages—or are *you* the automatic document feeder? Before we get into the specifics of scanning multi-page documents, we need first to introduce types of scanners relevant to scanning multi-page documents. The main two types you will come across are flatbed and sheet-fed.

Flatbed Scanners

Flatbed scanners are the most popular. They come in a variety of sizes, from some that are hardly larger than a small stack of paper to professional high-speed optical scanners. These scanners all have a flat piece of glass as their scanner bed on which you place the item to be scanned.

The smaller, slim-line flatbed scanners use a "scanner head." This consists of a row of optical sensors and lights (LED, or Light Emitting Diode) on a bar the width of the scanner. The "scanner head" moves down the length of the page to scan the item. The scanner head both illuminates the page and senses the reflected image. This system is inexpensive to manufacture and provides excellent results and resolution. This system is known as CIS (Contact Image Sensor). As the name suggests, it is a "contact" sensor, meaning that the page or item being scanned needs to be in contact with the glass bed for the image to be in focus.

When scanning books, where the pages curve up toward the spine, you may not get a clear scanned image when the page is several millimeters off the scanner bed. In fact, it may not produce an image at all.

CAUTION

Do not press down too hard to flatten a book or item being scanned. Most of the scanner glass beds are only held on with double-sided sticky tape. You run the risk of pushing the glass right through.

Also, when cleaning the glass, *always* place the cleaning fluid on the cloth. Never pour or spray it directly on the glass as it can run under the glass and dissolve the glue.

The other types of flatbed scanners are those that are several inches high. These have a lamp and mirror to reflect the image. The reflection is then focused through a lens onto a CCD (Charge Coupled Device) sensor. These sensors provide a greater resolution and image quality than the CIS sensor, because the image is focused through a lens, just like a camera. The scanner has a "depth of field." In other words, you can scan 3D objects as high as an inch or so and still get a clear image. We have seen bakery laboratories scan moldy bread this way. They placed a black velvet cloth over the bread to keep out stray light. The poor staff who used the scanner afterwards had to clean the scanner glass. You can even use it to scan flower arrangements, as shown in Figure 9.1.

Figure 9.1
3D scan of a water iris flower from our garden fishpond

Flatbed scanners that use the CCD sensor are great for scanning single pages and books or items that do not sit completely flat on the scanner glass, as opposed to sheet-fed scanners, where you can only feed one page at a time past the scanner head.

Some accessories for flatbed scanners can make your life easier. A film and transparency unit will allow you to scan photograph film, both negatives and slides. An Automatic Document Feeder usually replaces the scanner lid and moves the paper past the scanner head. Often, ADF accessory units cost as much as the scanner; however, some inexpensive scanners have a good ADF built in. The scanners with a built-in ADF often cost less than purchasing a scanner and ADF accessory separately. The more pages per minute the scanner and ADF can handle, the higher the cost.

Sheet-Fed Scanners

Sheet-fed scanners range in price from under one hundred dollars into the thousands. These scanners feed the pages past a fixed scanning head. You can't use them to scan books or other items other than single pages, as they don't have a glass flatbed on which to lay your items. A single page at a time is passed over the scanner head, like the sheet feeder of a photocopier.

A sheet-fed scanner with a document tray is ideal for scanning multi-page documents. Many of these scanners do not take up much room on your desk. The less expensive ones don't have an ADF tray, requiring you to drop or feed each page separately. The more expensive ones have the document tray and can hold up to a hundred pages and scan at twenty pages per minute or more.

If you will be scanning a high number of pages, you really need a scanner with an ADF. Work out how many pages a day you are going to scan and the amount of time you want to spend scanning them. Some of the lower-cost scanners can take over sixty seconds to scan a full-page, color document. The more expensive scanners can even scan both sides of the original at the same time in color at twenty pages (forty images) per minute. Scanners that can scan both sides at the same time are called duplex scanners.

TIP

Say you plan to scan 200 pages a day and the pages have color images you want preserved. A cheap scanner that takes sixty seconds to scan a color page will take over three and a half hours to do the job. A ten-page-per-minute scanner with an ADF will do the job in twenty minutes, and you don't need to feed each page into the scanner. If you are going to be scanning and OCR'ing large numbers of pages, make sure you have a high-performance PC to handle it. If you have a fast scanner and a slow PC processor, the process will be slow, as the scanner will lag behind the PC.

Do you want to scan books and other items as well? If so, you will need a flatbed scanner with an ADF.

If you intend to do lots of scanning, you may find that two twenty-page-per-minute scanners are cheaper than one forty-page-per-minute scanner, and, of course, you have a backup.

If you have a flatbed scanner with no ADF and lots of pages to scan, what can you do? Well, OmniPage has thought of this. There is an Option Setting to automatically start another scan after so many seconds have elapsed. You set the time between scans. This gives you time to lift the lid, turn the page or place the next page on the scanner, and close the lid before OmniPage automatically starts the next scan. This saves you from having to press the Finish/Additional button after each page. You can concentrate on being the ADF.

Setting Up Automatic Scanning

Now that we know a little about the hardware we're working with, let's take a look at setting up Scanner options to work with multi-page documents.

Set Scanner Options

Before you get started, you will need to set the Scanner options to tell OmniPage to automatically scan pages.

1. On the toolbar, click the AB Options button.
2. Click the Scanner tab (Figure 9.2).

Figure 9.2
Setting the Scanner option to automatically scan the next page—the option you want to set is "Flatbed"

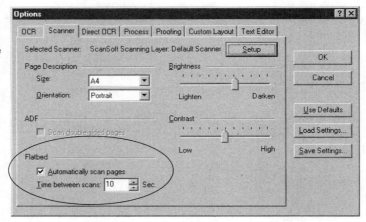

3. In the bottom left-hand side, click Flatbed to select Automatically scan pages. The default for this setting is off. When you select this option, "Time Between Scans" becomes active. Notice that the default time between scans is set to ten seconds. It is best to start with this time delay. You can change this at any time. As you get quicker at changing the pages, make it shorter. If it is too short a time for you to change the pages, make it longer.

After each page is scanned, OmniPage will begin the OCR processing and display the dialog box "Auto Scan Next Page from Flatbed" (Figure 9.3). This dialog box will be on the screen for the time you have set in "Time Between Scans." When the time delay is reached, OmniPage automatically begins the next scan. When you have scanned all the pages, click the Stop Scanning button.

If you drop the book you are scanning or need more time to prepare the page, just click the Pause button. The dialog box will stay on the screen. When you are ready to continue, click the Scan Now button.

Figure 9.3
Flatbed Auto Scan
Next Page dialog box

Automatic Document Feeder (ADF)

The best way to scan multi-page documents is with an Automatic Document Feeder. Simply load pages in the correct order into the ADF and click Start. OmniPage will begin to request pages from the scanner. If you have a scanner with an ADF attachment—provided you set up your scanner at the time of installation of OmniPage with the scanner wizard—all the pages in the ADF will automatically keep scanning until the ADF is empty.

NOTE

When using the AutoOCR toolbox to scan long documents with an ADF or the Flatbed option Automatically Scan Pages, OmniPage starts the zoning and OCR process as soon as the first page is scanned. This slows the scanning process of the next page, because OmniPage is busy OCR'ing the first page. The same will happen for subsequent pages. Depending on the speed of your PC, this can make a big difference in the time it takes to scan a document, especially when scanning color documents. See Table 9.1 for scan times.

Table 9.1
This table compares the time it takes to scan pages vs. the time it takes to scan *and* OCR pages, for black and white, grayscale, and color. These scan times are on a PC Pentium-III, 850 MHz, 256 MB RAM. The scanner is an Epson 1640SU-USB interface without an ADF.

Time in Mins:sec	Scan B&W		Scan Grayscale		Scan Color	
	Scan only	Scan / OCR	Scan only	Scan / OCR	Scan only	Scan / OCR
Page 1	0:15	0:15	0:18	0:18	0:30	0:30
Page 2	0:15	0:15	0:18	0:23	0:30	0:40
Page 3	0:15	0:15	0:18	0:25	0:30	0:40
Total inc. time between scans	1:00	1:15	1:15	2:00	2:00	2:30

CHAPTER 9

As you can see, when scanning just black and white, it took 15 seconds to scan each of the three pages, and in the same 15 seconds it could OCR the page as well. When we scan in color, it takes 30 seconds to scan a page without OCR. The first page is scanned and OCR'd in 30 seconds, but, because the PC is still busy OCR'ing the first page, it takes 40 seconds for the second and third pages to be scanned. If you are scanning many pages and depending on the speed of your PC, the scanning time can amount to several extra minutes, because the PC is busy doing the OCR. One way to cut down this wasted time is to use the ManualOCR toolbox and just scan all the pages in one shot. Then, let OmniPage do the OCR while you do something more productive.

1.   Use the ManualOCR toolbox to scan all the pages.

2.   When finished scanning all the pages, click the Save Results button to have OmniPage perform the OCR process and save the entire document.

NOTE
If you click the Perform OCR button, only the page currently selected will be processed.

3.   Or, use the Schedule OCR feature discussed later in this chapter. With Schedule OCR, you can scan all the pages and save as a multi-page image file (TIF or DCX). You can schedule OmniPage to scan and process pages after you have left work for the day.

Using Blank Pages to Separate Chapters or Sections

Here is a neat way to quickly break up a long document into separate files. Let's say you are scanning a book of one hundred loose pages and it consists of five chapters. You could scan the whole lot and save as a one hundred page Word document. Another way would be to scan the five chapters separately and save as five Word files. An even better way is to insert a blank page between each chapter or section of your document and scan the entire one hundred pages in one go. When you save the results, use the Advanced File Save option (Figure 9.4), "create a new file at each blank page." The saved files will have the name of your file with a number for each chapter or section—for example, "filename0001.doc, filename0002.doc." This is an easy way to break up large documents into smaller, more manageable files. If you are working on a large document in Word, it can be broken up into smaller files, allowing more than one person to work on the complete document at the same time. You can then use the Master document function in Word to recombine all the individual files into one document. Also, if Word crashes, and it probably will when you are using a very big file and you have a deadline, there's a good chance only one chapter will be damaged, not the entire one hundred pages.

Another place where this "blank page" can be handy is if you had a large number of photographs that you wanted as one photo per file. You could create a zone template of one graphic zone for the whole page (or use the Custom layout, One graphic, in Chapter 13—Advanced Options). Scan in each one separately and then go through the file save process for each. Or, place a blank page between each photo, scan them all in one take, and have OmniPage save to separate files.

Figure 9.4
The Advanced save option "Create a new file at each blank space"

TIP
When scanning long documents, if you have not manually placed a blank piece of paper between chapters or sections, scan in a blank page. On the menu, click File > Save Image. Save the image with the file name "Blank Page.tif." Then, using the Manual OCR toolbox, scan in all your pages. To separate the chapters, keep loading the Blank Page.tif file as many times as you need. In the Thumbnail view, click the blank page and move it to the desired location to create the breaks between the chapters.

Scanning Double-Sided Pages

With an ADF, you can scan double-sided pages. To set this option:

1. On the standard toolbar, click the AB button.
2. Click the Scanner tab.
3. In the ADF field, click Scan Double-sided Pages.

With this option set, OmniPage will scan all the odd page numbers through to the end of the document. The software will then direct you to turn the document over and scan all the even-numbered pages. When finished, OmniPage will interleave all pages in the correct sequence.

CHAPTER 9

If you have a duplex scanner, one that can scan both sides at the same time (which would make you lucky, as they are quite expensive), do not select this setting. This is because the duplex scanner will automatically send both sides of the page to OmniPage at the same time and in the right order. Please read the user manual that came with your duplex scanner for the correct setup.

Automatically Prompt for More Pages

Use this option if you have a document with more pages than the capacity of your ADF and you don't want to "break" the batch of pages you are scanning. If you don't have an ADF, you can have OmniPage automatically prompt you for more pages to allow you to manually scan all the pages of your document. This is similar to the Flatbed setting in the Scanner options. You can use the "Flatbed" option or the "Automatically Prompt for more Pages" option, or you can have both activated. I prefer to have both off all the time, unless I am doing a specific long document, as when I use the "Flatbed" option.

This setting is not in the Scanner options, but in the Process options.

1.   On the standard toolbar, click the AB Button.
2.   Click the Process tab.
3.   Click Automatically Prompt for more Pages to select it, as shown in Figure 9.5.

Figure 9.5
Option setting to
Automatically Prompt
for more Pages

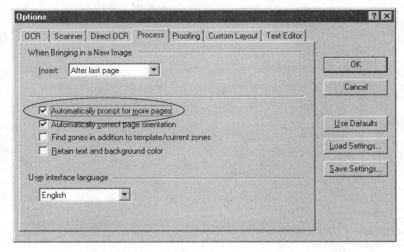

When the ADF is empty, you will get a prompt to load another batch of pages. These pages will be included in the current document. You can also use this option when scanning single pages without an ADF. (See Figure 9.6.)

When the ADF is empty or you have finished scanning a single page, a dialog box lets you add further batches or pages and tell OmniPage when all pages are scanned.

Figure 9.6
Continue Automatic
Processing dialog box

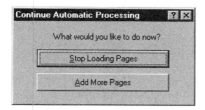

Scanning a Multi-Page Document

With the basic concepts of scanning multi-page and long documents understood, let's do an exercise. For this exercise, we will use five of the sample pages from the appendix of this book. The files are:

1.   Test.tif
2.   Spexmple.tif
3.   Mpexmple.tif
4.   Tpexmple.tif
5.   Xmas100.tif

You will also need a blank page of paper to scan.

In this exercise, we will use the blank page to split our five-page document into two separate "documents." We will place the blank page between pages three and four. Our result will be two saved files—one that's three pages long and another that's two pages long.

Check the Scanner Settings

First, we need to set the Scanner options.

1.   On the standard toolbar, click the AB Options button.

Figure 9.7
The Options button on
the standard toolbar—
this is the same as
selecting Tools,
Options

2.   Select the Scanner tab. If you have an ADF, make sure "Scan Double-Sided Pages" is not selected, as our pages are not double sided.
3.   For this exercise, you are going to "be" the ADF. Click the Flatbed option, Automatically scan pages. Ensure the time delay is set to 10 seconds. You can change this at any time.
4.   Click OK to set these options.

Now, let's set up the toolbox.

AutoOCR Toolbox

As you want OmniPage to automatically draw the zones, click the AutoOCR toolbox (Figure 9.8). When the process has finally finished, if the results are not quite as you would like, you can always go back and redraw the zones and rerecognize the pages.

Figure 9.8
The AutoOCR toolbox

Next, tell OmniPage how to get and process the pages.

1. As you are scanning black and white pages from the book, set the Get Pages option to Scan B&W.

2. Set the OCR options. You are scanning several pages of different layouts; set Perform OCR to Automatic.

3. Click the down arrow of Perform OCR.

4. Click Automatic.

Next, tell OmniPage how to export the results. You want OmniPage to automatically save the files at the end of the OCR process.

1. Click the down arrow of Export Results.

2. Click Save as File.

Scanning the Pages into OmniPage

Now that we have set up all the options, let's scan in the pages.

1. Place the first page in the scanner.

2. Click the Start button; OmniPage will start the scan of the first page.

3. When it has finished the scan, the "Auto Scan Next Page" dialog box displays. You switched this on in the Scanner options. You have ten seconds to remove the page and replace it with page two.

4. Proceed calmly, ten seconds is a long time. Open the scanner lid, remove the first page, and place the second page face down and positioned correctly.

5. Gently close the scanner lid. If you drop the lid or close it too quickly, the rush of air can blow the page out of the scanner or cause it to be crooked.

NOTE

If the page has pictures or graphics and the page is scanned slightly crooked, the saved document will have crooked pictures. Remember, the saved text will always be straight lines, but the pictures will be exactly as they were scanned. You can fix this by cropping the graphic to a straight square or rectangle with the Draw Rectangular Zone. You will, of course, lose part of the picture. You can also use the picture toolbar in Word to crop and resize the graphic.

6. Notice that as soon as the page is scanned in, OmniPage displays the scanned page in the Thumbnail view and starts the zoning and recognition process.

7. Wait the ten seconds, and OmniPage will start to scan your second page. When the scan is complete, replace page two with page three. If you find you have plenty of time left after replacing the page, you can click the Scan Now button if you don't want to wait.

8. Repeat until all the pages are scanned. When the last page has been scanned, click the Stop Scanning button. (If you don't tell OmniPage to stop scanning, it will continue to scan whatever is in the scanner until you stop it. Sometimes, you may not click the Stop Scanning button quickly enough. If this happens, be ready to click it when it next displays, and delete the unwanted page in the Thumbnail view.)

9. When you have scanned the last page, you can start fixing the words displayed in the Proofreader. You can do this while OmniPage is still recognizing the remainder of the pages.

TIP

When using the Proofreader, you don't need to move the mouse to click the buttons; you may find it quicker using the keyboard.

When the Proofreader displays a word for checking, the word is highlighted in the "Change To" box. If you look closely, the Ignore button is the Active button. You can tell this, as it is "highlighted" with a darker border. This means that, if you press the Enter key, it is the same as clicking the button. If the word is correct, just press Enter to move on to the next word for checking. If the word needs changing, as soon as you type in the "Change To" box, the Active button changes to the Change button. When you have typed in the correct word, just press Enter to move on to the next word. If you have a few corrections, it is much quicker working from the keyboard than from the keyboard and mouse.

Once all the pages have been scanned in, processed, and proofread, and you have checked that the zones produce the results you need, it's time to select the layout for the saved document.

CHAPTER 9

Document Layout View

For this exercise, select True Page in the Text Editor, as we won't be editing the document in Word.

Remember, the format of the saved document depends on the "view" you select in the Text Editor view.

In the Text Editor view, click the True Page icon at the bottom of the view. All the paragraphs and blocks of text will be in frames. The original layout of the document will be retained.

For practice, check out the effects of the other layout views.

Retain Flowing Columns

You would use the Retain Flowing Columns view if you wanted to retain as much as possible of the original layout and you wanted to do a lot of editing of the document. Most of the time, the text will be in flowing columns. Just be careful when you have manually drawn zones or when some text spans two or more columns. Some paragraphs of text will be in frames, which can make editing a bit more difficult.

Retain Font and Paragraph

You would use the Retain Font and Paragraph view if you want all the text in one column, retaining the font attributes. The paragraphs and graphics will be in one column in the zone order, the little number in the top left corner of the zones (remember the reordering of zones in Chapter 4?). This makes editing and rearranging of the text and pictures very easy.

No Formatting

You would select No Formatting if you want all formatting removed. This is useful for exporting to spreadsheets and importing into databases.

Now that you have seen the effect of the different layouts on the results, let's save the document.

Exporting the Results of the Multi-Page Document

Once the OCR Process and the proofreading are complete, the Save As dialog box displays. Most of the time when you have been saving your documents, you have used the Basic save options, where to save it and in what file format. What we are going to do this time is to use the Advanced save options to have our scanned document automatically saved as three separate documents. Then, we will save the five scanned pages as a single five-page image file for use in the next section.

1. In the "Save In" box, check that the Training folder you created is selected.
2. In the File name field, type "Multi."
3. In Save as Type, select Word or your word processing application.
4. Click Save and Launch, if it's not already selected.

5. Click the Advanced button to display the additional save features. Notice the button's name then toggles to Basic. Basic switches off the Advanced save features display.

6. Click the drop-down arrow at the end of the File Options field. A selection of three options displays. The selection of these options is only active for this save. It then reverts to the default of Create one File for all Pages. The options are:

▶ Create one File for all Pages. This is the default and the one you would use nearly all the time.

▶ Create one File for each Page. Use this if you have many single page documents, like letters or memos regarding a particular topic. Instead of scanning each one in and saving separately, you can scan them all at one time. By selecting this option when saving, OmniPage will automatically create as many single page document files as there were pages scanned.

▶ Create new File at each Blank Page. Great for dealing with long documents. This breaks the long document into manageable smaller documents.

Figure 9.9
Advanced save options, Create a new file at each blank page

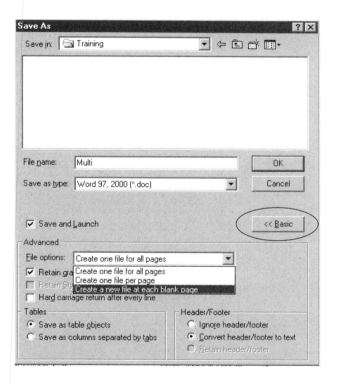

7. Select Create a new file at each blank page.

8. Click Save.

CHAPTER 9

You will see the save process creating the document. When the save is complete, Word will be launched and open two files: Multi_0001 and Multi_0002.

Once you get the hang of being the ADF, it's not too time consuming. However, if you intend to scan lots of large documents, investing in a scanner with an ADF is well worth it.

Let's see how long this took to scan. To find this information, click the Detail tab in the Document Manager window. We ran this exercise on a Pentium II 266 with 128 MB RAM, and it took eighty-six seconds to perform the OCR. If we had a one hundred-page document, it would take about thirty minutes to OCR. This is not counting the time it took to feed the pages into the scanner. If you have a document with numerous pages and your scanner has an ADF, you will be interested in the next option for scanning long documents. There is a way you can get OmniPage to do the OCR while you are not at the PC; OmniPage calls this Schedule OCR.

Save the current images you have just scanned for this exercise, as you can use them in the next section, Schedule OCR.

Switch to OmniPage, if you are not already there. On the menu bar, click File > Save > Image to save the five pages to one image file.

OmniPage has two file formats that support multi-page image files—Tiff and DCX. Notice that, in the drop-down box for file type selection, there are seven different Tiff file types. The ones marked with the red line (Figure 9.10) will support multi-page in black and white, grayscale, and color. The one that's circled in the figure (Tiff LZW) will give the best compression and smallest file size. The other Tiff file types that have "Group" in the name are types of fax compression and only support black and white, not grayscale or color, and their file size will be even smaller.

Save it in the folder C:\My Documents\Schedule OCR Input. Make the file name "Schedule sample" and select LZW Tiff for the file format.

Figure 9.10
Saving the Multi-page
Image file for the
Schedule OCR exercise

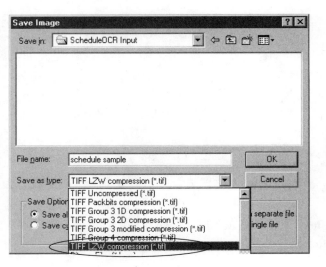

What Is Scheduling OCR?

Schedule OCR lets you tell OmniPage to start performing the OCR process at a preset time in the future. When that time arrives, OmniPage can process a number of prescanned image files or start up the scanner and ADF and begin scanning.

Now you know how to scan a multi-page document. You may be wondering how you can scan a document such as a book, manual, large report, or any other document that has many pages and not have to wait around to feed the scanner or wait for the job to finish. This is a job for Schedule OCR. OmniPage does not even have to be running, as it will automatically launch at the time you select within the next twenty-four hours.

How Does Schedule OCR Work?

It works like the In and Out trays on your desk. You place the OCR jobs to be processed in the In tray and tell OmniPage when to process them. When it's time to start the process, OmniPage starts in the background and begins processing the document. When finished, the job is saved in the Out tray.

At installation time, OmniPage created two folders for the In and Out trays. The In Tray folder is C:\My Documents\ScheduleOCR Input. The Out Tray folder is C:\My Documents\ScheduleOCR Output (Figure 9.11). By default, this is where OmniPage will look for and save your scheduled documents.

Figure 9.11
Schedule OCR Input
and Output folders

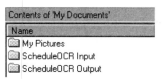

Just as you have job notes attached to each job in your In tray, OmniPage works in the same way. You attach a "job note" to tell OmniPage how to process that job; the instructions are:

- ▶ where to get the documents to process
- ▶ what the original documents look like
- ▶ what language and training files to use
- ▶ what the saved document format (layout) will be
- ▶ what file type to save as and where you want it saved
- ▶ when you want to start and what to do with the originals when finished

You can set any number of jobs to be processed unattended. The image files can be loaded from different computers connected to your network, processed, and saved as Excel or Word files on your computer or on other computers.

NOTE
For those of you who have used previous versions of OmniPage, Schedule OCR allowed you to use saved OmniPage format files. For version 9, it is *.met. For version 10, it is *.opd . OmniPage version 11 only allows image files. It does include PDF's and other image file formats not available in the previous versions.

To set up each job, OmniPage has an easy Schedule Wizard to guide you through six steps. The steps are similar to those for using AutoOCR and Manual OCR.

The document for the Schedule OCR can be from your scanner or from saved image files. If you have an ADF scanner, you can fill the ADF tray with the document to be scanned. Then, use the Schedule OCR option to scan the documents unattended, although we're not sure this is a good idea. You know Murphy's law: As soon as you turn your back, it would have a paper jam, unless you know you have a good scanner and an ADF that doesn't misfeed.

The best way to use Schedule OCR is to first scan only the document using the ManualOCR toolbox to create and save as multi-page image files in the Schedule OCR In box. Only load the images, don't OCR process them. This way, you spend the time scanning and not the time to scan and OCR. Also, you can have more than one scanner scanning the documents using a program that lets you save multi-page image files. Then use the PC that has OmniPage installed to do the Schedule OCR processing.

To create a "job" for OmniPage to schedule, you first need to create the image file of the original document.

1. Select the Manual OCR button.
2. Scan the pages or load the images.
3. Save the scanned images as one file.

It's a good idea to save the image files for scheduling in the Schedule OCR Input folder. This way, they are easy to locate. This is especially helpful when you start to get lots of files, as you will know where they are. It's also good housekeeping.

For the purpose of this exercise, you will need several pages of a document. We suggest you use the file of the five pages you scanned and saved in the previous section. The file you saved is "Schedule sample.tif." The documents that we used in the previous section were Test.tif, spexmple.tif, mpexmple.tif, tpexmple.tif, and xmas100.tif.

If you have not created the image file in the previous section, follow the steps below using the above files. You will find these in the appendix at the back of the book or on the companion Web site.

If you have created the image file in the previous section, use Windows Explorer to copy the file to the folder C:\My Documents\Schedule OCR Input. Then, go to the instructions below, under "Scheduling the Job."

Create a Multi-Page Image File for Schedule OCR

We are going over these steps in case you did not save the multi-page image file in the previous exercise, "Scanning Multi-Page and Long Documents." If you did save the file, then skip down to "Scheduling the Job."

If you do not have the file "Schedule sample.tif" do the following:

1. Click the AB Options button to take you to Options.

2. Click the Scanner tab.

3. In the Flatbed option, click Automatically scan pages, as shown in Figure 9.12. Check that the Time between scans field is set to 10 seconds. If you find it is too long or short, you can change it later.

4. Click OK to close the Options panel.

Figure 9.12
Flatbed Scanner time delay option for feeding pages every ten seconds

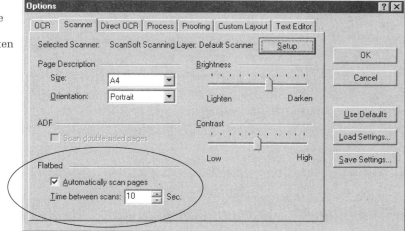

5. Select the ManualOCR button.

6. Click the drop-down arrow of the Get Page button.

7. Select Scan B&W.

8. Click the Get Page icon.

9. Scan all originals.

CHAPTER 9

Remember, the point here is just to get the originals scanned as images. The Schedule OCR process will do the OCR and saving. Once all the pages have been scanned, you will need to save them as a Multi-Page Image File. We need to save it in the Schedule OCR Input folder. To save the multi-page image file:

1. On the Menu, click File.
2. Select Save Image.
3. In the Save in field, select the folder C:\My Documents\Schedule\OCR Input.
4. In the File name field, type in Schedule2.
5. In the Save as type field, select "Tiff LZW compression."

Tiff LZW file format is the smallest file size for grayscale and color images. If the pages are only black and white, use TIF Group 4. For example, a color three-page A4 image file is about 2.2 MB. An image file of the same three pages in black and white and saved as Tiff Group 4 is 100 K. That's about twenty times smaller.

1. In the Save Options field, select Save all pages (default).
2. In the File Options field, select Save all pages to a single file (default). For this exercise, you want all the pages saved in one file, as shown in Figure 9.13.
3. Click OK.

Figure 9.13
File type options for saving the scanned document as a multi-page image file

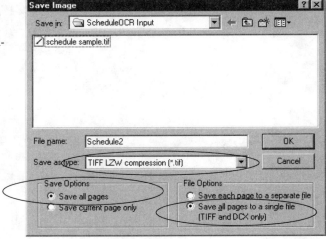

Now that you've saved the document as a multi-page image file, you can schedule it as a job for OmniPage. You can create as many image documents as you like, then schedule them to be processed. Let's look at scheduling a job.

Scheduling the Job

The first step is to add a job. Click the Add Job button to launch the OCR Scheduler wizard (figures 9.14 and 9.15). The wizard will step you through a series of six screens, asking questions about how you want this particular job processed. You can always change the settings later before processing. This is like setting up the "job note" for processing. Let's consider the steps involved in working with the Schedule OCR Wizard to schedule a document to process at a later time.

To open the Scheduler In box:

1.   On the menu bar, click Process.

2.   Select Schedule OCR.

Figure 9.14
The Process menu with the option Schedule OCR selected

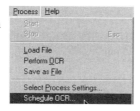

Figure 9.15
The Schedule OCR InBox

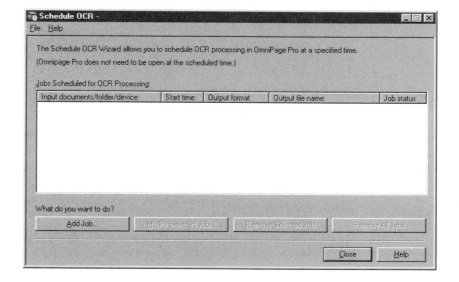

CHAPTER 9

Screen 1: What Document Do You Want to Schedule for OCR Processing?

Select the source of the document (Figure 9.16).You can select from a single file, all the files in a selected folder, or the scanner. Just remember, if you are going to scan the document unattended, make sure you have a good ADF. The default is the single file option.

Figure 9.16
Schedule Wizard
Screen Step 1

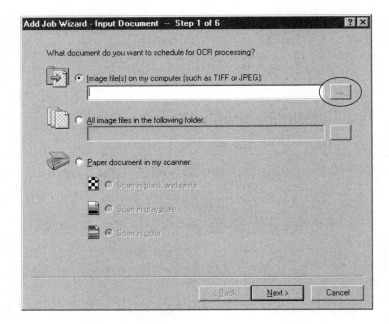

1. Click the button at the end of the Image file field, as shown in Figure 9.16. When the dialog screen pops up, locate the folder C:\My Documents\Schedule OCR Input and select your multi-image file Schedule sample.tif or Schedule2.tif, as seen in Figure 9.17.

Figure 9.17
Schedule OCR Input
dialog box to select the
document to schedule

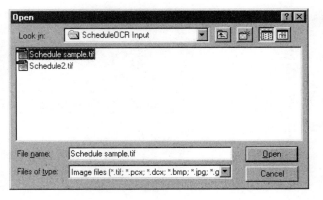

2. Click Next to describe your original document.

Screen 2: What Does Your Input Document Look Like?

The next step is to tell OmniPage what the document looks like (Figure 9.18). This sets the Perform OCR process options, which decides how OmniPage will draw the zones.

    1.   Use the default, "Let OmniPage Pro Decide (auto)."

Figure 9.18
Schedule Wizard
Screen Step 2

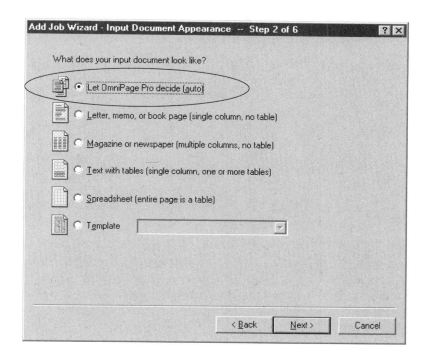

    2.   Click Next to set the language and dictionary options.

Screen 3: What Language Does Your Document Contain?

The third step in the Schedule wizard sets up the languages in your document, the OCR method to use (more accurate or faster), the training file if required, and the dictionary. These are the settings from the OCR and proofing sections in the OmniPage Options panel.

The default language is English. Select the other languages that may be in your document by clicking in the boxes, as shown in Figure 9.19. For best results, leave the OCR method as More Accurate. If you have created a training file (see Chapter 13), you can select it here. If you have a user dictionary of words that are not in the standard Windows proofing dictionary, select it here. You may have words that are specific to your industry that you have added to your user dictionary. The easiest option here is to accept the defaults, then click Next to describe the layout of the saved results.

CHAPTER 9

Figure 9.19
Schedule Wizard
Screen Step 3

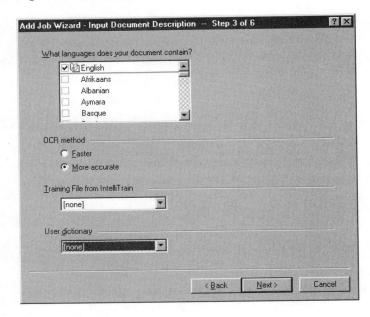

Screen 4: How Much of the Document's Appearance Do You Want to Retain?

This sets the output format. The options here are what you would select in the Text Editor view. The default is True Page. Remember, True Page saves the document using frames to position the blocks of text on the page so that it looks like the original. If you want to edit the saved document, you will want to choose one of the other options. For this exercise, accept the default, True Page (Figure 9.20), and click Next to select the file type to save the document.

Figure 9.20
Schedule Wizard
Screen Step 4

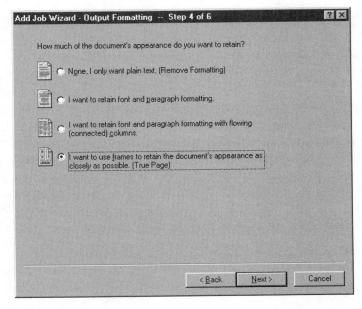

Screen 5: Select a File Type for Your Output Document

This screen asks for the file type that you want to save your document as. The options are the same as in the Export results dialog box. Choose the file type of your word processor. In Figure 9.21, we have chosen Word 97, 2000 (doc). An option on this screen tells OmniPage to create one file, one file per page, or a new file at each blank page. These options are from the Advanced options in the Export results dialog box.

By default, OmniPage will save the document in the Schedule OCR Output folder. You can overtype the location and the file name, or you can click the button on the right side of the file location field, which opens the Save As dialog box (Figure 9.21).

TIP

If you can't find the files after Schedule OCR has run, the first place to look is in the folder C:\My Documents\ScheduleOCR Output. You may have forgotten to select where to save the document. You can always check the log file in C:\My Documents\ScheduleOCR Output. If you don't give the job an output file name, OmniPage will assign filenames Job 1, Job 2, and so on, in sequence.

Figure 9.21
Schedule Wizard
Screen Step 5

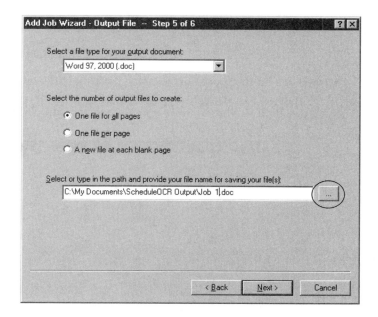

In step 5, we are going to set this job up to save as Word 97 document(s) in the Schedule OCR Output folder and give a name to our saved document(s).

In the Wizard screen 5, do the following:

1. Select the file type as Word 97, 2000 or your word processor application.

2. Leave the option as One File for all Pages.

3. Click the Path and file name button. This will open the File Save dialog box (Figure 9.22).

4. For this exercise, select the default location C:\My Documents\Schedule OCR Output.

5. Type in the file name "schedule exercise."

6. Click Save.

Figure 9.22
Schedule OCR Output

7. The next screen that pops up is Screen 5 again, showing the path and file name you have just selected, as shown in Figure 9.23. Click Next to go to the last step, which is when to tell OmniPage to start processing this job.

Figure 9.23
Schedule Wizard
Screen Step 5

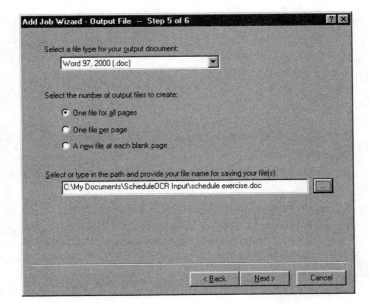

Screen 6: When Do You Want to Start Processing This Document?

The last screen (Figure 9.24) tells OmniPage what time to start the OCR process. This can be any time in the next twenty-four hours. OmniPage does not have to be running at the time, as Windows will automatically launch OmniPage in the background. You won't see the usual OmniPage window, just a gray window displaying the progress of the job. This screen also asks what you want to do with the Original image file—delete it or keep it. It is far safer to keep the original than delete it; this is the default option. You may have to reprocess the document, so keeping the original is a good idea. Always check the results before deleting your input image files. Finally, you can create a log file of the process. This will tell you when the job started, where the job was saved, how long it took, and any errors associated with it.

For this exercise, you are going to set the job to begin two minutes after you finish scheduling it. To do this, look in the bottom right-hand corner of your computer screen for the current time on your computer, and add two minutes.

Now, to set the time to begin processing:

1. In the Time field, click the hours and type in the current hour shown on your computer. Or, use the up and down scroll buttons on the right of the field. Click in the Minutes field and type in the minutes (current time plus two minutes). If you use the scroll arrows for the minutes, it scrolls in fifteen-minute increments.

2. Leave the other settings as the defaults.

3. Click Finish.

Figure 9.24
Schedule Wizard
Screen Step 6

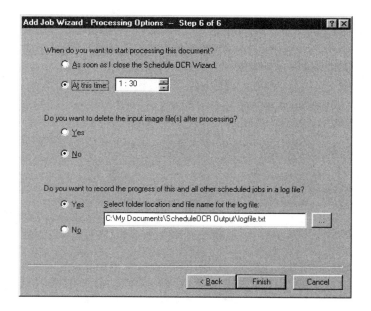

Congratulations, you have just scheduled an OCR job to run in two minutes. The Schedule OCR screen (Figure 9.25) now shows the job and its details. Once you have done this a few times, it's an absolute breeze to move through the setup.

Figure 9.25
The job in the
Schedule OCR list

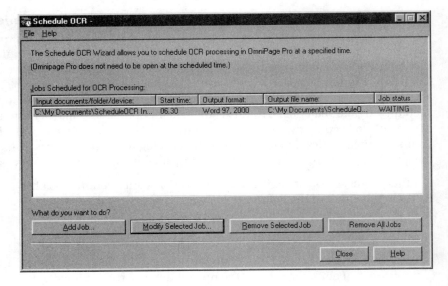

Modifying and Running the Scheduled Job

If you like, you can change any of the Schedule OCR job details before it runs.

1. Click the job to select it.
2. Click the Modify Job button, as shown in Figure 9.26. The six tabs on the Modify Job screen are the six steps the Schedule Wizard took you through.

Figure 9.26
The Modify Job
Options dialog box

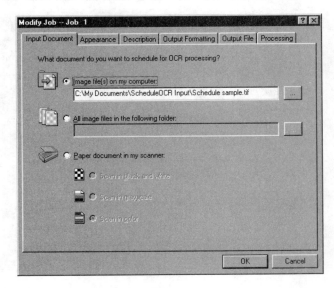

3. Click OK for now; you can experiment with these later.

Now that you have scheduled the job and set all the options, it is ready to run.

Close OmniPage and Wait for the Job to Run

Close OmniPage. When the two minutes have elapsed and the computer clock has ticked over to the time you set to start the OCR job, OmniPage will start up in the background. You won't see the familiar OmniPage desktop, just a small gray window—"Scheduled OCR Running"—that shows the progress of the job(s). The progress events that display in this window are written to the log file you selected in step 6. This way, you can refer to the statistics of each job when they have completed. The log file will be saved, as shown in Figure 9.27.

Figure 9.27
Shows the Scheduled OCR Running message log

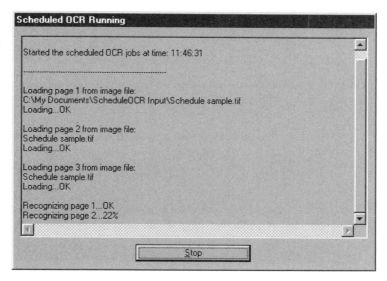

NOTE

If the Scheduled OCR Running screen doesn't display, the screen may be behind other applications you have open. If so, hold down the Alt key on the keyboard and press the tab key to cycle through your open applications. When you have highlighted "Schedule OCR Running," release the Alt key. As the task is running in background mode, it doesn't display on the windows task bar. Figure 9.28 shows the tasks running in picture format, and displays the current task selected.

Figure 9.28
The job is running

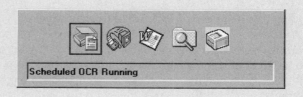

Reviewing the Results

Let's review the results of the job just completed. To review the status of a scheduled job:

1. Launch OmniPage.
2. On the menu, click Tools.
3. Click Schedule OCR to open the Schedule OCR list of jobs.
4. Have a look in the job status column and you will see that your job status is Completed.
5. Open your saved word document "schedule exercise.doc."
6. Use your Windows explorer to open the folder C:\My Documents\Schedule OCR Output.
7. Double click the document "schedule exercise.doc" to open.

If the result is what you wanted, you can move or save the document to another folder where you keep all your work. On the other hand, if it is not what you wanted, you can reschedule the Input Image file and use other settings. For example, you might change the original document description or other options.

NOTE

The Schedule OCR settings are not written back to OmniPage Pro. All the settings except where to get the image file are passed on as the default settings for the next Schedule OCR job.

If OmniPage Pro is being used at the same time a Schedule OCR job is timed to start, Schedule OCR is started in the background.

If you schedule each job to start as soon as the Add Job Wizard is closed, multiple instances of Schedule OCR will run in the background. This may impact the performance of your PC if you are using it.

With Schedule OCR, auto-zoning always runs. If you are using a zone template and the option "Find zones in addition to template zones" is turned off, auto-zoning will not be run.

Any settings not available in the Add Job Wizard take their values as set in OmniPage Pro. The most important setting is whether IntelliTrain will run or not. IntelliTrain is the function by which OmniPage creates a training file of characters it has trouble recognizing. Please refer to Chapter 13 for more details.

If you type in image file names rather than select them, check to be sure the name and path are correct. An incorrect entry will cause a job error.

You have learned more about scanners, ADFs, and working with long documents. Now, instead of doing the whole scan and OCR process and saving each document file, you can just scan the documents, save as a multi-page image file, and use the Schedule OCR to have OmniPage do all the work after you have gone home for the day!

10

Saving, Publishing, and Sending Documents

Throughout this book, we have talked about saving our scanned documents as Word or Excel. Each time you save the document, there are a number of options you can use. Among these are the various options available through Export Results: You can save as a file, send as mail, and copy text to the clipboard to paste into another application. In this chapter, we will explore these options.

Save as a File

The Save As dialog box has a Basic and an Advanced selection of options. Figure 10.1 shows the Advanced save options. The Advanced button toggles between Advanced and Basic, depending on which is currently selected.

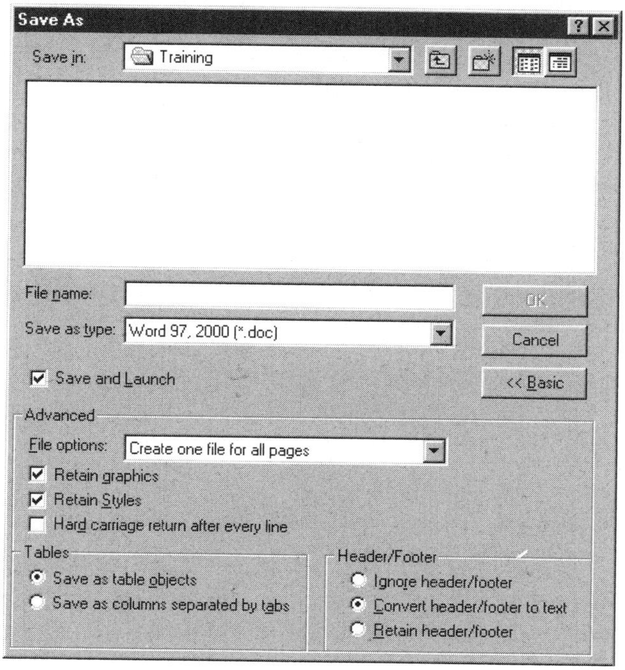

Figure 10.1
The Advanced save options

Basic

Basic allows you to choose the file type and whether or not to launch the application associated with that file type. Most of the time, this is all you will use.

Save and Launch will launch the application and open the document you just saved; throughout this book, we have saved as Word and Excel file types. If you choose other file types, it will launch the matching application.

Advanced

The Advanced options give you much greater control over how the document is saved. It's also a good place to start looking when your files are not being saved correctly. The settings in the Advanced options stay set just like the options in Tools > Options. If someone changes your OmniPage settings, those settings will be retained, and the next time you use OmniPage you may not get the results you expect. Let's look at each option in turn.

The options as shown in Figure 10.1 are the Advanced default settings. It is best to leave the settings in their default configuration. This covers 90 percent of the way you will want to save documents.

File Options

Here, you can choose to save the entire document as one file, as a separate file for each page, or as a new file each time OmniPage encounters a blank page in the original document.

Retain Graphics

Users are commonly confused about the Retain Graphics option. Without Retain Graphics selected, the pictures are not exported and will not display in Word and other applications. If your pictures are not being exported, make sure this setting is on. A quick way to fix it is to use the Options defaults to reset all options. Remember, on the menu, click Tools > Options or, on the standard toolbar, click the AB Options button. Then, click Use Defaults; this is a good way to set everything back to square one. You can click Retain Graphics to select it; however, without checking every setting, you don't know what a previous user may have switched on or off.

Retain Graphics will export the graphic zones to your document. With it switched off, it won't. However, the image zones will still show in OmniPage Text Editor view, so you won't realize it has been switched off until you open the saved document.

Retain Styles

OmniPage creates styles to format the text within each paragraph. Retain Styles saves and exports these styles into Word and other applications that support styles. The style defines only the paragraph layout, tabs, line spacing, and alignment. It does not include any font formatting.

Retain Styles applies only when using the Text Editor views Retain Flowing Columns, True Page, and Retain Font and Paragraph Formatting.

You can create, apply, and modify styles in OmniPage Text Editor view, although we find it much easier to change the layout and styles in Word.

Hard Carriage Return after Each Line

Why would you want to use this? Isn't this what we use word processors for?

During one of our courses, a gentleman wanted to scan his wife's poetry, which she had typed years ago. The poems just didn't look the same when all the text flowed on the same line. Poetry is a good example of when you might wish to insert hard carriage returns after lines. For example:

> *There was a young maid from Bright*
>
> *Who used to travel faster than light.*
>
> *She left one day in a relative way*
>
> *And arrived the previous night.*

Looks and sounds better than:

> *There was a young maid from Bright Who used to travel faster than light. She left one day in a relative way And arrived the previous night.*

Generally, you would leave the hard carriage return option off.

Tables

There are two options for saving tables. We find the default, Save as Table Objects, covers most situations. The other option, Save as Columns Separated by Tabs, is for applications that did not support table objects, such as PowerPoint or Microsoft Publisher. OmniPage knows which applications do not support table objects, so the option defaults to Save as Columns Separated by Tabs.

Header and Footer

The Header and Footer option looks for repeating text on multi-page documents. It is active only when there are two or more pages in the document.

All four Text Editor views allow you to either Ignore the Header and Footer or keep them (Retain Header/Footer).

The Text Editor view Retain Flowing Columns gives you all the other options. So it includes Convert the Text to Header and Footer. These options are useful when you don't want to keep the footer information from the original document. An example is when you want to use your own headers and footers, or to insert something other than what is in the scanned document.

Using the PDF File Format

Did you know you can OCR PDF files and create PDF files? PDF (Portable Document Format) is one of the new image file formats that OmniPage can recognize.

PDF documents are a special type of image file made using Adobe Acrobat Writer. OmniPage can now save files in the Adobe PDF format. Many manuals and company documents are distributed as PDF files. They provide a compact way of sending and storing all types of documents, including pictures, photos, graphics, and line art drawings. Many companies choose to scan catalogs and other products and company information, and they make those documents available on the Internet in PDF format.

Acrobat distributes the software required to read PDFs free; it is available for easy download on the Web (www.adobe.com). The free Acrobat Reader means everyone with a computer can read the document. You don't need to worry about whether the recipient has Word 2000 or Wordperfect, etc.

Recognizing PDF Files

If you want to insert part of an existing PDF document into a Word document, you can copy and paste only from the visible page of the PDF document. You cannot copy and paste the whole document or multiple pages. Nor can you copy and paste pictures or keep the PDF layout.

With OmniPage, however, you can load the entire PDF document and perform the OCR on the whole document, or on just the pages you select or the zones you draw. OmniPage will also retain the layout and pictures of the original PDF document.

OCRing a PDF document is no different than scanning paper documents. Instead of scanning in the document, you use the Load Image option. Then, follow all the steps you have learned in this book for scanning and OCR.

Saving Your Scanned Document as PDF File Format

This is a great new feature in OmniPage Pro version 11. It is especially useful when you don't have the Adobe Acrobat writer application and want to create Adobe PDF files. Here's an example: One of our clients wanted to send overseas advertisements from newspapers. The ads didn't need to be converted to text, as nothing was to be changed. The ads were in color, so faxing was no good. They could have scanned each ad and converted to JPG image files, lowered the resolution, then e-mailed all the separate image files. Instead, they scanned all the ads with OmniPage using a template of a single graphic zone over the entire page and saved in PDF format. This created one complete file of all the pages in color, and because it was in PDF format, the file was small. They were then able to e-mail the PDF file from within OmniPage.

Try this:

1. Launch OmniPage.
2. Select the AutoOCR toolbox and Load Image file.
3. Use the three-page sample image file "Sample_multi.tif," located in your "My documents" folder.
4. When it has completed the OCR process, select Acrobat PDF in the Save as File type field.
5. Select the Save and Launch option.

The original file "Sample_multi.tif" is 6.7 MB—far too large to e-mail.

The saved PDF file is only 73 KB. That's nearly a hundred times smaller. The PDF file is perfectly readable, both on the screen and when printed.

Now, try saving in the different PDF file formats.

The Four PDF File Formats

There are four variations of PDF format you can select. Below, we have listed alongside the variation the actual file size, along with attributes, of the three-page sample document "Sample_multi.tif" when saved in the various formats. The first two PDF formats allow you to edit the PDF document using the Adobe Acrobat writer, a purchasable application that is not to be confused with the free Adobe Acrobat Reader.

Adobe PDF (73 KB)

This standard Adobe format contains color images and text. It is exported with the color images and text as they appeared in the Text Editor view in the True Page layout. You can do text searches and edit the PDF file when saved in this format. Figure 10.2 shows the first page of the PDF file; see how all the text is black, the extra blue border around the photo is gone, and the photo caption that was white text against a blue background is now black text and no background? Figure 10.3 is an enlargement of the last paragraph on page 2. Notice how all the characters are clean and sharp. This is because in this format, the text is displayed as text rather than as the scanned image of the text.

Adobe PDF with Image Substitutes (83 KB)

This is similar to the first option (Adobe PDF). However, the words containing reject and suspect characters display as images, appearing as they did in the original document, so you can edit them if need be. The PDF file can be viewed, edited, and searched. See Figure 10.4; it is the same paragraph as Figure 10.3, but it was saved as Adobe PDF with Image Substitutes. Here, the two words "pensiero" and "dorate" contained suspect characters in the Proofreader. The words were not converted to text. Instead, small images of each word were inserted in their place in this PDF format.

Figure 10.2
Page one of the document appears the same when saved as "Adobe PDF" and "Adobe with Image Substitutes" formats, no colored text

"Va pensiero, sull'ali dorate!" So much
for having to explain where the name
came from. Back in Argentina where he'd
grown up, Alex and his fellow cadets had
a teacher who was a big opera fan and
made them listen to Verdi's Nabucco
until they

"Va pensiero, sull'ali dorate!" So much
for having to explain where the name
came from. Back in Argentina where he'd
grown up, Alex and his fellow cadets had
a teacher who was a big opera fan and
made them listen to Verdi's Nabucco
until they

Figure 10.3
Enlargement of last paragraph on page 2 saved
as "Adobe PDF"

Figure 10.4
Enlargement of last paragraph on page 2 saved
as "Adobe PDF with Image Substitutes"

Adobe PDF with Image on Text (804 KB)

This is the image of the original document "overlaid" on the text. This format allows for text
searches, but the text cannot be copied, pasted, or otherwise modified. You can see in Figure
10.5 that the color text of the original document is retained, as are the color border around
the picture and the photo caption of white text on blue background. See how the text is not
as clear as in the first two options? This is because the text is being displayed as an image
rather than as a text font character. Compare the same paragraph (Figure 10.6) of text with the
first two PDF options. The text is not as sharp and clear as in Figures 10.3 and 10.4.

Adobe PDF with Image Only (720 KB)

This format is similar to PDF with Image on Text, except it is the image of the original
document only. The text cannot be searched or edited. As you can see, the file size is smaller
than with the Image on Text option. Again, the text is not clear because it is being displayed
as an image (Figure 10.5).

Figure 10.5
"Adobe PDF Image on
Text" and "Adobe
Image Only" retains the
colors of the text and
layout exactly, as the
entire page is an image

Figure 10.6

Enlargement of the last paragraph on page 2 saved as "Adobe PDF Image on Text" and "Adobe Image Only;" all the "text" is an image of the original scanned document

"Va pensiero, sull'ali dorate!" So much for having to explain where the name came from. Back in Argentina where he'd grown up, Alex and his fellow cadets had a teacher who was a big opera fan and made them listen to Verdi's Nabucco until they

Saving as HTML

Saving as HTML is very handy for quickly making Web pages and JPG image files suitable for the Web and e-mailing, while still retaining much of the detail and image quality.

When you save as HTML, text and images are saved separately from one another. The HTML text is then encoded with instructions saying where the images are and what their file names are. The separate image files are saved in a new subfolder, "filename_Dir," beneath the folder in which you save the HTML document (where "filename" is the name of your HTML file). When you save many HTML documents to the same folder, OmniPage creates a new subfolder each time you save an HTML document (Figure 10.7).

Figure 10.7

Subfolders are created for each saved HTML document

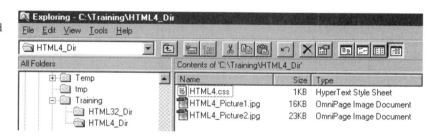

When you save in HTML, the resolution of your graphics is automatically reduced to 150 dpi and is compressed by 15%. This makes the files smaller and easier to e-mail. As an example, one of the small photos of the file "Sample_multi.tif" is reduced from a 233 KB tif file to a 16 KB JPG file.

The usual way to prepare photos for e-mailing is to scan them in an image-editing application, reduce the resolution to 150 or 75 dpi, and save as a JPG, specifying the compression. When you scan with OmniPage, these details are taken care of for you.

When you use the saved HTML document, always remember to send the document *and* the subfolder containing the image files; otherwise, your recipients will get just a blank box with the word "Picture" but no image.

OmniPage supports two different HTML formats: HTML 3.2 and HTML 4.0. Most recent versions of Web browsers support HTML 4.0, which handles a greater variety of document layouts than the earlier version 3.2. Version 4.0 supports style sheets, scripting, frames, embedding objects, improved support for right to left and mixed direction text, richer tables, and enhancements to forms, offering improved accessibility for people with disabilities. A good Web site for learning more about HTML is theW3C site: http://www.w3.org.

Let's do a quick exercise of saving one of the installed sample files in HTML 3.2 and 4.0 to see the difference.

Save a Document as HTML 4.0.

We will load the three-page sample file "Sample_multi.tif," as it will be quicker than scanning a three-page color document. Launch OmniPage, using the AutoOCR toolbox to Load Image. Perform OCR as Automatic and Export Results as Save as File. Click the Start button and, when prompted to load the image file, navigate to your C:\My Documents\My Pictures folder and select the file "Sample_multi.tif." Let the process complete and close the Proofreader if it displays.

1. In the Save As dialog box, select Save the Document in the Training folder you created.
2. In the file name field, type in "HTML4."
3. In the Save as Type field, select HTML 4.0.
4. Ensure the option Save and Launch is selected.
5. Check that the option Retain Graphics is selected. Click Basic > Retain Graphics.
6. Click OK.

Depending on the Text Editor layout selected, you may get the warning message shown in Figure 10.8. This is because HTML 4.0 supports the OmniPage export only as True Page. Just click OK and OmniPage will change the Text Editor layout before saving.

Figure 10.8
When saving as HTML 4.0 and the Text Editor layout is not selected to True Page, this warning message displays

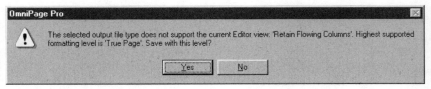

As you selected the Save and Launch option, your Web browser will be launched and the saved file "HTML4.htm" will be opened. It will look like Figure 10.9. The Web browser used in this exercise is Internet Explorer 5.0. See how it has retained the original layout, tables, and images very well? Scroll through the document to see how it handled the other two pages. It did a pretty good job, didn't it?

Figure 10.9
The sample file "Sample_multi.tif" saved as HTML 4.0

CHAPTER 10

Save a Document as HTML 3.2

1. Go back to OmniPage by clicking the OmniPage button on the Windows task bar.

2. In OmniPage, click the Additional button and select Export Document Again.

3. Save the document in the same folder, Training.

4. In the file name field, type in "HTML32."

5. In the Save as Type field, select the file type as HTML3.2.

6. Click OK to save and launch your browser.

This time, the warning message box did not display, as the HTML 3.2 exporter doesn't require the pages to be in True Page view.

Have a look at what you get this time. Figure 10.10 shows the result. You can certainly see the difference! It's not as good as HTML 4.0. This is because HTML 3.2 wasn't designed to handle complex layouts.

Figure 10.10
The same document saved as HTML 3.2 format

Just be careful when saving the two different formats; if you are scanning numerous single-column documents, you may not notice much difference with HTML 3.2, except that there is no blank line spacing between paragraphs. Then, when you scan a complex multi-column document and save as HTML 3.2, you may wonder what went wrong. The format will not be the same as the original. Always check the result in your current Web browser.

Next, let's consider another important option for exporting the results of your scanning.

Send as Mail

To e-mail from within OmniPage, set the Export Results as Send as Mail. Using this option instead of saving your document as a file, OmniPage e-mails the scanned document as an attached file. You can use any of the file types as an attachment *except HTML*. You choose the type of file attachment before OmniPage saves your document and attaches it to your e-mail. OmniPage automatically links to your default e-mail application. Your mail application must be MAPI compliant. MAPI stands for "Mail Application Programming Interface." Nearly all popular e-mail applications are MAPI compliant, including Outlook, Outlook Express, Netscape Communicator, and Eudora.

When the OCR processing is completed, OmniPage pops up the Send Mail dialog box, as shown in Figure 10.11. You can select the attachment file type you want from the drop-down box and specify options for how the attachments are created. You can Create one Attachment for all Pages (the default and usually the best option), Create one Attachment Per Page, or Create New Attachment at Each Blank Page. These options are the same as in the Advanced file save options. Click OK.

Figure 10.11
Selecting the file type
of the attachments and
number of attachments

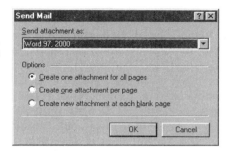

Next, your mail application appears with the attachment(s) ready for you to create the message
(Figure 10.12). The subject for the e-mail is automatically created. You can change by over-typing
before sending. The subject name will be one of three different names: If the document has one
attachment, the subject is either (1) "Untitled from OmniPage" or (2) the file name you used
when the document was last saved; or if the document has more than one attachment, the subject
is (3) "Attached files" (Figure 10.12). The attachments are named "Snd.doc" (or the extension
appropriate to the file type you chose). If more than one attachment is created, they become
"Snd_0001.doc," "Snd_0002.doc," etc. Fill in the e-mail address of the person you want to send
to, click Send, and you're done—you've scanned and e-mailed the document, pictures and all.

NOTE

Once the e-mail message window is open, you can't get back to OmniPage until
you either send the mail or close the e-mail message. This is because OmniPage
is linked to the message until it is sent or closed.

Figure 10.12
The unaddressed e-
mail with attached files
and subject filled in

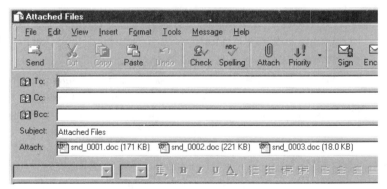

CAUTION

Do not send HTML attachments when you use Send as Mail. Once you have
used the Send as Mail option with an HTML attachment, you will *not* be able to
use the Send as Mail option again. To get around this, you will need to delete
the HTML folders created for the e-mail attachment. See below for details.

E-Mailing HTML Warning

OmniPage creates a temporary folder named "Send" to hold the e-mail attachments it is preparing to send. Once it has sent the e-mail, the contents and folder are automatically deleted. When using the Send as Mail export option, all images are sent in the attachment—except when using an HTML attachment. When OmniPage creates an attachment as, say, a Word document, the images are embedded within the document. HTML, on the other hand, saves images separately, in a subfolder named Snd_dir. Images in the subfolder are not sent when the HTML document is e-mailed. After sending the e-mail, OmniPage attempts to delete the subfolder "Send" containing the HTML file, but since the folder is not empty—it has a subfolder containing the image files—it cannot be deleted. The next time you try to Send as Mail, you will get the message: "Error in format exporting" (Figure 10.13). The quick fix for this is to delete the subfolder "Send" and its subfolder "Snd_dir." These two folders are in the Windows folder; their location depends on the Windows operating system you are using.

The steps on how to do this and where to find the folders are next.

Figure 10.13
Error message when attempting to send a second e-mail as an HTML attachment

The "Send" folder is found in different locations in different operating systems. Navigate to the folder location using Windows Explorer and delete the folder "Send" and the subfolder "Snd_dir." In the list below, substitute your disk drive letter and point to the folder on your PC where you have Windows installed.

▶ **Windows 95**—C:\Windows\Application data\Scansoft\OmniPage\Send

▶ **Windows 98**—C:\Windows\Application data\Scansoft\OmniPage\Send

▶ **Windows ME**—C:\Windows\Application data\Scansoft\OmniPage\Send

▶ **Windows 2000**—C:\Winnt\Documents and Settings*"Your Logon user name"*\Application data\Scansoft\OmniPage\Send

▶ **Windows NT**—C:\Winnt\Profiles*"Your Logon user name"*\Application data\Scansoft\OmniPage\Send

Copy to the Clipboard

When you use this Export Results option, the recognized text is *not saved;* the entire document is just copied to the clipboard. You can then paste the recognized document into another open document or file. On the down arrow of Export Results, click and select Copy to Clipboard, as shown in Figure 10.14.

Figure 10.14
Export results: Copy to
Clipboard

Some examples of when you may want to use this option are:

▶ When you are working with an application that does not accept Direct OCR.

▶ When your document file type is not in the Save As list.

▶ When you are using an image-editing application and you want to import some text. Use Copy to Clipboard and paste into the image-editing program's text tool.

▶ When you are using an application that uses text boxes.

Copy to Clipboard retains text formatting such as bold and italics only when you paste into an application that supports RTF (Rich Text Format). Otherwise, only plain text will be pasted. The graphics will be retained if the application supports inserting images.

Be careful if you are pasting a multi-column, recognized page into your single-column document. It can change your whole document into multi-column, just as it does when using Direct OCR. If you are doing this, remember to insert a section break in your document before pasting in the recognized text.

The clipboard can only hold one thing at a time, so if you copy something else to the clipboard, you will lose the OmniPage clipboard's results. If you do this, it's easy to get it back: Just go back to OmniPage and click the Finish button or Export Results to re-export the results again to the clipboard.

If you want only part of the recognized text, you can do this in two ways:

1. Once the document has been recognized, highlight the required text and pictures in the Text Editor window. Use Edit > Copy to copy the selected text to the clipboard, then paste to your destination document.

2. Draw zones around the text you require. Process the zones and use the Export Results option Copy to Clipboard. We use Copy to Clipboard when, for example, we need to extract text from marketing brochure PDF files. We load the PDF brochure using the Manual OCR toolbox. This is a great feature for extracting data from PDF files.

That's how easy it is to export data via the clipboard.

11

Managing Documents and Images with PaperPort

Have you ever gone looking for a particular document on your computer? You *know* you saved it to a particular folder, but you just can't find it! It happens to all of us. We all lead busy lives, and we all promise ourselves that *tomorrow* we'll clean up and organize all the documents and images on our hard drives. But when tomorrow comes, we're busy with more pressing things, and the PC housekeeping doesn't get done.

There are ways to find those misfiled documents—we'll learn an easy way to do this from within OmniPage —and there are simple methods you can apply to help keep your documents in good order. In this chapter, we'll consider an easy, helpful method of organizing your hard drive, creating a filing system, and archiving documents and images. We will look at using Windows Explorer and another product from the makers of OmniPage, PaperPort. PaperPort, as you will see, is a fantastic way to keep track of your documents. Of course, you still need a filing methodology to make sense of your files.

Developing a Method for Filing Documents

The key is to file your scanned documents and images—in fact, all of your files—in an organized way using appropriate folders. Think of your hard disk drive as a large metal filing cabinet with many drawers. Each drawer is a folder. Within each drawer are other folders called subfolders. Before you file any paper-based document in your filing cabinet, you plan how to organize the drawers and folders. Next, you name the filing drawers and label the tabs that will be placed on the hanging folders. You make decisions about any color-coding or how many folders you will need for your clients or papers. You might organize the filing cabinet so that there is one drawer for each client, or maybe one drawer per project.

Your Computer's Filing System

So, in terms of our analogy, your hard drive—typically, your drive labeled C—is the filing cabinet. The folder on the C drive called Program Files is the "drawer" that contains all of your programs. Within that drawer, each program has its own folder.

For example, C:\Program Files\Scansoft\OmniPagePro11.0 is a subfolder within the Program Files drawer as shown in Figure 11.1. This is the folder where OmniPage is automatically installed. On your PC, you'll see how most of your programs are installed in the programs file folder. This is so you and Windows know where all the program files are; rather than having them all over the place, they are stored in one logical location. It is a good idea to ask yourself when filing documents, "If I wanted to find this later, where would I logically think I had filed it?"

Figure 11.1
Windows Explorer's
hierarchy of folders

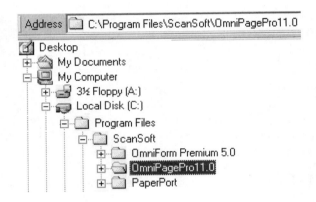

Folders and Subfolders in Windows

The methodology you apply to your manual filing system is the same when organizing your hard disk drive(s).

Windows creates a My Documents folder, and in this folder it creates a My Pictures subfolder. This is a good place to start creating subfolders to store all your scanned images, photos, and documents, as shown in Figure 11.2. You may already be doing this. The My Documents folder is an excellent place to store your documents and images, so when you do a backup you just need to back up My Documents and its subfolders. Then, you will be confident you have backed up all your documents.

Figure 11.2
Filing drawers and
folders

This is the filing drawer in
your filing cabinet

This is the folder within the
filing drawer in the filing cabinet
(a subfolder of My Documents)

Creating a Subfolder in Windows Explorer

To create a subfolder, simply click the parent folder beneath which you want to create a new
subfolder. On the Windows Explorer menu, click File > New > Folder, as shown in Figure 11.3.

Figure 11.3
Click File > New >
Folder

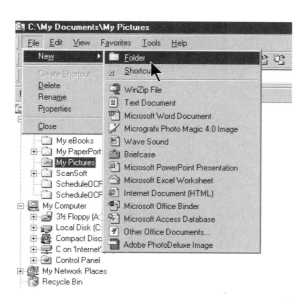

On the right-hand side of the Windows Explorer view, a new blank folder displays with the cursor ready to enter a name for the folder. Type a name for the folder. Repeat these steps for as many folders as you need to store your photos, as shown in Figures 11.4 and 11.5. For your scanned documents, create subfolders in the My Documents folder.

Make sure you do not have too many folders hanging off the top level—i.e., multiple levels of subfolders within folders. The more subfolders you have, the longer it takes to locate files because there are so many layers of subfolders to click through. There is nothing more annoying than having to continually double-click the subfolders, drilling down to locate the image or file you need. While you can set the Document Default Folder in Word to a specific folder and lock it in during that session, you are not always going to be working in the same folder every day. However, if you have an easy-to-use methodology that takes away the need to remember where files are located, then your housekeeping nightmare becomes a pleasant dream.

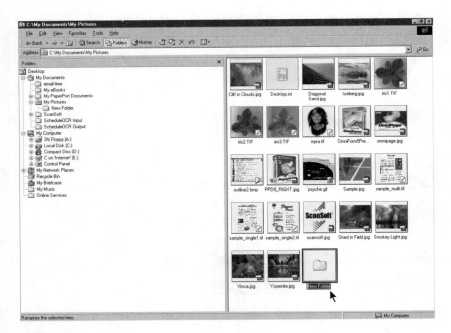

Figure 11.5
A newly created folder, with its folder name

Figure 11.4
In Windows 98, ME, and 2000, you can turn on View to show thumbnails—this makes it easy to see all your images

File Organization with PaperPort

If you are anything like us, you have lots of paper-based documents and computer files. In our training business, what we need is a quick, flexible filing system that indexes, allows for visual recognition and annotation of files, and also makes it easy to do quick searches for a variety of files and file types. Could you use such a system, too?

Well, there is such a program. It's called PaperPort Deluxe 8.0. It was developed by the same people who make OmniPage—ScanSoft, Inc. PaperPort is a Personal Document Management software program. PaperPort Deluxe 8.0 is the leader in digital document management software, indispensable in organizing your documents, pictures, spreadsheets, and other files. With PaperPort, you can view all your files in the folders as thumbnail previews to allow visual recognition of files. Its indexing system allows for flexible filing schemes and quick searches through a variety of files and file types, and it has annotation capabilities for taking notes on files. It has built-in forms capability and Web-based management and collaboration for your business and personal documents and images, and much more.

PaperPort is like having your own personal librarian. Imagine your hard disk drive (or network drive, or the Web) is the library consisting of all your files (books); the librarian has an index to show where each book is on the shelf. In the old days, libraries used to have a card filing system. Each book was represented by a card, on which was printed the book's title, author, date, brief description, category, and, most importantly, the location of the book in the library. PaperPort is that card filing system, and much more. You are in charge of how you arrange and organize the reference cards. PaperPort organizes files and folders and reads, remembers, and retrieves information from virtually any source, including word processor documents, spreadsheet files, faxes, scanned documents, and more. It collects information from a variety of sources such as hard drives, scanners, digital cameras, e-mail, and the Web. You can annotate files, colorcode folders, and search by title and content. When you want to find, say, a letter you sent to Michael, and you can't remember where you saved it, just type "Michael" into the PaperPort search menu and it will instantly show you all the files containing the word "Michael" ranked in order by the number of times the word appears in the document.

You still can use Windows to create, move, and delete files and folders; however, PaperPort lets you find them easily on your PC. In fact, anyone who has a lot of files and folders on their PC and doesn't have the time to arrange them in any order could use PaperPort to reorganize them. You can even create folders in PaperPort and they will appear in Windows Explorer.

Document Sharing

You can store your documents locally and share with others over the Web without requiring the IT overhead structures and high costs of larger, more expensive image and document management systems. It allows business users to work in a shared environment. This significantly increases the filing system organization and productivity by reducing the amount of time spent manually searching for documents.

Thumbnails

PaperPort shows large, clear thumbnails of all your documents and photos. Each thumbnail appears with an icon identifying the program in which it was created, or with which it is currently associated, with the exception of PaperPort image items (.max) files. This makes it easy to quickly see and find all different types of files on your computer.

CHAPTER 11

Archiving and Sending Documents

What about documents that can't be effectively OCR'd—documents that have lots of drawings such as service manuals or product brochures and specification sheets, even old manuscripts or books and handwritten letters? They can be archived with PaperPort. We had a gentleman attend one of our training courses who wanted to put all of his wife's handwritten recipes on computer for their grandchildren. In this case, it is not appropriate to use OmniPage, as there is no printed text, and none of the information in the recipes needs to be changed, but PaperPort is a good product for jobs like this. PaperPort also OCRs documents. However, the OCR engine is not as powerful as OmniPage's. To OCR a document, once it is scanned, just drag and drop it onto your Word processor Icon Link at the bottom of the PaperPort desktop, and the recognized document will open. Or, you can drag it to your fax link to automatically fax it.

You can open a file in preview mode or with its application, view the file in thumbnails, view part of the document, even annotate the document before e-mailing it. Yes, you can e-mail from within PaperPort. As we said before, you can do some of these things in Windows Explorer, but PaperPort is much faster, and you have all of the links to quickly fax, e-mail, OCR, and more using the PaperPort link bar. You can do all this just by dragging and dropping onto the link bar at the bottom of the PaperPort desktop.

The PaperPort Interface

Let's have a look at the PaperPort desktop (Figure 11.6).

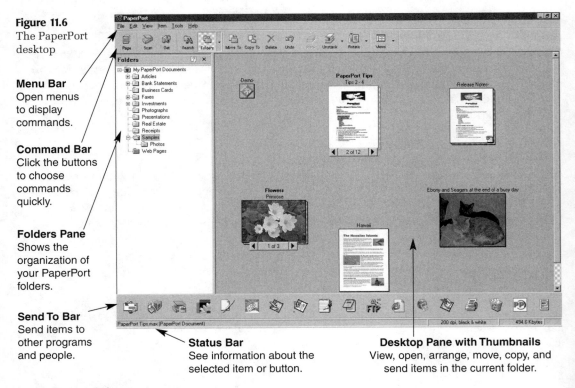

Figure 11.6
The PaperPort desktop

Menu Bar
Open menus to display commands.

Command Bar
Click the buttons to choose commands quickly.

Folders Pane
Shows the organization of your PaperPort folders.

Send To Bar
Send items to other programs and people.

Status Bar
See information about the selected item or button.

Desktop Pane with Thumbnails
View, open, arrange, move, copy, and send items in the current folder.

The PaperPort desktop consists of four main areas:

- ▶ The Command toolbar, at the top
- ▶ The Folders pane, on the left
- ▶ The Desktop pane, on the right
- ▶ The Send To bar, on the bottom

The Command Toolbar

The Command toolbar contains most of the commonly used functions (they are also accessible from the menu bar). These functions include "getting" the files into PaperPort from a number of sources, such as your hard disk, scanner, digital camera, and more. The command bar is also used for searching, as well as stacking and unstacking files.

The Folder Pane

The Folder pane on the left displays the folder hierarchy you have set up within PaperPort. This is where you organize your folders, import folders, create new folders, and colorcode them.

The Desktop Pane

The Desktop pane is where the action is. It's where the files of the selected folder are displayed as thumbnails. Notice the thumbnails are larger than the ones in Windows Explorer. Notice also that the thumbnails of text documents display the text layout and images of the first page of the document. The text thumbnails in Windows Explorer show only an icon of the application. In the Desktop pane, you can stack and unstack files, add annotations, add search criteria, open in the PaperPort viewer, or open in the file's original application.

The Send To Bar

The Send To bar contains icon buttons that are links to applications you have installed on your PC, such as OmniPage, Word, Excel, Fax, E-mail, Adobe PDF Writer, etc. You use the Send To bar by selecting a file or files from the Desktop pane and dragging to the application. This takes a copy of the file(s) and sends it to that application; for example, it e-mails the file if you drag it to the e-mail icon.

To help you get started with filing, PaperPort creates a subfolder of My Documents called "My PaperPort Documents," which includes all of the initial folders set up in PaperPort (Figure 11.7). There are some sample files you can move around, index, search, print, re-index, and OCR in the sample folder.

CHAPTER 11

Figure 11.7
The PaperPort folder
displayed in Windows
Explorer

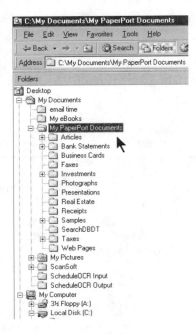

To Display Thumbnails

Thumbnails make it easy to organize your disk drives because you can see what the file consists of, rather than just a file name. To display thumbnails, on the command bar, click the Views button and then click Thumbnails.

Before you can work with a file (in PaperPort, they are also referred to as "items"), you must first select its thumbnail on the desktop. A red line appears around a file item to indicate that it is selected. Here are some of the things you can do with thumbnails on the PaperPort desktop:

▶ Click a thumbnail to select it.

▶ Drag a thumbnail to reposition it on the desktop.

▶ Drag a thumbnail to a folder to move the file to that folder.

▶ Double-click a thumbnail to view the file.

▶ Press the Ctrl key and double-click a thumbnail to open the item in its source program.

▶ Right-click a thumbnail to display the shortcut menu.

▶ Drag and drop on top of another file (item) to stack similar documents together. The files still stay as individual files. It's like putting a bulldog clip on several paper documents associated with a particular project.

▶ Drag a thumbnail to the Send To bar to send a copy of the file to another program.

Organizing Existing Folders and Files on Your PC

There is much you can do to organize your files. The first step is to add your existing folders to the PaperPort desktop. Then, you can copy, move, rearrange, and rename folders to group and organize your scanned images, documents, and files. You can colorcode your folders to help classify them and drag and drop items and folders from the PaperPort desktop to any folder. You can also set up an index and search criteria to help find files.

PaperPort folders are simply Windows folders that you want to use with PaperPort. PaperPort displays folders in the Folders pane on the left side of the PaperPort desktop, as shown in Figure 11.8.

Figure 11.8
PaperPort Folders pane

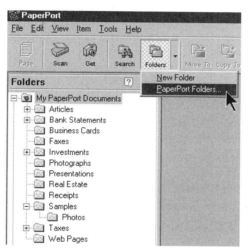

Adding Folders

You can add any folder on your computer as a PaperPort folder. You can then use that folder and all its subfolders with PaperPort. You can also add network folders and folders on external devices attached to your computer. When you add an existing folder, PaperPort assigns it a name based on the Windows folder name. For example, if you add a folder named E:\Lesson1 from your CD-ROM drive or network drive to PaperPort, it names the folder "Lesson1 on E:"

To add a folder to the Folders pane:

1. On the Command bar, click the Folders button to display the Folders pane.
2. On the Command bar, click the down arrow on the Folders button.
3. Click PaperPort Folders.
4. In the PaperPort Folders dialog box, click Add (Figure 11.9).

Figure 11.9
The Add Folders
option

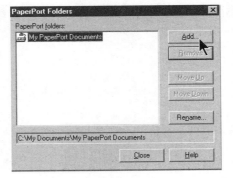

5. In the Add Folders dialog box, navigate to and then select the folder you want to add (Figure 11.10).

Figure 11.10
Selecting CD-ROM
drive folder to add to
the PaperPort Folders
pane

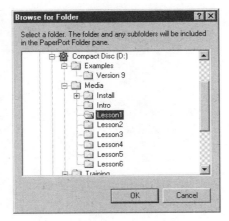

6. Click OK.

7. The folder now appears in the PaperPort Folders pane (Figure 11.11).

Figure 11.11
The CDROM Drive
folder has been added
to the PaperPort
Folders pane

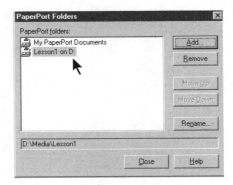

The potential number of items or files you can keep within a folder depends on the amount of disk space available on your computer. You can also use Windows Explorer and other Windows tools to help manage your PaperPort items.

NOTE
You can have up to sixty-four PaperPort folders. There is no limit on the number of subfolders. Just remember what we said earlier—having too many subfolders makes it messy to manage and takes longer to navigate to the required location.

Renaming, Removing, and Reorganizing Folders

You can rename PaperPort folders, but remember that any changes you make in PaperPort apply just as if you had made the same change in Windows Explorer. To rename, remove, and reorganize PaperPort folders, you use the PaperPort Folders dialog box (Figure 11.12). Just click the Folders button, then PaperPort Folders. Click the folder you want to rename, remove, or reorganize and click the appropriate option button.

Figure 11.12
How to remove, rename, or move up or down to reorganize folders

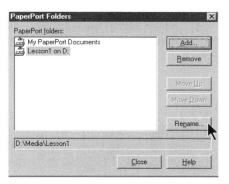

Subfolders, which are located within PaperPort folders, are named with the actual Windows folder names.

NOTE
You can move, rename, and copy subfolders and the changes will be reflected in Windows Explorer.

Renaming Folders

To rename a subfolder, click Tools > PaperPort Folders, click the folder you want to rename, then click Rename. The cursor appears inside the folder name, ready for you to enter the new name. Press Enter when you are finished typing the new name. When you rename a subfolder, you also change the Windows name for that folder.

Removing Folders

You can also remove a PaperPort folder and any subfolders from the Folders pane at any time. Click Tools > PaperPort Folders, click the folder you want to remove, then click Remove. A warning appears asking if you are sure you want to remove the folder.

NOTE

A PaperPort folder is removed only from the Folders pane. The actual folder and its contents will still reside on your computer or external device.

Reorganizing Subfolders with Drag and Drop

To move subfolders to other subfolders or to other PaperPort folders, simply click the subfolder and drag it to a new location in the Folders pane. Subfolders within a folder are always listed in alphabetical order.

TIP

To be prompted when moving or copying a subfolder, click and drag the folder with the right mouse button. The Move prompt or Copy prompt will display.

Reorganizing Folders in the PaperPort Folders Dialog Box

My PaperPort Documents is always the first PaperPort folder in the Folders pane and cannot be rearranged. In the Folders dialog box, use the Move Up and Move Down buttons to move the selected folder one position at a time, as shown in Figures 11.13 and 11.14.

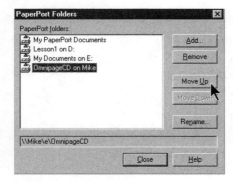

Figure 11.13
Using the Move Up button to rearrange a folder

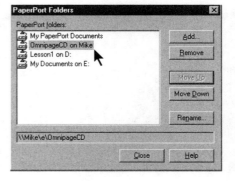

Figure 11.14
The moved folder in its new location

Color Coding Folders

One of the many features we really like is colorcoding—it's a great way to organize your folders. Although the default folder color is manila, you can change the color of any existing folder to one that helps you better organize your items. Color-coding is useful when you want to find items quickly by importance, based on your own personal color preferences. Let's look at how to do that now.

In the Folders pane, select the folder or subfolder whose color you want to change. Then, right-click and select Properties from the shortcut menu. The Folder Properties dialog box displays (Figure 11.15). Click the down arrow of Color, scroll through the colors, and select your preference. The folder becomes the color selected (Figure 11.16).

Figure 11.15
The colorcoding selection box for folders

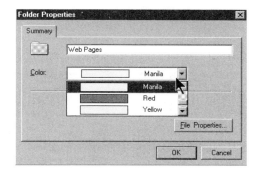

Figure 11.16
The folder with the preferred color

Working with Items

The key to organizing items (files) in PaperPort is filing documents and images in appropriate folders. You can drag and drop items from one folder to another or from the desktop into any folder you want.

To move an item to a folder, select the item you want to move on the desktop and drag and drop the item onto the folder in the Folders pane.

To copy items from one folder to another or to the desktop, select the item you want to copy on the desktop. Hold down the Ctrl key as you drag and drop the item to the desired folder. The original item remains in the original location. The name of each item appears above the thumbnail when you display the Thumbnail view. In a multi-page item, the name appears above the individual page names. The more descriptive the name, the easier it is for you to quickly locate the item. In Figure 11.17, we selected the Samples folder and copied the photo of Ebony and Seagers to the subfolder Photos.

Figure 11.17
The File Import selection box

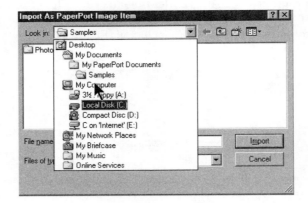

Importing Files

Instead of adding the original Windows Explorer folder that has "Ebony and Seagers" filed, we just selected the destination folder, on the Command menu clicked File > Import, navigated to the original Windows Explorer folder, double-clicked the photo, and dropped "Ebony and Seagers" right into our destination folder. You see it's not always necessary to add folders to get just one file into the PaperPort desktop folder (Figure 11.18). Then, to put a name to the photo, simply click in the title above the photo and type.

Figure 11.18
To import an item, select the folder, then click "File Import"—no need to add a folder if you only want to get one item from a Windows Explorer folder

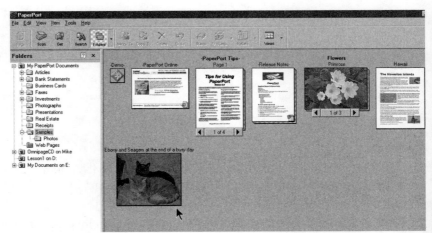

Working in Page View

If you double-click the photo, it opens in Page View. This is how you view pages in a document within a folder. Page View is a fast way to view everything on the PaperPort desktop, including one or all the pages in a document within a folder or images on the desktop. If you want to view only one page within a document, go to the appropriate page by clicking on the page slide bar on the desktop (Figure 11.19). Then, on the Command bar, click Unstack; the pages are tiled so you can see the name of each page or file (Figure 11.20). Then, simply click Page on the Command bar and you can annotate.

Figure 11.19
To select a page within a document, make sure you have the right page before you open it with its original software application—you may want to annotate the page before you e-mail it, in which case you have to select it and unstack the pages

Figure 11.20
Multiple pages in a document that have been unstacked—one Page has areas on the page that have been highlighted in Page View; you can see the highlighter icon where the areas have been highlighted, while the original document in Windows Explorer remains as it was originally saved

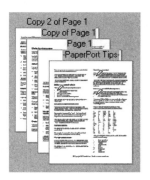

While in Page View, if you want to go to other pages or images on the desktop folder, simply click Item and the next item on the desktop appears. You can go backwards and forwards through the desktop (Figure 11.21). To get back to the PaperPort desktop, click Desktop on the Command bar. You can also annotate a document or image.

Figure 11.21
The "Item" button navigates to other pages or images on the desktop folder

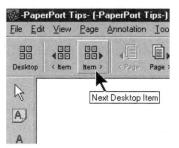

Annotating Documents and Images

Using PaperPort's annotation tools, you can add notes and text, highlight text, draw lines and arrows, or stamp a picture onto a PaperPort image item. You can select an annotation tool from the Annotation toolbar whenever you display a PaperPort image item in the Page View window. This is very useful when e-mailing documents that require areas on the page to stand out to alert the recipient.

The annotations are not applied to the original document. They only show in the PaperPort desktop. The annotation tools include:

▶ **Select Annotation.** Selects, moves, or resizes annotations on the page.

▶ **Note.** Adds a resizable note much like a sticky note.

▶ **Text.** Adds a line of text with a transparent background.

▶ **Highlighter.** Highlights any part of the page.

▶ **Scribble.** Draws freehand lines or marks on the page.

▶ **Arrow or Line.** Draws straight lines, with or without arrowheads, on a page.

▶ **Stamp**. Pastes a graphic on the page, much like using a rubber stamp.

To add a note, display the PaperPort image item in the Page View window (Figure 11.22) and click the Note button on the Annotation toolbar.

Figure 11.22
To annotate work in Page View

Figure 11.23
Click desktop to go back to the folders—the image displays an annotation icon

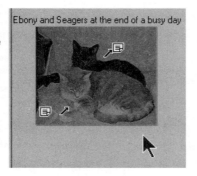

Searching and Finding Files

Sometimes you cannot remember an item's name, but you do remember words within the document. Index Search lets you find items by specifying words in the document as well as the name of the document and other properties. Before you can perform an Index Search, you must add your items (files) to the SimpleSearch index. The PaperPort OCR program converts the items (files) to text and builds an index of words in those files. You need to build the index and update it periodically. You can update the index yourself or let PaperPort do it for you whenever your program is idle.

Although you can use Windows Explorer to search for files containing the text you are looking for, PaperPort is much faster and ranks the files it finds. Windows Explorer reads through all the files on the drive or folder you have selected, so, depending on where they are on your PC, it can take quite a while. I searched for "PaperPort Online" using Index Search; it took five seconds to bring back six documents ranked in order. After twelve minutes in Windows Explorer, I gave up; it had only found one and was still looking.

There are two ways you can find files on your PC:

> ▶ **File search**. Searches the file attributes for your search criteria.

> ▶ **Index Search**. Searches the file attributes and any text within an item for your search criteria. An Index Search requires you to build and periodically update the SimpleSearch index.

When the file(s) are found, they are displayed ranked by the number of times your criteria appears in the file(s).

Adding Search Criteria to Items

You can assign item properties to PaperPort image items (.max files) and then use the properties as search criteria to find items in PaperPort. On the desktop, select the item, right-click, and select Properties to display the Item Properties dialog box (Figure 11.24).

Figure 11.24
Setting up keywords on a document

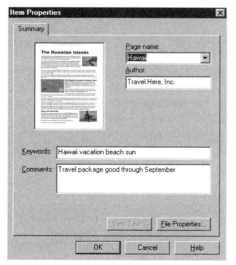

Finding Files

PaperPort provides different features to help you find your PaperPort items. For example, you can quickly find an item by visually browsing through thumbnails on the desktop. When you are searching through many folders and items, you use SimpleSearch.

SimpleSearch provides many options for specifying where and what to look for when finding an item, including indexed text content. The information you want to find is referred to as search criteria. You can look for items either by their item properties or text content.

NOTE

SimpleSearch adds text with a resolution of between 150 and 600 dpi to the SimpleSearch index. The SimpleSearch process does not index content of files in the BMP, JPEG, GIF, TIFF, or Access database MBD formats.

Finding Items by Their Properties

When you search by item properties, you can specify these criteria: author, added comments or keywords, text in annotations, or the URL of a captured Web page.

Finding Words in an Item

To search for words within an item, you need to add the item to the SimpleSearch index and select Use Index for searching. When you search using the index, you can find items by their properties, content, or both.

Adding Items to the SimpleSearch Index

The SimpleSearch index uses PaperPort's OCR software to extract and copy textual content from your items, and then creates a database of the words or phrases in those items, much like the index of a book. Item properties such as name and author are also added to the index. Although creating an index is time consuming, searching for items in the index will be much faster than searching file by file.

Using PaperPort options available from the Tools menu, you can specify whether you want SimpleSearch to run automatically each time you add a new item or modify an existing item. You can also set how long PaperPort should wait before starting the update process. You can manually update the SimpleSearch index for all files, a single file, or all files in one or more folders. It is good practice to update the SimpleSearch index on a regular basis to shorten the length of time required to complete the process.

To Add a Single File

On the desktop, right-click the file. The shortcut menu pops up. Click Add to SimpleSearch. The SimpleSearch Indexer displays (Figure 11.25).

Figure 11.25
The SimpleSearch
Indexer pops up as
soon as you click "Add
to SimpleSearch"

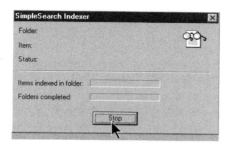

To Add All Files in a Folder

Make sure no items are selected on the desktop. In the Folders pane, right-click the folder
and click Add to SimpleSearch.

To Add All PaperPort Items During a Search

On the Command bar, click the Search button. In the Search pane, click Update Now.

TIP

The first time you update the SimpleSearch index, depending upon the number
of items you have added to PaperPort, it might take several minutes. To use
other programs while PaperPort updates the SimpleSearch database, hold down
the Alt Key and press the Tab key or Ctrl and Esc to move between different
programs.

Once the SimpleSearch index is updated, you can search for files. Use the Search pane to
enter search criteria and select options, as shown in Figure 11.26.

Figure 11.26
Search pane for setting
up search criteria

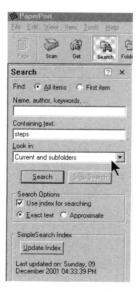

CHAPTER 11

Searching for Files

After indexing a drive or folder and subfolders, you can search for files. A file search is based on item properties only. You enter the file properties in the Name, Author, Keywords box. You would have to have item properties for every file in the Folders pane. If you have many files and folders, this is time consuming. The best way is to index the drive and folders first, and then do the search. An Index Search references PaperPort's SimpleSearch index to find actual text contained within a file or the file properties. You enter the file properties in the Name, Author, Keywords box and the text content in the Containing Text box (see Figure 11.27).

Figure 11.27
All the files containing the word "steps" with a thumbnail of the first file ranked according to the number of times "steps" appears in the document

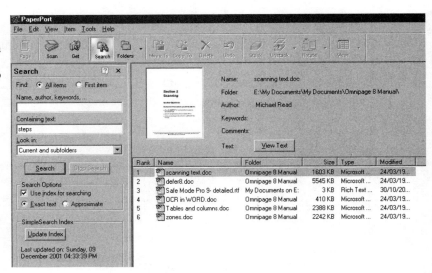

We indexed a network drive with a few subfolders, then did a search on all files in the current folders and subfolders for files containing the word "steps." The result shows all the files ranked in order of the number of times "steps" appears. There's also a thumbnail of the files and a button to click to view the file where the criteria appears (Figure 11.28). Clicking in View File takes you back to the list of files with the file highlighted, as shown in Figure 11.29. Click the Page option on the Command bar to view the whole document. If this is the file you want to open to edit in its associated software application, make sure you are not in Page View. Go back to the desktop, point to the file, hold down the Shift key, and double-click the file. The application launches and opens the file.

Figure 11.28
The file with the search
criteria highlighted

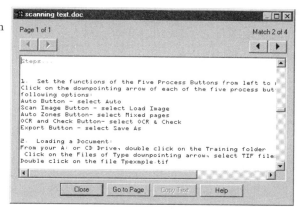

Figure 11.29
The list of files found
with the word "steps;"
the one ranked highest
is highlighted

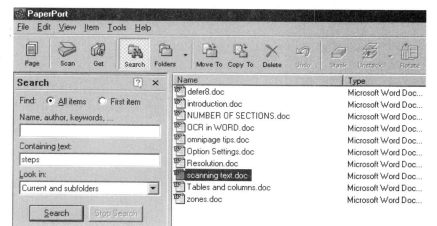

Set Up a Search Criteria

On the Command bar, click the Search button to display the Search pane, and specify your search criteria. Click Search to start the search. You may not remember where your files are, so use the SimpleSearch index to find the actual text contained within a file or files. Enter the text content in the Containing Text box. SimpleSearch returns a list of all the files that match the criteria you specify.

If you select First Item, PaperPort finds the first item that matches the search criteria and automatically selects it on the desktop. To find the next item, press F3.

If you select All Items, PaperPort displays the Search Results pane in the desktop and lists all the found items, as shown in Figure 11.27. Double-click a listed item to select it on the desktop. Right-click a listed item to display a shortcut menu. The shortcut menu allows you to select Open in Folder, View, or Properties for that item.

Click View Text to see the words found in the text of the selected file.

Other Uses for PaperPort

▶ Download pictures from your digital camera

▶ Crop and touch up images

▶ Send files to other applications—fax, for example

▶ E-mail

▶ Customize and reorganize the Send To bar at the bottom of the desktop

▶ Convert images to text

▶ Scan and fill out forms

▶ Scan straight to the PaperPort desktop

▶ Capture Web pages

▶ View documents even when you don't have the originating program (PaperPort has built-in viewers that allow you to easily view files created in most popular programs)

▶ Web-based management and collaboration of your business and personal documents and images, using PaperPortOnline™

PaperPort gives you the latest technology for organizing your drives, files, and folders. When you purchase PaperPort, the user manual, "usrguide.pdf," is installed in the PaperPort folder. It is an excellent reference guide with examples.

12

Form Scanning with OmniForm

Just as we use a hammer to knock in a nail and a spade to dig a hole, we use specific computer applications to perform specific jobs. We use a word processor to edit documents and a spreadsheet for calculations. However, sometimes we try to use the spade to knock in a nail, and that doesn't work very well. It sort of does the job, but it also makes a big mess.

In the sample documents at the back of this book and in the introductory chapters, you can see that certain kinds of documents are ideally suited for OmniPage. If you are scanning a document in order to edit the text, to create an electronic copy, or to incorporate text/graphics into other documents, OmniPage is the appropriate application.

If you're scanning forms, then the right application is OmniForm. Does your document have lots of lines or checkboxes? Are there areas on the page where specific information is to be filled in? Examples are legal documents, real estate documents, credit application forms, survey forms, bank forms, employment forms, product data forms, and order forms.

In this chapter, we'll cover using OmniForm's built in Forms Assistant to scan your forms and documents that look like forms. We'll learn how to fill in a form on screen, how to print and e-mail a form, and how to easily transfer data to your database or spreadsheet from the completed form. OmniForm is a very powerful and comprehensive software application made specifically for forms. Before they discover OmniForm, many users try to scan their forms with OmniPage, get frustrated, and eventually give up. But remember, it's all about using the right tool for the right job.

Introduction to OmniForm

OmniForm is a complete solution for creating, filling in, and managing electronic (digital) forms. It is the easiest way to convert your paper forms, design new forms, fill out forms and distribute forms in a variety of formats, and publish forms on the Web. OmniForm has its own database for storing form data. You can even export data to your own ODBC database such as Microsoft Access, as you will see later in the chapter.

CHAPTER 12

OmniForm is a separate purchase, another application to use with your scanner. Think of it as you might a special saw blade for your electric saw. When you bought your saw (scanner) it came with a blade (application) to cut wood. Now, you are buying a different blade to cut brick. Same saw, different blade for a different job. You could use the wood saw blade that came with the saw, but it won't do the job.

Figures 12.1 and 12.2 show examples of different types of forms.

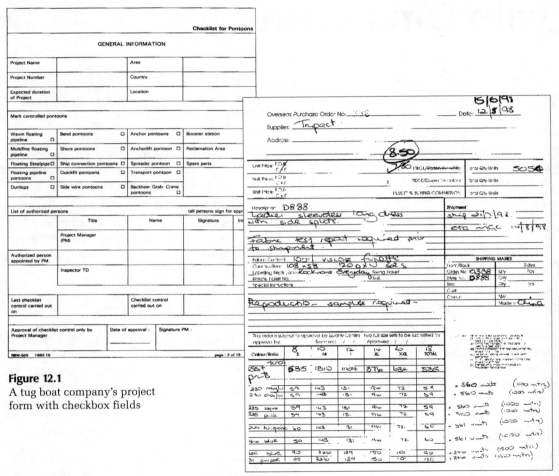

Figure 12.1
A tug boat company's project form with checkbox fields

Figure 12.2
One of our clients' order forms

Figure 12.2 illustrates an example of mistaken expectations. This client thought OmniPage would be able to scan the form and OCR the handwriting. It came out a terrible mess. The client was very frustrated and couldn't understand why OmniPage couldn't scan her form and maintain the proper format. When she attended one of our training courses, she discovered it was more properly a job for OmniForm.

Using OmniForm

Using OmniForm is very easy, even though it is a very powerful application. OmniForm has excellent wizards to get you started. You can create your first basic single form in about five minutes. Once you are familiar with designing forms, you can move right up to designing complex forms that access external databases for lookup tables, multi-page forms, and more. There are two major components of OmniForm: the Designer and the Filler. And you can publish and manage your forms on the Web using Online Forms.

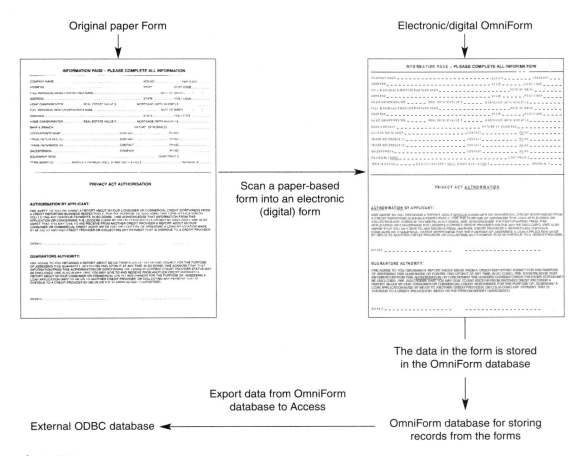

Figure 12.3
The creation and flow of data
when using OmniForm

Use OmniForm to scan the form and create a digital copy of the original. The form can then be filled in on a computer and printed. OmniForm can perform calculations on the filled fields. You can print forms on demand, so there is no costly bulk printing of forms that are often not used, and you can change the forms when you need to. The forms can even be filled in at remote locations.

Let's look at the process of designing the form using the built-in Wizard. This Wizard is a bit like the Wizard function of OmniPage; it asks you questions about your form and the fields. Then, we'll look at the options for saving and filling in the form. Finally, we'll learn how to save the data and what can be done with it.

The OmniForm Desktop

The OmniForm desktop has three tabbed views that allow you to create, fill in, and publish forms. You can easily click between Form Designer, Form Filler, and Online Forms (Figure 12.4).

Figure 12.4
The three views of the desktop

▶ Use Form Designer to create new forms from scratch and to modify an existing form's design. For basic forms, simply follow the prompts in the Forms Assistant. The Forms Assistant will guide you through four screens before scanning and creating your form.

▶ Use Form Filler to fill out new form records and search through each form's database.

▶ Use Online Forms view to instantly publish and manage forms on the Web using ScanSoft's online forms hosting service—eOmniForm.com. This is an easy way to publish your forms on a secure Web site. It does not require any complicated setup or technical knowledge. All you need is a connection to the Internet. After publishing your forms with eOmniForm.com, anyone with a Web browser and Internet connection can fill them out. The process for publishing forms on eOmniForm.com is very simple: eOmniForm.com provides you with the Web address where your form is published. Send this Web address to the people you want to fill out your form. Collect the form data from the Web using the Online Forms view. The data is added as new records in your OmniForm database. ScanSoft offers some limited free publishing and storage on eOmniForm.com.

Let's scan a form.

Form Designer

In this exercise, you will be using a credit application form, the file "form2.tif," as shown in Figure 12.5. You can find the file in the appendix or it can be downloaded from the Web site (see Introduction).

We're going to use the Forms Assistant (Wizard) in showing you the steps to create an electronic form from a scanned page.

Figure 12.5
"Form2.tif"

INFORMATION PAGE – PLEASE COMPLETE ALL INFORMATION

COMPANY NAME .... ACN NO .... YEARS EST ....

ADDRESS .... STATE .... POST CODE ....

FULL INDIVIDUAL/DIRECTOR/PARTNER NAME .... DATE OF BIRTH ..../......./

ADDRESS .... STATE .... POST CODE ....

HOME OWNER/RENTER .... REAL ESTATE VALUE $ .... MORTGAGE (WITH WHOM?) $ ....

FULL INDIVIDUAL/DIRECTOR/PARTNER NAME .... DATE OF BIRTH ..../......./

ADDRESS .... STATE .... POST CODE ....

HOME OWNER/RENTER .... REAL ESTATE VALUE $ .... MORTGAGE (WITH WHOM?) $ ....

BANK & BRANCH .... NATURE OF BUSINESS ....

ACCOUNTANTS NAME .... CONTACT .... PH NO ....

TRADE REFERENCE (1) .... CONTACT .... PH NO ....

TRADE REFERENCE (2) .... CONTACT .... PH NO ....

SALESPERSON .... COMPANY .... PH NO ....

EQUIPMENT DESC .... COST PRICE $ ....

TERM (MONTHS) .... MONTHLY PAYMENT (INCL. STAMP DUTY & FID) $ .... RESIDUAL $ ....

PRIVACY ACT AUTHORISATION

AUTHORISATION BY APPLICANT:

I/WE AGREE TO YOU OBTAINING A REPORT ABOUT MY/OUR CONSUMER OR COMMERCIAL CREDIT WORTHINESS FROM A CREDIT REPORTING BUSINESS RESPECTIVELY, FOR THE PURPOSE OF ASSESSING THIS LOAN APPLICATION OR COLLECTING ANY OVERDUE PAYMENTS; IN SO DOING , I/WE ACKNOWLEDGE THAT INFORMATION FROM THIS APPLICATION OR CONCERNING THE LENDERS CURRENT CREDIT PROVIDER STATUS MAY BE DISCLOSED. I/WE ALSO AGREE THAT YOU MAY GIVE TO AND RECEIVE FROM ANOTHER CREDIT PROVIDER A REPORT ABOUT MY/OUR CONSUMER OR COMMERCIAL CREDIT WORTHINESS FOR THE PURPOSE OF ASSESSING A LOAN APPLICATION MADE BY ME/US TO ANOTHER CREDIT PROVIDER OR COLLECTING ANY PAYMENT THAT IS OVERDUE TO A CREDIT PROVIDER.

SIGNED ....

GUARANTORS AUTHORITY:

I/WE AGREE TO YOU OBTAINING A REPORT ABOUT ME/US FROM A CREDIT REPORTING AGENCY FOR THE PURPOSE OF ASSESSING THIS GUARANTEE OR FOR RELYING UPON IT AT ANY TIME, IN SO DOING, I/WE ACKNOWLEDGE THAT INFORMATION FROM THIS AUTHORISATION OR CONCERNING THE LENDERS CURRENT CREDIT PROVIDER STATUS MAY BE DISCLOSED. I/WE ALSO AGREE THAT YOU MAY GIVE TO AND RECEIVE FROM ANOTHER CREDIT PROVIDER A REPORT ABOUT MY/OUR CONSUMER OR COMMERCIAL CREDIT WORTHINESS FOR THE PURPOSE OF: ASSESSING A LOAN APPLICATION MADE BY ME/US TO ANOTHER CREDIT PROVIDER; OR COLLECTING ANY PAYMENT THAT IS OVERDUE TO A CREDIT PROVIDER BY ME/US OR THE PERSON HEREBY GUARANTEED.

SIGNED ....

1. Launch OmniForm. Click Start > Programs > Scansoft OmniForm 5.0.

2. The Form Assistant prompts you to choose an activity (Figure 12.6).

Figure 12.6
Forms Assistant screen 1 displays after closing "Tip of the Day;" its options include: Scan a Form or Image File; Fill in a Form; Print a Form; Search a Form for Information; Work on a Form's Design; or Create a New, Blank Form

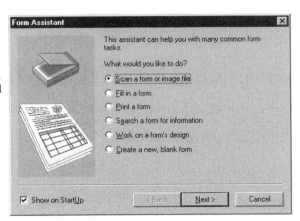

CHAPTER 12

3.   Click Scan a Form or Image File and click Next.

4.   Click Scanner, as shown in Figure 12.7. If you are scanning a color form, simply click the option I'm Scanning a Color Form. Click Next.

Figure 12.7
Screen 2 asks that you choose an existing file or acquire an image from the scanner

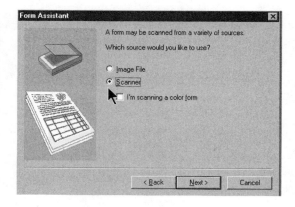

5.   Select the paper size for your original form. Is it a legal form, an A4 form, or a Letter form? We will select A4 (see Figure 12.8). Click Next.

Figure 12.8
Screen 3 asks you to choose from three page sizes

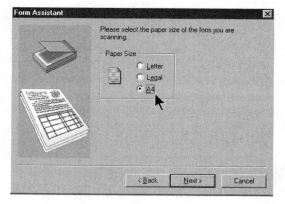

6.   The next screen to pop us asks you what you want to do with the form once it is scanned. Click "I want to have control over the form's design," as shown in Figure 12.9.

7.   Click Finish.

Figure 12. 9
Screen 4 offers two options: You can choose to have full control over the form's design, or just fill out the form

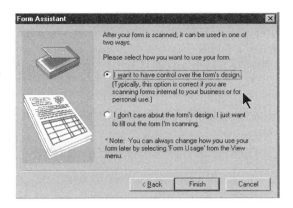

OmniForm designs the form based on the text and the fields from the original, as shown in Figure 12.10. You can see the progress of the form analysis by the yellow bar moving down the page.

Figure 12.10
OmniForm designing and recognizing the scanned form

The next screen to pop up is the Proofreader box; for now, click No.

Figure 12.11
The Proofreader prompt box displays after the scanned form is recognized

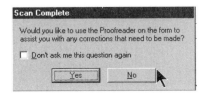

CHAPTER 12

OmniForm has a fantastic proofreading feature that is easy to use. It helps you perfect your forms. The Proofreader has ten separate screens that assist you in areas such as spelling, color adjustment, text formatting, and field tabbing. A window pops up on the left-hand side, guiding you through the many things you can do to improve the design of the fields. For example, you can change the tabbing order of the form (the order in which the cursor proceeds when users press the Tab key) simply by clicking on the field name in the Proofreader window and clicking the Move Up or Move Down arrow buttons (Figure 12.12).

Figure 12.12
Fields with markers highlighting the "tabbing order"

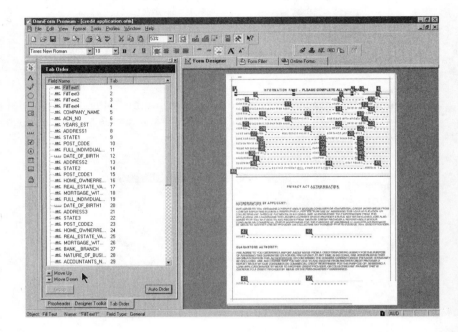

The Proofreader box pops up. For now, click No. We won't go through the proofreading. You can also use the tools in the Proofing toolbar to make corrections and changes to your form. You can always switch it on at any time while in Form Designer by clicking Tools > Proofreader. The screen splits in two. On the left side is the Proofreader Wizard; on the right is the Form. The Wizard makes it easy to proofread.

In Figure 12.13, you can see that OmniPage has recognized the text, placed the text in its original position, and created yellow boxes for data entry. These yellow fields can be moved and deleted, and properties can be set for each field to control validation and filling. In order to see the yellow fields, you must ensure they are switched on. To do this, click View > Highlight Fillable Fields.

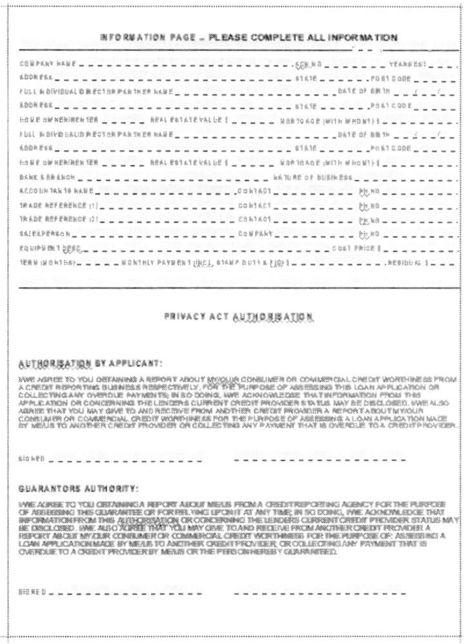

Figure 12.13
The new form with
fields highlighted

Let's see how to use the fields in the form.

1. Point to the yellow field to the right of the heading "Company Name."

2. Right-click to see the properties of the field. This is the Fill Text Definition selection box.

3. Click Object Definition. Every element on the page of a form is classified as an object. You will see in Figure 12.14 that OmniPage has named this field the same as the text to the left of it, "Company Name."

Figure 12.14
The Fill Text Definition
box for formatting the
field the cursor is in

CHAPTER 12

4. Click OK.

5. Repeat steps 2 and 3 for the Date of Birth field (Figure 12.15).

Figure 12.15
The date field highlighted and the Fill Text Definition box for making a change to the date format— OmniForm has detected the word "date" in the field name and, therefore, sets the field to a date type field

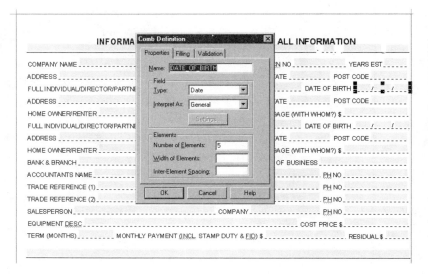

6. You can also format fields. Click the down arrow of the field Interpret As and select "DD/MM/YY." This changes the way the date will display and allows dates to be entered in only that format (Figure 12.16).

Figure 12.16
Changing the interpretation of the field to a different date format

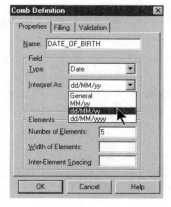

7. Click OK to accept that date format.

Before you save the form, let's quickly take a look at the different field types and their attributes you can use in your form. We won't be designing a form in this chapter; however, it's worth knowing the type of fields OmniForm uses.

▶ **Fillable Text Fields.** You can enter characters in a fillable text field (Figure 12.17) such as letters, numbers, symbols, and dates. On the menu, in the View options, make sure Highlight Fillable Fields is selected. If it's not, the fillable fields will not be highlighted in yellow.

Figure 12.17
A field for
alphanumeric text

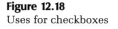

Name _____

▶ **Checkbox Fields.** These are commonly used for Yes/No questions and for selecting an item in a group (Figure 12.18). Click a checkbox to fill it. A filled checkbox field can contain a check mark, an "x" mark, or a solid fill. Checkboxes might be grouped so that only one can be selected at a time. In this case, selecting one checkbox automatically deselects other checkboxes in the group.

Figure 12.18
Uses for checkboxes

Yes ☑ No ☐

Yes ☒ No ☐

Yes ◼ No ☐

▶ **Comb Fields.** A comb field (Figure 12.19) is a fillable text field that is broken into separate segments for entering a set number of characters, like fields for entering a credit card number. You can enter any characters in a comb field that are appropriate to the field. Comb fields are commonly used for phone numbers, credit cards, zip codes, and postal codes. You do not have to tab to each element (box) in a comb field. Just type the data, and the cursor automatically moves to the next comb element.

Figure 12.19
Comb fields

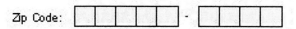

Zip Code:

▶ **Circle Text Fields.** You may use these on questionnaires where you circle your response (Figure 12.20). Click a circle text field to make a selection. Circle text fields might be grouped so that only one can be selected at a time. In this case, selecting one circle text field automatically deselects other circle text fields in the group.

Figure 12.20
Circle fields

1   2   3

CHAPTER 12

▶ **Fillable Graphic Fields.** A fillable graphic field allows you to insert a graphic into a form. You can import an existing graphic file or scan a picture directly into the field using a TWAIN-compatible scanner. OmniForm imports the graphic into the form field.

▶ **Table Fields.** A table field consists of cells that can be fillable text fields. You can enter characters in these cells just as you would in regular text fields. A table can also have checkboxes. Tables can do calculations and are great to use on order forms. You can perform calculations using any field on the form.

After you have made changes to the format of the form, you need to save the form, then you can fill it in with the appropriate data.

To save a form, on the standard toolbar, click the Save button, or choose File > Save. If this is the first time you have saved the form, the Save As dialog box appears. Choose the folder to save the form in, the file type (see below for more about file types), and file name. Click OK.

When you save a form, the default file extension is OFM. An OmniForm Form is automatically set up with its own searchable database. As new records (blank forms) are filled out for the form, each record is stored in the database.

There are four different file formats in which you can save your form (Figure 12.21).

▶ OmniForm Markup Language (OFML)

▶ Hypertext Markup Language (HTML)

▶ Adobe Portable Document Format (PDF)

▶ Microsoft Word Rich Text Format (RTF)

Figure 12.21
The Save As dialog box and file types for saving forms

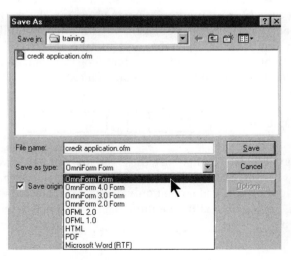

There is also a separate option in the file menu to Save as Mailable Filler. This creates an executable file of the form. The recipient can open and fill the form in without having OmniForm on his or her computer; all that is required is Windows.

You may want to post your form on the Internet or an intranet. Before you save your form in HTML file format, we recommend you preview the form in your Internet browser to make sure it looks the way you want it to. Do this by clicking File > Preview in Browser (Figure 12.22).

Figure 12.22
How to preview an HTML form in your Internet browser

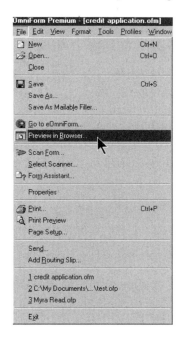

For this exercise, we will save it as an OmniForm Form (OFM). On the menu, click File > Save As. In the Save In field, navigate to the training folder; in the Filename field, type "credit application;" leave Save as Type the default OmniForm Form, as shown in Figure 12.23.

Figure 12.23
Save the exercise as an OmniForm Form

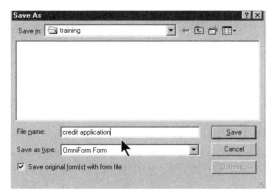

Form Filler

OmniForm automatically saves form records as you fill them in. Saving occurs after various actions, such as moving from one record to another, printing or closing a form, and before importing or exporting data.

You use the Form Filler view to fill out new blank forms and search through each form's database. Form Filler view allows you to enter data on forms, manage form records in its database, import and export the saved data on the form, print forms, and e-mail forms. You view a form in Form Filler by clicking the Form Filler tab, or by selecting View > Form Filler from the menu.

OmniForm includes a feature called User Profiles. It's great for forms that require the same information to be entered each month, such as employee data, insurance information, credit reports, travel details, etc. OmniForm guides you through creating profiles. Figure 12.24 shows one of the guided user profiles you can set up. Once a user profile is set up, the user's personal details or unchanging information is repeated each time they fill in the form and is automatically entered. You can even add attachments, such as receipts to expense forms.

Every OmniForm form has its own OmniForm database associated with it. An OmniForm database is a collection of information stored as individual records. Each record is a completed form.

Figure 12.24
One of the predesigned
User Profiles

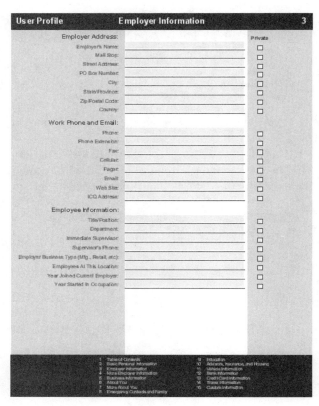

Next, let's fill in the form we have just scanned with the appropriate information.

To enter data, click the Form Filler tab, as shown in Figure 12.25. This will open your form in Fill mode; here, you can only enter data in the specified fields.

Figure 12.25
Click the Form Filler
tab to be able to enter
date into the fields

Figure 12.26 shows the view users will have. It does not allow them to change the form layout or existing text, only enter data in the defined fields. Now, you can start filling in the data. Experiment with filling in all the fields. Tabbing is the quickest way to move from field to field. If you want to go back a field, press Shift+Tab. You can also select a field by clicking the mouse on the required field. The selected field will have a fine dotted line around it.

Figure 12.26
Form Filler view with
fill-in fields
highlighted

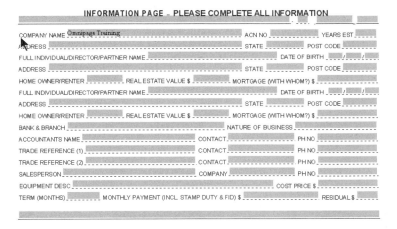

To display a new data entry form for the next record and save the data, simply click Records > GoTo > New (Figure 12.27). A new blank form displays, and you are ready to enter more data.

Figure 12.27
Creating a new record
using the same form

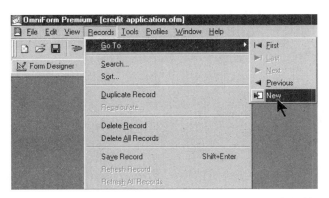

CHAPTER 12

You can also navigate through the form records with the Fill toolbar (Figure 12.28). If it's not on, click View > Toolbars > Customize > Fill.

Figure 12.28
The easy-to-use database navigation toolbar

For this exercise, practice creating three new records and enter the data. Leave the "Company Name" as "OmniPage Training" because, on the second form, as soon as you type "O," the rest of the company name will be entered for you. This is called Type Ahead, and it is made available under Tools > Options. Click the Filling tab, then click Enable Type Ahead. Fill in the form fields with any data you like; make it meaningful so that, when you export the data to an external database later, you can clearly recognize the data.

It is good practice to check the logical flow of the tab order—making sure the fields are logically grouped and that those most often filled in are at the beginning and the less frequently used are at the end of the tab sequence. Give the form to your colleagues and others to test and get their feedback. Good form design will lead to easier acceptance and greater ease of use; it can make or break the form.

NOTE
OmniForm automatically saves information you enter when filling out forms. You do not have to save the form record each time you enter data.

Before you print the form, have a good look at it by zooming in (Figures 12.29 and 12.30).

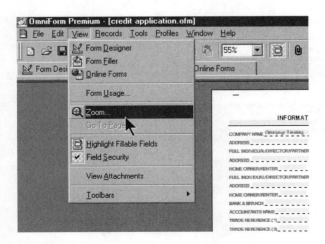

Figure 12.29
How to zoom into the form to check for errors

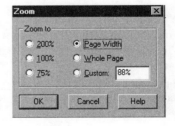

Figure 12.30
Magnification options for zooming

Printing Forms

You can print forms with different page sizes, margins, orientation, and color. Preview the form before you select any page settings. If you preview it first, you can see what needs to be changed and save on paper. Of course, if you were designing a new form with Designer, you would set up the page during the design stage.

We always print a hard copy, as it is sometimes easier to read on paper than on screen. We always do this before we e-mail or distribute any form. It makes it easier to check that you haven't forgotten anything and that the form looks the way you want it to.

Page Options must be set up or altered before printing the form. We will look at that shortly.

Print Preview

On the standard toolbar, click the Preview icon. You can print from within Print Preview, as shown in Figures 12.31 and 12.32.

Figure 12.31
Print Preview button
on the standard toolbar

Figure 12.32
Check Print Preview to
be sure the page
margins look OK

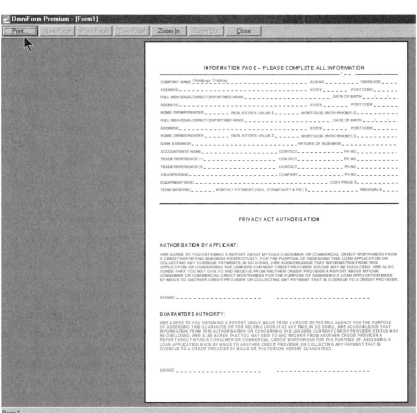

CHAPTER 12

Let's look at Page Settings prior to printing the form, using the Print menu.

Page Settings

To change page settings before printing a form:

1. Open the form in Form Designer. If the form is already open, simply click the Form Designer tab.
2. In the File menu, click Page Setup.
3. The Page Setup dialog box appears (Figure 12.33).

Figure 12.33
Page Setup options

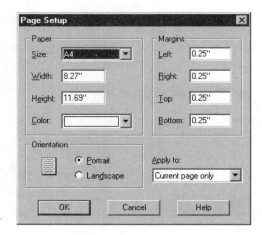

4. Select the desired options.
5. Click OK to apply your options and close the dialog box. For this exercise, we will leave the options as set.
6. To save these changes to your form, click Save before closing the form.

You can choose what you want to print. You may have some preprinted forms and only want the data entered to print on the form, not the form itself. You may just need to print the form, since you don't have a hard copy of it, or you may want to send it around to other departments to get their ideas on its design. You need the form and the data on it. Here is how you choose one of the three options.

Three Options for Printing the Form and Data on the Form

You print your form with the data entered from the Form Filler view. When you are printing from Form Filler, you can print Form and Data, Data Only, or Form Only. Selecting Data Only just prints the information you have entered in the fields. This is useful if you want to print data on a preprinted form.

1. Open the form in Form Filler if you want to print data in the form.
2. On the standard toolbar, click the Print button or choose Print in the File menu. The Print dialog box appears (Figure 12.34).

Figure 12.34
Options for "What do you what to print?"

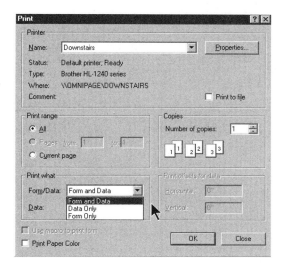

3. Select the desired options for printing. We will select Form and Data for this exercise. You can also choose whether you want to print all the records, just the current one, or a range of records (Figure 12.35). For this exercise, we will select Current Record Only. This is the default and should already be selected.

4. Click OK to start printing.

Figure 12.35
Options for "What data do you what to print?"

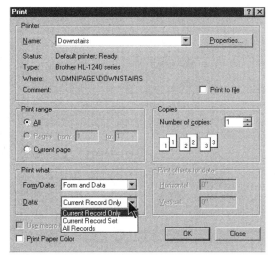

OmniForm prints your form with the selected settings.

CHAPTER 12

Transferring Data from OmniForm to an External Database

You fill in data and manage records with Form Filler view. Every form has its own database associated with it. The first time you open a form and fill in information, that form becomes the first record in the database. Anyone with access to the form can create new records in the database.

The data from the OmniForm database can be exported to an ODBC-compliant database. You can export to Microsoft Access, dBASE, Excel, FoxPro, Paradox, DB2 (IBM), Oracle, Sybase, and Microsoft SQL Server, and you can export text-based and CSV files.

You must have a database set up first in order to export data to it. You export the data from the form's database to a table within the external database. If there is no existing table in the external database, OmniForm will create it for you, except for DBII, Oracle, Sybase, and SQL Server.

You can import data into your form database from these sources:

▶ Another OmniForm database

▶ An OmniForm Mailable Filler file (either HTML or EXE)

▶ Any supported ODBC database source (available sources depend on the installed database drivers)

You must first export data from another database in order to import it into OmniForm. You cannot import data into OmniForm if data protection is turned on for the form.

In this exercise, we will export the data from our form's database to a new table in Microsoft Access. Before we do, we will need to set up a database for this exercise.

Launch Microsoft Access. In the Create a New Database field, click Blank Database. In the Save In field, navigate to your training folder. In the Filename field, type "training database." Click OK. The new database is created and ready to receive the data from the form.

You transfer data from OmniForm to your database through the File option on the menu bar of OmniForm (Figure 12.36).

1. On the menu, click File > Export.

2. Click New. The Export Data Setup dialog box appears (Figure 12.37).

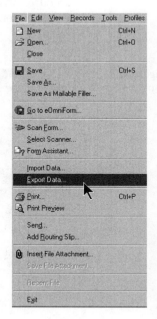

Figure 12.36
How to begin transferring data to an external database

Figure 12.37
Previously saved
database exports

3. In the Export To field, click the down arrow and select ODBC database (Figure 12.38). ODBC stands for Open Database Connectivity. ODBC is a common database protocol that many applications can access. Installed ODBC database drivers appear in the Available Data Sources list box. Depending on your database driver, you can export up to 255 fields at a time.

Figure 12.38
ODBC databases to
choose from

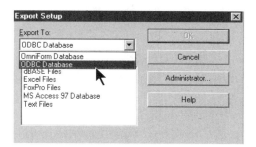

4. Select your database application from the available sources. We will select Access 97, as this is the one we have installed on our system right now, as we write this book. Double-click Access 97 or your database to select it. The type of dialog box that appears next depends on the type of database application you have selected. For example, the Export As dialog box appears if you selected to export to an OmniForm database (Figure 12.39).

Figure 12.39
The dialog box for
saving an OmniForm
database

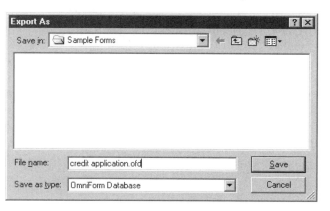

CHAPTER 12

5.   Because we selected ODBC, the Select Database dialog box appears and asks us to select a database. Navigate to your training folder and double-click "training database.mdb" (Figure 12.40).

Figure 12.40
The Select Database dialog box displays when ODBC database is selected

6.   The next screen asks you to select a name for the table that will store all the records from the form in the training database. Type "credit application" for the name of the table (Figure 12.41).

Figure 12.41
The name of the exported table in the external database

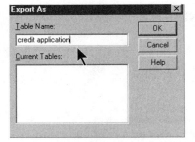

7.   Click OK. This will create the new table.

8.   Now, you have to select the fields you want to export. We will need all fields for this credit application, so highlight all the fields in the Fields in: Form 1 field. Scroll to the top of the list and click the first field name. Scroll down to the last field name in the list, hold down the Shift key, and left-click to select all fields. To select specific fields, Shift-click to select multiple adjacent records, or hold the mouse button and drag the cursor over adjacent records. Ctrl+click to select multiple nonadjacent records.

9.   Now, we need to add the fields to the Fields to Export. Click the Add button to add all the field names to the Fields to Export. This ensures that all the field names will appear as the header at the top of the table (Figure 12.42). That's all for this step, so click OK.

Figure 12.42
Field names in the
OmniForm database on
the left and the ones on
the right will be added
to the table in the
external database

10. The next screen (Figure 12.43) requests us to make a decision on what we
want to do with the records we have just exported. Click Run to start
exporting the data as specified.

Figure 12.43
Once the field names
have been added for
export, you then
choose whether you
want to export the data
to the table in the
external database, go to
the Save options, or
cancel this step

11. When you export data from OmniForm, you can save and reuse your export
selections for future exports. To save your settings during export for future
use, click Save. A dialog box prompts you to enter a name for your saved
export selections, as shown in Figure 12.44. Click Save and Run.

Figure 12.44
When you choose the
option to save, you are
prompted to save the
export for future use
and the data is entered
into the table in the
external database—
Save and Exit, on the
other hand, does not
transfer the data to the
table in the external
database; it just saves
the export setup for
future use in
OmniForm

CHAPTER 12

Now, the records are exported to your database. Let's check out what our new table, "credit application," looks like with the record from this form.

To view records in your external database:

1.   Launch your database application. We will launch Microsoft Access.

2.   Navigate in the list of databases to find "training database." Double-click to open.

3.   Click the Table tab; it is selected by default.

4.   Double-click the table "credit application" to open.

You will see all the field names in the header and the information you entered for each record on the form. Figure 12.45 displays data in just the "Company Name" field. That's because that's all we typed on our form. If you added more fields, they will be displayed in your table.

NOTE

The Export function does not append data to an existing table; it replaces all the data in an existing table. Therefore, use a temporary input table in your external database in which to export the OmniForm data. Then, in your external database, use the Append functions to append the data to the appropriate database table.

				COMPANY_NA	ACN_NO	YEARS_EST	ADDRESS1	STATE1	POST_CODE	FULL_INI
FillText1	FillText3	FillText2	FillText4							
				Omnipage Trair						

Figure 12.45
The table in the Microsoft Access database

That's how easy it is to scan and fill in a form and export the data from the form's database to an external database.

E-Mailing the Form

You can save a form in a number of formats. PDF format is a small file size, suitable for e-mailing. A Microsoft Word RTF creates a form document in Microsoft Word. Or, you can create a self-running executable (EXE file) mailable form by selecting File > Save As Mailable Filler. With the Mailable Filler option, recipients don't need OmniForm or any other application to open the form. They just need Microsoft Windows.

You can e-mail a blank form to be filled in by the recipient, the data and the form, or you can e-mail the data only. In this case, the recipient must have OmniForm or OmniForm Filler installed to open the e-mailed form.

OmniForm Full Version (not an upgrade) comes with Mailable Filler, allowing you to send forms to people who do not have OmniForm.

OmniForm includes a trial license for a specified number of Mailable Fillers. The details of this license are described in an insert in the package. After you have used all your licensed number of uses, you need to purchase additional licenses.

NOTE:

When sending a Mailable Filler, it attaches both an HTML file and a self-running executable file (EXE) to your message. You do not have to send both file formats. If you know which format is supported by the recipient's e-mail, you can delete the other attachment. (The HTML version is recommended for e-mail systems that do not allow executable file attachments.)

To send a form as an e-mail attachment:

1. Open the form you want to send. To send the form and data, click the Form Filler tab, not the Designer tab.

2. In the File menu, click Send. The e-mail options appear. The options available depend on whether you are sending the form from Form Designer or Form Filler. Figure 12.46 shows options when sending from Form Filler. Figure 12.47 shows options when sending from Form Designer.

3. Select the required option. If you are sending form data only, click Range and specify the range of records you want to send. We have only one record in our exercise. If you do not specify a range, OmniForm will send all records.

4. Click OK.

Figure 12.46
E-mail options from
Form Filler view

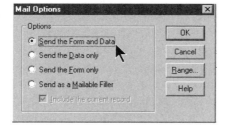

Figure 12.47
E-mail options from
Form Designer view

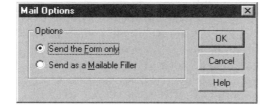

5. Most of the time, your e-mail application will pop up automatically with the form attached (Figure 12.48).

Figure 12.48
After you have chosen the e-mail option, a blank e-mail message pops up with the form attached

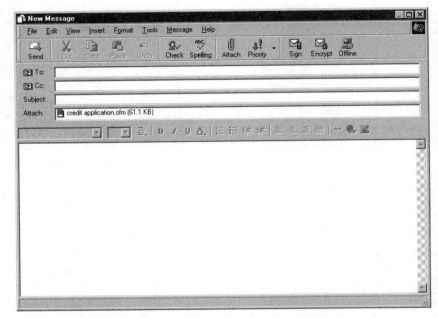

6. Create your message and click Send.

More OmniForm Features

Take a look at additional helpful features of OmniForm:

▶ You do not need a scanner to make forms electronic. OmniForm can import and design from fax files.

▶ Special characters and symbols can be inserted into a form. On the menu, simply click Insert Symbol.

▶ When filling in a shared form, make sure you are seeing the latest data by clicking Records > Refresh Records.

▶ The AutoFill Wizard allows you to fill forms with information from external databases. Select a Comb or Fill Text element and, in the Format menu, select Object Definition. Click the Filling tab and select Enable AutoFill. Then, click AutoFill Wizard and follow the instructions.

▶ You can set up your form to automatically fill fields using the Type Ahead option. Click Tools > Options. Then, click the Filling tab and click Enable Type Ahead. As you begin to enter a word on the form, OmniForm automatically completes the word for you, if there is previously filled information that matches the word you are entering. For example, if you had previously entered the name Myra in a field, as soon as you enter M in another field, OmniForm would automatically enter Myra for you.

▶ Have you ever had to squeeze your name and address into a form field? Well, now you can shrink text to fit fields. The text you enter may not always fit in the text fields on a form. To fix this, OmniForm can automatically shrink your text to make it fit in the fields. Click Tools > Options, and select the Filling tab. Click Automatically Shrink Text to fit Within Fields to select it.

▶ You can copy logos from a scanned form to newly created forms. This command is only available if you saved the original scanned form image at the time you saved the newly designed form. You will find the option Save Original Form(s) with Form File in the Save As dialog box. Click the Form Designer tab. Click View > Form Image. Select the graphic tool from the Designer toolbar; draw a selection box around the logo by holding down the mouse button and dragging the cursor around the area. Release the mouse button. The selected logo appears as a graphic in your converted form. Drag the graphic to the desired location in the form.

▶ To automate data entry and reduce errors, you can define calculations for fillable fields. Calculation fields can display today's date, the sum of selected fields, the square root of a number, and dozens of other functions. In the Tools menu, click Calculation to display the Calculation toolbar. You can also have drop-down lists for selecting things like states or product names. You can restrict data entry to a data range. You can also look up information from external databases—product codes or parts lists, for example.

▶ When exporting data to an external database, in the Select Database dialog box, click Exclusive to limit access to one user at a time, so that no one can access the database while you are trying to update it with the export. When finished exporting, the database is available in Shared mode. It can be accessed simultaneously by multiple users.

▶ There are thirty-one sample forms in C:\My Documents\Scansoft OmniForm 5.0\Sample Folder that you can use or redesign to meet your own needs.

▶ If you want to publish a form to your own Web site, provided you have the technical know-how for publishing Web forms, simply click Tools > Publish to a Web Site. A Wizard guides you through the steps.

▶ You can set up a form database so that multiple people can access it and fill forms in at the same time. Open the form and click the Form Designer tab. In the File menu, click Properties. Click the Sharing tab and select the shared option. Then, you must save and close the form before sharing can take place.

▶ You can turn oval, rectangle, graphic, and text elements on a form into hyperlinks. Hyperlinks can jump users to Web sites, other documents, and applications. Click the Form Designer tab, select the form element, and, on the menu, click Format > Hyperlink.

▶ OmniForm supports the new "euro" currency symbol. To use this symbol, click Tools > Options. Then, click the International tab. Finally, select the current form and Use Euro Currency Symbol.

▶ OmniPage supports the following graphic formats: BMP, GIF, JPEG, PCX, TIFF, Macintosh PICT.

CHAPTER 12

Form Scanning Tips

If you scan typeset, high-quality printed paper forms, text recognition and form conversion accuracy should be very high. With lower-quality pages, text recognition might not be as accurate. Following are some ways for improving scanning forms and recognition performance.

▶ **Original Document Quality**. OmniForm recognizes characters in almost any font, from 6 to 72 points; however, the print should be reasonably clean and crisp. Characters must be distinct; they should be separated from each other and not blurry or overlapping. The document should be free of notes, lines, or doodles. Anything that is not a printed character slows recognition, and any character distorted by a mark will be unrecognizable. The document font should be nonstylized; for example, OmniForm may not recognize the "Zapf Chancery" font accurately. For best results, underlined text should have the lines placed below the text and not touching the text. It is difficult to recognize underlined text because the underline overprints the descenders on the letters (g, j, p, q, and y), changing their shape.

▶ **Placement of Original**. Make sure each document is positioned correctly in your scanner and is not crooked. If there seem to be many errors, it may be simply that the page is not straight in the scanner.

▶ **Scanner Glass Clarity**. The sheet of glass on the flatbed scanner must be clear. If it gets dirty, wipe it gently with a soft, damp, lint-free cloth or tissue. Be sure it is completely dry before you put pages on it. See your scanner documentation for more information on proper scanner maintenance.

▶ **Lightweight Paper**. Some originals that you scan may be on lightweight paper. If you have a double-sided original, the text on the underside may come through. This can interfere with scanning accuracy. Just place a matte black piece of paper on top of the page. A shiny piece of black paper may reflect the light back through the page, which is just what you want to avoid.

For those of you who have OmniForm, we hope this chapter has given you some more useful information. For those of you who don't, thanks for taking the time to read this chapter; you are now aware there is a software application specifically for scanning forms. As an informed OmniPage power user, when your colleagues have problems and are trying to scan a form with OmniPage, you can introduce them to OmniForm.

13

OmniPage Advanced Configuration Options

After using OmniPage for a while, you may have clicked Tools > Options on the menu bar or clicked the Options button on the toolbar and wondered what all those choices were about. You may have tried to use them but were unsure how to proceed. There are common problems and issues that users encounter that are solved by some of these option settings. In this chapter, we will explore the settings in the OmniPage Option Settings dialog box. We have touched on some of these in previous chapters, but now we'll take a comprehensive look at these option settings.

The quickest way to access Options is from the standard toolbar. It's the button with the little AB in it, just below and to the right of Help. You can get there from the menu bar as well; just click Tools > Options.

The Options dialog box consists of seven different process tabs: OCR, Scanner, Direct OCR, Process, Proofing, Custom Layout, and Text Editor (Figure 13.1).

Figure 13.1
The OmniPage Options dialog box

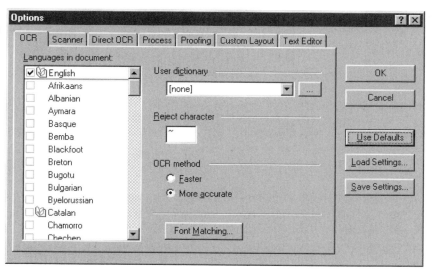

Let's take a look at each tab in turn.

OCR Tab

The OCR tab allows you to select the Languages in the document, the User dictionary, the Reject character, OCR method, and Font Matching. Everything in OCR settings is concerned with the actual recognition of the characters of your scanned or loaded document.

Languages in the Document

The language by default is English. OmniPage recognizes 114 different languages, from Afrikaans to Zulu. All 114 languages fall into three main character set groups: Latin, Greek, and Cyrillic. Latin is the character set most commonly used for the supported languages; the characters in this book, for instance, are Latin characters. Greek and Cyrillic are completely different character shapes.

When reading Greek and Cyrillic text (Figures 13.2 and 13.3), OmniPage will recognize English letters mixed in with them. The Text Editor will display the recognized text in the correct language. You can read, delete, and proofread even if your computer has no Greek or Cyrillic font files or code page support. You cannot add text, though, if you do not have the language font or code page support installed on your computer. If you do add text, it will be in English characters and font. Greek and Cyrillic (Windows) language support is needed to correctly handle the exported text in your word processor and to add text in the Text Editor window. The languages, code pages, and fonts are set up in the Windows Control Panel.

Figure 13.2
Greek characters—
OmniPage also
supports recognition of
characters needed for
reading Ancient Greek

α β γ δ ε ζ η θ ι κ λ μ ν ξ ο π ρ ς σ τ υ φ χ ψ ω ϊ ϋ ό ύ ώ

Figure 13.3
Languages written
using Cyrillic are:
Russian, Bulgarian,
Byelorussian, Chechen,
Kabardian,
Macedonian,
Moldavian, Serbian,
and Ukrainian

Б в г д е ж з и й к л м н о п р с т у ф х ц ч

OmniPage also comes with seventeen different language dictionaries: Catalan, Czech, Danish, Dutch, English, Finnish, French, German, Greek, Hungarian, Italian, Norwegian, Polish, Portuguese, Russian, Spanish, and Swedish. To help in the recognition process and to provide suggestions in the proofreader, these dictionaries are used along with your own personal user dictionaries. In the languages window, little "book" icons appear beside the languages that have a dictionary.

NOTE

Be careful when recognizing documents with mixed character sets. We were testing a document that was in English with some Greek characters in it. We selected English and Greek in the OCR Language in the document setting. The font was Times New Roman. The result? Some of the English "a" characters that were standing alone came out as a Greek α. So "a Cat" came out as "α Cat," and other Greek characters were inserted where they shouldn't have been.

If you select multiple languages, all characters of those languages are used for recognition. If you select more than one language with dictionary support, all the dictionaries are used, so you may get suggestions from more than one language.

When you select a language, all special characters of that language—such as accents, cedilla, and the umlaut—are included, and the recognized text will have them.

In Text Editor view, words that are not in the dictionary will be underlined in red and words containing suspect characters will be underlined in blue. These markers can be turned on of off by selecting the Text Editor tab in Options Settings and clicking Show in the field named Markers.

OCR Method

OmniPage 11 can use two recognition engines. A recognition engine is the part that does the OCR work for OmniPage. Each engine has a different way of looking at and assessing the characters' shape. Selecting the Option Setting OCR method "More accurate" switches both of them on, and they each have a go at recognizing the character shape. They then compare notes and come to an agreement on what the character should be. Sometimes this more than doubles the time required to recognize the text. It's doing twice as much work, but it's more accurate. Dual-engine recognition is available for Danish, Dutch, English, Finnish, French, German, Italian, Norwegian, Portuguese, Spanish, and Swedish. The faster option uses only one recognition engine. If the quality of the original is good and you are in a hurry, the "Faster" option may do just as good a job in half the time.

For example, the recognition times for the three-page sample file "Sample_multi.tif," installed with OmniPage, were:

1. **Faster** (one recognition engine)—3440 words per min, 34 seconds to recognize the document, 37 suspect words, 100% (no rejected characters).

2. **More accurate** (both recognition engines)—1713 words per minute, 68.5 seconds to recognize the document, 6 suspect words, 100%.

The PC used was a Pentium II 266 MHz, 256 MB RAM. We used the AutoOCR toolbox, with one language—English—selected.

User Dictionaries

User dictionaries are your own dictionaries that you use for spell checking your documents. Usually they contain special names, industry specific words, jargon, etc. You can create your own user dictionaries for OmniPage.

OmniPage uses its seventeen built-in dictionaries to assist during the recognition process by giving the recognition engines a bit more confidence when recognizing a character. They are also used to give suggestions during proofing. You can use a user dictionary as well at the same time. You can have any number of user dictionaries, but only one can be loaded at a time.

You can create your own dictionaries, select which one to use, and add words from other dictionaries or files into your own. As you continue to use OmniPage, you can continue adding words to your user dictionary using the proofreader. Whenever you come across a word that's not in OmniPage's dictionary or yours, just use the Add button to add it to the dictionary. This will improve OmniPage's recognition capabilities, because it will have more words to check against.

- **Starting a User Dictionary**. In the Text Editor view, when the OCR Proofreader dialog box appears, click Add. If you have no user dictionary loaded, you will be asked for a file name for the new blank dictionary. You can also start a new dictionary by opening the User Dictionary Files dialog box in Tools (click New). You will be asked for a file name for the new dictionary. When you proofread documents, you simply click the Add button to add words to this new dictionary.

- **Loading or Unloading a User Dictionary**. In Option Settings, click the OCR tab. In the User Dictionary field, click the down arrow and select the dictionary to use. Or in Text Editor view, when the Proofreader displays, click the User Dictionary down arrow. Select a dictionary file to load, or select "none."

- **Editing a User Dictionary**. You can add words to a loaded user dictionary by clicking the Add button in the OCR Proofreader dialog box. By clicking the Edit button, you can add you own words. Delete words or use the import function to add words from a text file.

The Reject Character

The reject character is used when the recognition engines are unable to recognize a character. The default character that displayed in its place is a red tilde (~). In the Text Editor view, when proofreading, you can easily replace the tilde in the document with the correct word(s). In the Option Settings, OCR tab, Reject Character field, you can change the reject character; however, we recommend leaving the tilde as the default. It's unlikely you would have a tilde character in your document, a fact that makes them easy to search for.

Font Matching

This is really cool. OmniPage not only OCRs the text; it will try to save the recognized text in the original font or as close to it as possible. When OmniPage recognizes a character, it determines its shape. OmniPage then scans the font maps you have added to the list from the ones installed on your PC to find the font that best matches the character. The default maps to nine standard Windows fonts that are located in Windows' font folder.

To add more fonts, in Options Settings, OCR, click the Font Matching button. In the Font Mapping window, select additional fonts from the left-hand side and click the Add button. If you want to remove any fonts, select them on the right-hand side and click the remove button, as shown in Figure 13.4.

Figure 13.4
Selecting additional fonts to be used in matching the fonts of the original scanned document

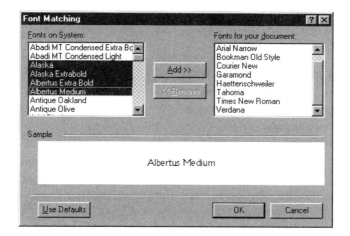

Adding fonts is a little like registering applications for use with Direct OCR. In Font Mapping you add (register) additional fonts to be used in your saved document.

Scanner Tab

Scanner options are the only part of OmniPage that actually affect the scanner (Figure 13.5). All other settings control the OCR process and saving. So you can see that the scanner is just a small part of OCR. Many people use the term "scanning" when they really mean the whole process, from running documents through the scanner to OCRing and saving them using OmniPage, or scanning pictures using an image application such as Adobe Photoshop. When something goes wrong they say, "The scanner's not working," when, in fact, the problem may have more to do with the application program than the scanner itself. The scanner merely takes the picture, and in Scanner Options you adjust the controls to get a good picture, just as you would with a camera.

Figure 13.5
Scanner options

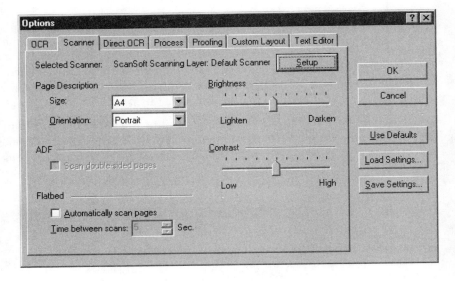

There are five sections to the scanner options.

Selected Scanner

The Setup button runs the Scanner Setup Wizard, which we covered in detail earlier in the book. You must select a scanner for OmniPage to work correctly. Many users bypass this as they think that, because the scanner works OK with other programs, they don't need to select a scanner. OmniPage does not communicate directly with the scanner but through an intermediate background program that communicates with the scanner driver and then with the scanner.

You can also use the Setup button to turn on the display of your scanner's native user interface. This gives you greater control of the scanner settings.

Page Description

OmniPage is concerned with two aspects of the pages it scans—their size and their orientation.

Page Size

Defines the page size you are scanning. The options displayed are dependent on your scanner. Generally, they are A4, Letter, and Legal. If your scanner is capable of scanning different sizes, you can set them up when running the Scanner Setup Wizard.

Page Orientation

In Portrait orientation, the width of the page is the smaller dimension. Most likely, the majority of the documents you scan will use this orientation. In Landscape orientation, the width of the page is the larger dimension.

Nearly all scanners are portrait scanners. So how do you scan a landscape page? OmniPage can automatically turn the page around for you, or you can do it yourself after it is scanned into OmniPage. Provided you have selected the Process setting option (see the Process option later in this chapter) called "Automatically correct page orientation," you can leave the page orientation set to Portrait and OmniPage will automatically turn the pages around.

ADF (Automatic Document Feeder)

This option will be available if your scanner has an ADF function and you selected the ADF function during the Scanner Setup Wizard. Set this option to activate the ADF; you can then put a batch of pages in the scanner and OmniPage will keep scanning until it is empty. You can also set this option when scanning double-sided pages. Scan the even-numbered pages first; when you reach the end of the batch, OmniPage will prompt you to scan all the odd-numbered pages, then it will collate the pages in the correct order. If you are lucky enough to have a duplex scanner that scans both sides at the same time, don't set this option on, as it will confuse OmniPage. Duplex scanners send both sides to OmniPage at the same time and in the correct order.

Flatbed

This option is for you if you don't have an ADF and you have to you manually feed the pages—in other words, if *you* are the ADF. After selecting this option, you can adjust the time between scans, so that when one page has finished scanning you don't need to click the Scan more pages button. You just have to be quick enough to change pages in the length of time you have specified. OmniPage will keep scanning at that interval until you tell it to stop. It's a bit like the Sorcerer's Apprentice.

Brightness and Contrast

These two options on the right-hand side in the Scanner Options tab are like those on a photocopier, where you can make the copy lighter or darker. Adjusting these controls can make a marked improvement in the OCR result of poor-quality documents or documents with dark backgrounds. Experiment to get the best result. Scan the document and check the quality in the Original Image view. Not all scanners allow the manual brightness and darkness to be changed, in which case the controls may be grayed out or have no effect.

Brightness

When scanning a document with light, thin, or broken text, moving the brightness towards Darken can improve the recognition.

Contrast

Use the slider to manually adjust the contrast between light and dark on scanned pages. Move the slider to high for light text on dark backgrounds.

CHAPTER 13

Direct OCR Tab

Direct OCR enables you to access OmniPage, OCR a document, and paste the recognized text into the application you are currently working in. For example, if you're writing a Word document and you need to incorporate several paragraphs and a picture from a magazine, with Direct OCR you simply place the page in the scanner and click File > Acquire Text from the Word menu. OmniPage will launch in the background and present the Original Image view with the scanned page. You can then draw zones around the text and pictures you want and click the Perform OCR button. Once the OCR process is complete, the text and pictures will be inserted into the document at the cursor location.

Direct OCR is activated by selecting Enable Direct OCR in the top left corner of the Direct OCR tab. OmniPage inserts two additional options in the file menu of the registered applications. These are Acquire Text and Acquire Text Settings.

You must register the software applications in order to use Direct OCR. Make sure the software application is open before you register. On the Direct OCR tab, you will see the names of unregistered applications in the field called Register Applications. Select the application to register and click Add. To remove an application, select it in the field called Registered and click Remove.

The two process options Draw zones automatically and Proofread OCR define what will happen when selecting Acquire Text. We prefer to leave Draw zones automatically unselected, as we like to select the text and pictures we need from the page before scanning and OCR. Leaving this selected is like using automatic processing in the AutoOCR toolbox—you end up getting the whole page.

These settings can all be changed in the Acquire Text Settings dialog box in the registered software application you are working in.

Figure 13.6
Direct OCR options—
we prefer to leave
"Draw zones
automatically"
deselected and draw
the zones we need
before OCRing

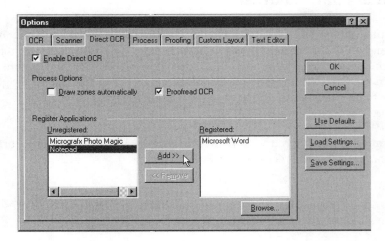

Process Tab

The Process settings are used to further define what to do with the scanned pages and to modify the zoning and OCR process. The setting When Bringing in a New Image is an intriguing one. When adding new pages, it tells OmniPage where to put the pages; if you are not careful, the order can become quite mixed up.

Figure 13.7
Process options

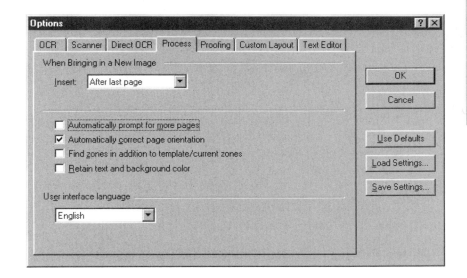

When Bringing in a New Image

This determines where the new pages will be added to your current document. It's best to leave as the default, After last page, to avoid any strange ordering of your pages. You can choose After last page, After current page, Before current page, and Before first page. Remember you can always reorder your pages by dragging and dropping in the Document Manager Thumbnail view.

If you have the option Automatically prompt for more pages or the Scanner Flatbed option Automatically scan pages set to a set number of seconds, OmniPage scans all those pages as one batch and will retain the correct sequence within each batch.

Here are the results for each option when scanning five pages, a single page at a time:

▶ After last page   1, 2, 3, 4, 5
▶ After current page   1, 5, 4, 3, 2
▶ Before current page   2, 3, 4, 5, 1
▶ Before first page   5, 4, 3, 2, 1

As you can see, page ordering becomes messy when you have changed from the default After last page. When OmniPage scans the pages, you will have noticed the first page stays as the current page, even when there is more than one page. That's why we recommend leaving After last page as the default and then moving the pages if required.

Figure 13.8
Where to insert the new images?—it's best to leave as default "After last page"

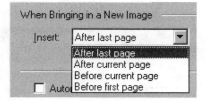

If your scanned pages display out of order, someone may have changed this setting. Like all the other settings, it will remain set until changed. You may wish to click the Use Defaults button to restore to the standard settings.

Automatically Prompt for More Pages

Use this option if you want to scan multi-page documents using a flatbed scanner. A dialog box appears after each page, prompting you to "Add more pages" to this batch, "scan," or "stop loading pages" and "start processing" the document (see Figure 13.9). This feature is useful if your document exceeds the capacity of your ADF. You can continue loading pages in the same batch. This option is only available when using the AutoOCR toolbox. The Manual OCR toolbox expects you to scan pages individually. If you have Automatically scan pages selected in the Scanner tab, you will not be prompted for more pages.

Figure 13.9
Continue Automatic processing to load more pages

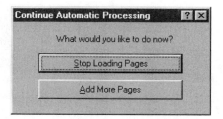

Automatically Correct Page Orientation

Select this option to have OmniPage Pro 11 check orientation and automatically rotate the image by 90, 180, or 270 degrees before recognition. All the pages are automatically straightened (deskewed) if necessary. If you have a document with text in both orientations—a large chart for example—OmniPage may rotate the page several times until it finds the orientation at which it can read the most text with the fewest errors. The text in the other orientation will not be recognized correctly. If you have pages like this and you don't need to change any of the text, it is best to grab the entire page as a graphic or manually re-draw zones around the unrecognized text and select as a graphic zone.

Find Zones in Addition to Template/Current Zones

Use this option to have OmniPage look for text and graphics that are not in either the current zones or template. This is very handy when you are using a template, and sometimes there may be additional text or graphics on the page outside the template that you want included. If you are re-processing the page because you changed or have drawn zones in addition to the automatic zones, the dialog box will display. It gives you the option to "Use only current zones," "Discard current zones and find new zones," or "Keep current zones and find additional zones," as shown in Figure 13.10.

Figure 13.10
Zoning Instruction to process or reprocess the page

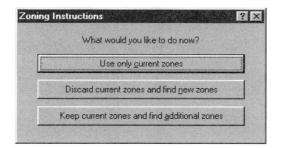

When using the Manual OCR toolbox, select the "Find zones in addition to template/current zones" option to display the Zone Instructions dialog box each time you click the Perform OCR button. This allows you to have zones found automatically in addition to the current zones. If you deselect this, the Zone Instructions dialog box will not appear, and all manual processing will be done with each page's current zones only.

Retain Text and Background Color

Select this option to have colored text and background detected, displayed in the Text Editor view, and kept when exported. If you deselect this, you still get the color pictures from the document but all the text will be black. You can change the color of the text and backgrounds in the Text Editor view.

Figure 13.11 is an example of the picture from page one of the three-page sample file "Sample_multi.tif" with the Retain text and background color option set off and on. The original picture has a blue border around the picture and text, and the text is white on a blue background.

Figure 13.11
The results of the
option "Retain text
and background
color" when viewed
in OmniPage Text
view—the left-hand
picture has the option
off and the right-hand
picture has the option
turned on

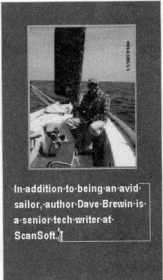

In the right-hand portion of Figure 13.11, you can see that when this option is set on there is a small white line around part of the text. This is not visible when the document is saved and exported.

Figure 13.12 shows the picture and text saved in a Microsoft Word document. OmniPage actually creates three objects in the Word document. All three are in frames. One frame is the total size of the original picture, border, and text and is filled in blue. The next is the text frame, which is also filled in blue with white text. The last frame contains the picture. They are all overlaid on the large blue frame. By clicking in the separate frames to select them, you can then click the frame border and drag to a new position, as we've done in Figure 13.12.

Figure 13.12
The frames in
Microsoft Word that
make up the
background and
colored text when
saving with the option
"Retain text and
background color"

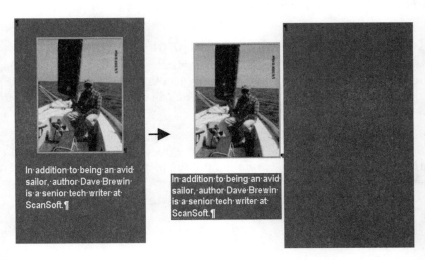

User Interface Language

This determines the language for the dialog boxes, views, and menu commands. OmniPage Pro 11 is delivered with the interface language appropriate to your country. The English version also has French and German language options (Figure 13.13). You can have fun with your colleagues by changing this to French or German; all the menu screens and messages will be in that language until changed back. You can also use it to brush up on your foreign language skills.

Figure 13.13
Change the user interface language—all the menus and messages will appear in the language you select

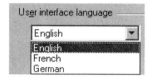

Proofing Tab

The Proofing tab contains the settings for the Proofreader (Figure 13.14) and the Training process. It also determines which training file to use.

Figure 13.14
The proofing options—Proofreader and the Training process

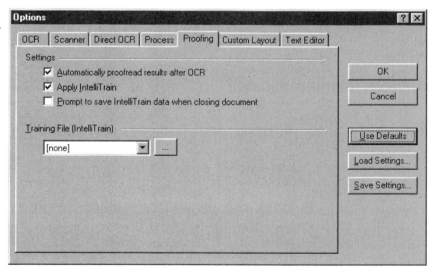

Automatically Proofread Results after OCR

With this option checked, the Proofreader will check the OCR results as soon as the process is completed. This option is on by default. It's a good idea to leave it on, as you should really check for any errors before saving, especially if the document is a long one.

Training OmniPage to Recognize Difficult Characters

The rest of the options on the Proofing tab deal with training OmniPage to recognize special characters that the program would not normally recognize.

OmniPage is a powerful pre-trained OCR product capable of producing good results without training. However, training can help OmniPage cope with text that is in an unusually styled typeface or that uses uncommon symbols, and the IntelliTrain process is how training is done. The training files are editable and can be stored for future use.

How IntelliTrain Works

A training file is like having a user dictionary of character shapes. OmniPage uses this dictionary of character shapes to assist in the recognition process. You determine what character OmniPage uses when it detects a certain shape. All this is done automatically in the background when you are doing the proofreading. When OmniPage detects a suspect or reject character and you type in the correction, the IntelliTrain module considers whether or not to add the corrected character's shape to the training file to help in future recognition.

You should use the training file only on documents that have characters similar to the ones in the document the training was created from. Using an inappropriate training file can have worse results than using no training file at all.

If you are scanning a long document and find that you are getting many errors on the same characters, turn on IntelliTrain and then rerecognize several of the pages with errors. When you make the corrections in the Proofreader, the corrected characters will be added to the training file. Once you have made the training file, check to see what characters have been added using the Edit training file dialog box, make any appropriate changes, and save the file.

Apply IntelliTrain

On the Proofing tab, select Apply IntelliTrain, and the IntelliTrain process will run during proofreading. When it runs, it considers using your corrections to solve other cases of unsure recognition in the document. Sometimes it will not add your corrections to the training file if it decides it won't help. This option must be on if you want to create a training file. If Apply IntelliTrain is on, it will also be used when using Direct OCR, even though you can't see this option in the Direct OCR options.

Prompt to Save IntelliTrain Data When Closing Document

Select this to be prompted each time you close a document in which your proofreading changes generated IntelliTrain data. This lets you save this data to a loaded or new training file for future use. If you choose not to be prompted and do not save the data, it will be applied to the current document only. Training data is always conserved in an OmniPage document, even if it is not saved to a training file. Of course you will only be prompted if you have selected the Apply IntelliTrain option as well.

Training File (IntelliTrain)

This drop-down list lets you choose the training file to use for recognizing this document and any future pages. To remove a training file, select "none." While a training file is loaded, any new training data is temporarily added to this file. Use the button beside the field to open the training file's Edit menu.

When you've selected Apply IntelliTrain, corrections you make during proofreading are used in the recognition of the rest of the document—without saving them in a separate training file. To use them on another occasion, you must save the training characters in a training file. If you do not save them in a training file, the unsaved training characters will be saved if you save the document as an OmniPage file, *.opd.

To Make and Save a Training File:

1. Open the Options dialog box by clicking the AB button on the standard toolbar. Click the Proofing tab. Click Apply IntelliTrain and prompt to save IntelliTrain data when closing document.

2. Select three or four pages from a long document that is giving you many recognition errors and whose typeface and quality is typical of the whole document.

3. Recognize and proofread the pages. The corrections you make during proofreading will be entered into the training file.

4. From the menu bar, click Tools > Training File. Open the Edit dialog box. Select "unsaved" and click Edit. This opens the training file so you can see the character shapes and what text characters will be used.

5. Double-click a character shape to select it; a small yellow box appears below. This is where you type in the text character for that shape.

6. Press Enter to apply the text character(s) to that shape.

7. If a character shape is incorrect and atypical, double-click it to select it and press Delete to delete it.

8. When all the character shapes that are useful are associated with their correct text characters, click Close to return to the Training Files dialog box.

9. Click Save and name the training file. This will then become the current training file and remain loaded.

NOTE
You can use the Training Files dialog box to change training files or to choose not to use one at all; click "none" to unload a training file. You can also make these changes from the Proofing panel of the Options dialog box.

CHAPTER 13

Editing a Training File

To edit your training file or to view its contents, click Tools > Training File > Edit. Or from the Options dialog box, click the Proofing tab and click the button beside the Training File field, then click Edit.

When the training file opens, as shown in Figure 13.15, the title bar has the name of the training file. The asterisk (*) in the title bar of the Edit training dialog box means that the training being displayed has not yet been saved. If a saved training file is being edited, its name appears without the asterisk.

The sixth and eighth characters "ni" and "r" have been marked as deleted, as have the first two characters on the second row. They do not disappear immediately; selecting and pressing the Delete key can restore them. Characters marked as deleted are actually deleted when the Edit Training dialog box is closed and the file saved.

You would want to delete the "ni" and the "r" shapes, as you can see the "ni" would get replaced by just the letter "i," and the partial "r" shape would get a text "m." Can you imagine the mess this could make of your recognized text?

Characters Not on the Keyboard

If the character to be "trained" is not on the keyboard, how can you type in what it should be? There are two ways to approach this. One is to substitute characters from the keyboard and then use search and replace in the saved document. The other is to find out what the ASCII code is for the character and use the appropriate ASCII Alt+number combination to enter it.

There are a couple of ways to find the ASCII number of a character. The easiest is to open Word and a blank document. From the menu bar, choose Insert > Symbol. Find the character you need and select it by clicking on it. Word will display the ASCII number of that character at the bottom of the screen on the status bar.

The other way is via Windows. Click Start > Programs > Accessories > Character Map. A table of characters will display; select the font you are using and then the character you want to train. The ASCII code of that character will be displayed in the lower right of the window as a combination of the Alt key and a number.

Armed with the character's ASCII code, you can now go back to OmniPage and the Edit training file window. Double-click the character you want to train to open its assigned value window. Hold down the Alt key and type in the number. Nothing will happen until you release the Alt key. Release the Alt key and the character will display in the assigned value window.

Substitute Characters

In Figure 13.15, the left-most character shape is currently selected and its edit box is open. This is a character that you can't type from the keyboard. We have typed in &&, as && will not ordinarily appear in a document. Once saved as a Word document, we can then search for && and replace it with the correct character. If you change the original text assigned to the shape, the changes are displayed in red.

Figure 13.15
Training file character shapes and the text characters associated with them

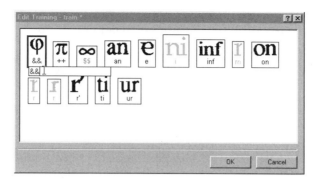

CHAPTER 13

TIP

To add new characters to an existing training file, load that training file first before applying IntelliTrain.

If your characters are being recognized incorrectly but without generating errors, you can't train OmniPage to recognize them correctly. For example, ® becomes © in the Text Editor view and it is not presented in the Proofreader dialog box as an error. Try turning off one of the recognition engines. Click the OCR tab in the Options Settings and select OCR Method Faster. Re-process your pages and you may be able to correct the errors.

If your document contains some Greek characters, such as those often used in math equations, try selecting additional languages on the OCR tab of the Options dialog box. Make sure you have both OCR engines on. In the field OCR method, click More accurate, as this tends to make the English characters take precedence over the Greek characters. Be warned: The text in the Text Editor view may look a bit messy, with differing font sizes and mixed characters. It's easy to fix, though; just select all the text and set to a single font and size.

Custom Layout Tab

When using the AutoOCR and Manual OCR toolboxes, the Custom Layout (Custom User Defined) setting appears in the drop-down box of Perform OCR. Perform OCR has five pre-configured Auto-Zoning options (Table 13.1). You select these from the drop-down box.

1. Automatic (default)
2. Single column no table
3. Multiple column no table
4. Single column with table
5. Spreadsheet

There are two other choices: Custom (user-defined) and Template, but they are not pre-configured. You have to create these settings.

Table 1 shows the predefined Perform OCR settings available from the drop-down box of Perform OCR. The layout description is the pre-set option. The columns in the table show the equivalent settings of the Custom Layout options. Use Custom Layout when your original document is not covered by one of the five pre-set layout descriptions.

Table 13.1
Five pre-defined "Perform OCR" options

Layout description	Flowing text	Tables	Graphics
Automatic	Auto	Auto	Auto
Single Column, no Table	One Column	No Tables	Auto
Multiple Columns, no Table	Auto	No Tables	Auto
Single Column, with Table	One Column	Auto	Auto
Spreadsheet	No Column	One Table	No Graphics

If none of the five preset values adequately describes your original document, you can select Custom Layout. It lets you specify the number of columns and whether or not your document has tables and graphics. These settings only take effect when you select Custom (user Defined) in Perform OCR, Describe Original. With Custom Layout, you can mix and match twenty-seven different ways to describe your original document—well, twenty-two; in fact it's fewer than that, as five are the predefined ones and some combinations of the settings in this panel override each other.

Using the AutoOCR toolbox or Schedule OCR for scanning long documents using a custom layout is most useful, especially when you want a minimum of user intervention and you can't check the zone types being created for each page.

Figures 13.17 to 13.23 are the first page of the sample file "Sample_multi.tif" (this file is installed with OmniPage in the My Documents\My Pictures folder). They show the results of each of the settings displayed in Figure 13.16. The Text Editor view is selected as Retain Flowing Columns. Experiment with mixing the options and comparing the results; it's the best way to learn about an application.

Figure 13.16
The Custom Layout tab in the Options Setting dialog box

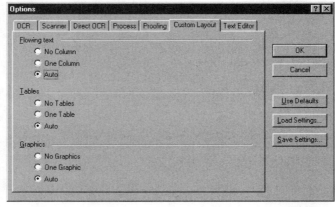

Flowing Text: Column Settings

Let's look at each of the three settings that describe how OmniPage will process the text on the page. "Flowing Text" refers to whether or not OmniPage will look for columns of text to flow from one column to another, or line to line, or treat the page as a single block of text like a letter or page from a book. You can tell OmniPage that your document has no columns or one column or to figure it out for itself (Auto).

No Column

If this is set, OmniPage recognizes only the graphics or tables on a page. The program treats all text found on the page as part of a table.

If the text is not part of a table, it will not be zoned or included in the recognized text. Choose this if your pages do not contain flowing text. Because the document in Figure 13.17 is a multi-column document, the only text that was recognized is the text in the table.

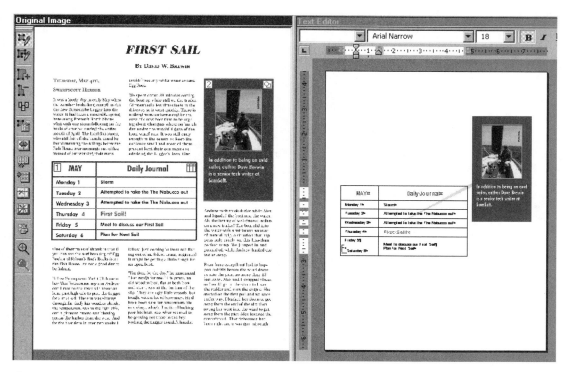

Figure 13.17
Custom Layout with Flowing text option set to "No Column" and the other two settings set to "Auto"

One Column

Choose this if the pages contain flowing text in a single column, such as in a report. You can see in Figure 13.18 the first two columns of text in the original document have been processed as if they were on the same line with a tab between them. Only the top three rows of the table have been recognized. The last three rows of the table in the original document have been included in the paragraph text in the lower half of the document. Also, the table and text zones have been allowed to overlap.

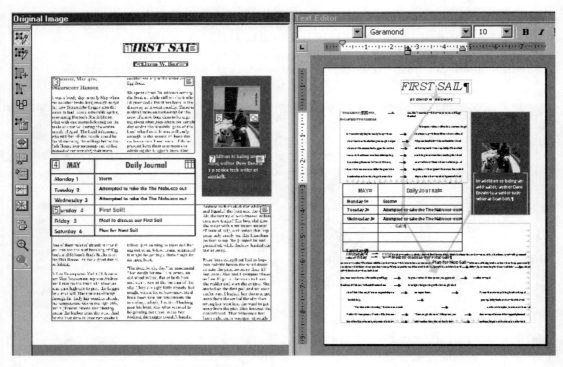

Figure 13.18
Custom Layout with Flowing text option set to "One Column" and the other two settings set to "Auto"

Auto

Choose this if the pages contain flowing text and are arranged at least partly in columns. The program will try harder to detect these columns (Figure 13.19). Use the Text Editor view to decide whether the text should be in one column or multiple columns. Setting all the options to Auto is the same as using the predefined Automatic setting in Perform OCR.

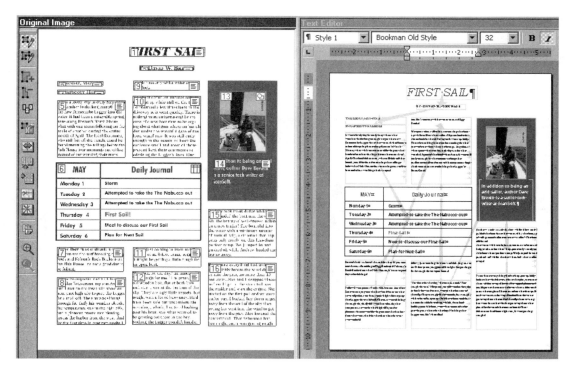

Figure 13.19
Custom Layout with Flowing text, Tables, and Graphics options all set to "Auto"

Table Options

Let's look at each one of these settings as they apply to the recognition of tables in your document. This option controls the part of OmniPage that looks for and processes tables. You can elect to turn it off and treat tables as tabbed columns of text, or treat the entire page as one table, or put it on Auto to locate individual tables on the page.

No Tables

Choose this to have all text areas treated as flowing text. Use it even if there is a table in the original and you want to keep its text but do not want it treated as a table. This means the text in the table will not be placed in a grid. The text may be kept in columns, or it may just flow, allowing you to reformat it as you wish. In Figure 13.20, the table has been zoned and recognized as separate blocks of text, *not* as a table.

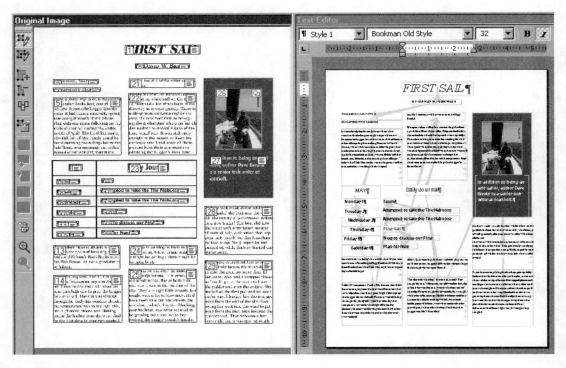

Figure 13.20
Custom Layout with Tables option set to "No Table" and the other settings set to "Auto"

One Table

OmniPage draws one zone over the entire page as one table, irrespective of graphics and columns (Figure 13.21). It is the same as using the Spreadsheet option in Process OCR.

Figure 13.21
Custom Layout with Table option set to "One Table" and the other two settings set to "Auto"

Auto

Choose this to let the program auto-detect tables. Use it for pages with more than one table and for documents containing some tables, but not on all pages.

Graphics Options

Here we tell OmniPage to look or not to look for graphics on a page. You can also tell OmniPage to treat the entire page as one graphic.

No Graphics

Choose this to prevent graphic zones from being detected. The resulting page will have no graphics zones. All auto-detected zones will be classed as text, and OmniPage will try to read any text in the pictures and graphics. Pictures will not be zoned or recognized. Selecting this for pages with line-art or diagrams may slow recognition. The text in line art or drawings will be recognized and may not be appropriate. Select No graphics if something you want recognized could be misinterpreted as a graphic. If you want to have text in diagrams recognized and the integrity of the diagram maintained, you may need to either select Auto or manually draw a graphic zone.

You can see in Figure 13.22 that the graphic has not been recognized.

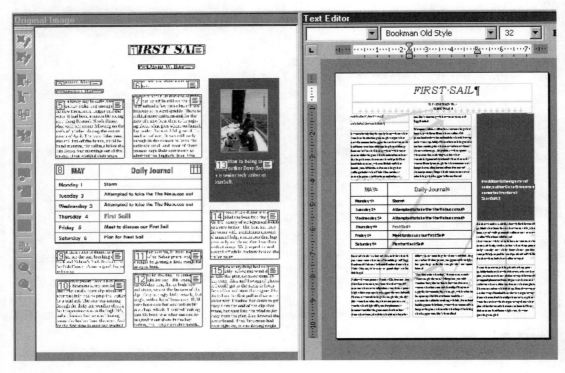

Figure 13.22
Custom Layout with Graphics option set to "No Graphics" and the other two settings set to "Auto"

One Graphic

Use this option to treat the entire page as one graphic zone. This can be useful when you are interested in capturing the pages as images with no OCR.

NOTE

Be very careful when selecting the "One Graphic" option, as it overrides the text and table setting and treats the entire page as a single graphic. It looks perfect in the Text Editor view, but it is only an image of the original page. The page has been zoned as a graphic around all the elements on the page. You will be unable to edit it because it is still an image. Choose this when you want to capture each page entirely as a graphic.

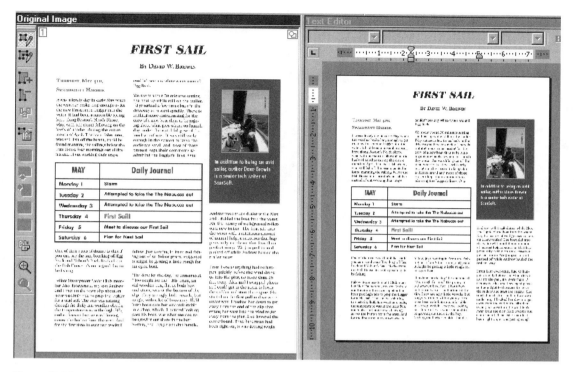

Figure 13.23
Custom Layout with Graphics option set to "One Graphic" and the other two settings set to "Auto"

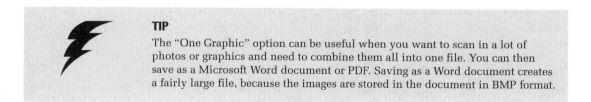

TIP

The "One Graphic" option can be useful when you want to scan in a lot of photos or graphics and need to combine them all into one file. You can then save as a Microsoft Word document or PDF. Saving as a Word document creates a fairly large file, because the images are stored in the document in BMP format.

Auto

Choose this to let the program decide what is a graphic and what should be recognized as text. Select this option if you have graphics on the pages or if only some pages in the document have graphics.

Text Editor Tab

The last tab in the Options dialog box is the Text Editor (Figure 13.24).

Figure 13.24
The Text Editor screen
display options

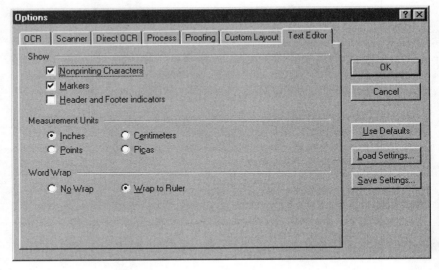

These settings determine what gets displayed and how it is displayed in the Text Editor view. When you make changes to these Text Editor settings, they take effect immediately on all existing pages in the Text Editor view.

Show

This gives you the option of turning on or off certain characteristics of the document in the Text Editor view. You can show the non-printing characters, the words found during proofreading, and any header and footer information that is found.

Nonprinting Characters

Select Nonprinting Characters to see them in the Text Editor view. Nonprinting characters are such things as the spacing dots between words, the end-of-paragraph mark, end-of-cell signs, and tab arrows.

Markers

Select Markers to display red wavy underlines for words that do not appear in any of the dictionaries in use. Blue wavy underlines are for words that contain suspect characters that OmniPage wants you to verify.

all· nonstylized· general·office,·

Figure 13.25
A word not found in a dictionary shows as a red wavy underline—the blue wavy underline indicates suspect characters within the word

Header and Footer Indicators

This option displays the header or footer markers from the scanned document. The header and footer markers will display only when you are in the No Formatting or Retain Fonts and Paragraph views in the Text Editor.

Measurement Units

Select the unit of measurement you want to use throughout the program. You can change this at any time, and the conversion will be done immediately on all the pages in the Text Editor view. Generally, you will be using inches, which is the default. European and Asia Pacific users often use centimeters. If you are a graphic artist or desktop publisher, you may prefer to work in points or picas.

Word Wrap

There are two options for Word Wrap.

No Wrap

When No Wrap is selected, the line breaks from the original document are maintained. In the Text Editor view with No Formatting selected, the original line breaks are always maintained, irrespective of this setting, as there is no ruler bar or margins to be changed.

Wrap to Ruler

Select Wrap to Ruler to have the text flow between the margins or within its frame. If you change the size of the margins or frames, the text will wrap to fill that space. If the text is in frames as in the True Page format and sometimes in Retain Flowing columns, the page will not expand if you reduce the width of the margins or frame. In these cases, you will need to make the frame longer to accommodate all the text. The setting is applied immediately to all recognized pages in the Text Editor view. The margins and layout of the Text Editor will be reflected in the saved document.

The three options below allow you to reset to the factory options, save any settings you want to use in the future, and load the settings to use again on another document.

Use Defaults

If things aren't working out as you expected in OmniPage, you can select Use Defaults in the Options dialog box to reset all the options. This isn't the solution every time something goes wrong, but it is a very good place to start. Many of the problems users experience with OmniPage are the result of either user error or someone's having changed settings without informing other users. When this happens, click Use Defaults. It sets everything back to the factory defaults. We can't stress enough how valuable this button is when things don't seem to be working correctly. As you can see, we have gone through seven different option-setting tabs and over seventy different settings. Trying to find which one is causing the problem can be a nightmare. Clicking Use Defaults is sometimes the best solution.

Load Settings

This is a real labor saver since, as we just mentioned, there are over seventy different settings. Once you have the settings working well for a particular type of document, you can save the settings for similar documents. Give the settings a name that's descriptive of what the template does. Then, next time you have to do the same job, just load the settings and, "hey presto," you're ready to go.

NOTE

At the time of this writing, some of the saved settings are not restored when using Load Settings. These are the toolboxes AutoOCR, Manual OCR, and OCR Wizard; the Get Page options Load File, Scan B&W, Scan Grayscale, and Scan Color; the Export Results options Save as file, Send as mail, or Copy to Clipboard.

The Perform OCR options are saved and restored, which is good, especially when using templates.

Save Settings

Use this button to save any options and settings so you can reuse them later. The settings are saved in an *.ini file in the folder C:\windows\Application data\ScanSoft\OmniPage. See Figure 13.26.

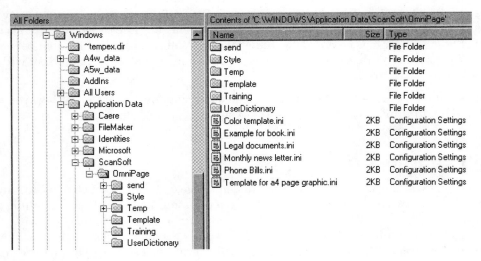

Figure 13.26
File location of saved settings files

14

Troubleshooting

In this chapter, we will consider some questions and technical support issues that arise for users of OmniPage Pro 11, PaperPort 8.0, and OmniForm 5.0. Because of the wide variety of computer configurations—the loaded applications (old and new), the different scanners and their drivers, and varying operating systems—sometimes the whole computer setup can cause an unfortunate interaction with OmniPage. ScanSoft tries to take into account all these variables to minimize and eliminate any adverse impact to their programs. Sometimes some slip through and we'll look at them here.

After installing OmniPage, locate the release notes/readme files and user manual. Read them, and, if you want to, print a hard copy for reference. The manual is in PDF format, and you will find it in the program application folder (a likely location is C:\program files\scansoft\omnipage\manual\manualeng.pdf). You will also find the release notes/readme files there, "readmeeng.htm," in HTML format.

Users have many questions about OmniPage Pro 11—too many to cover them all in one chapter. If you can't find the answer to your question in this book or this chapter, please log on to http://www.scansoft.com/support/. Click OmniPage, then Knowledge Base. Scroll down to the field Enter Search Criteria and type Pro 11, then click Go. If you have earlier versions of OmniPage Pro or OmniPage Limited Edition, type your version in the field named "What release do you have?" Then click Go.

Questions about OmniPage Pro 11

Why doesn't my software work?

Typically, there are three main causes:

▶ Often, it is because the program hasn't been installed optimally. See the next question.

▶ The scanner driver has not been installed to work with OmniPage. Even though your scanner works with other software such as Adobe Photo Deluxe, you still have to tell OmniPage which scanner driver to use and set it up. See Chapter 1, Document Scanning and OCR.

▶ Often the cause is not knowing the options and settings and when to apply them for the type of document being scanned and saved.

How do I install OmniPage to run optimally?

For Windows 95, 98, and ME, make sure you install OmniPage with only two tasks running—Systray and Explorer. Before you install software, hold down the Control and Alt keys and press Delete. The Windows Task List appears. Close all programs and tasks except these two (including your virus-protection program). When the software has been installed, you need to reboot the computer, so all the programs you closed will restore when the system reboots. For Windows 2000 and NT users, it can be a bit trickier. Close all programs, including the virus-protection program and any other background tasks. Also make sure you are logged on as the system administrator.

Common scanners are tested and tuned for use with OmniPage Pro 11. For a complete list of scanners that have been tested with OmniPage Pro 11, OmniForm, and PaperPort, visit http://www.omnipagetraining.biz or http://www.scansoft.com. You no longer set up scanner drivers for OmniPage Pro 11 with Scan Manager 5. You use the Scanner Wizard that pops up when installing OmniPage or the first time you attempt to scan a document. The Wizard automatically tests and optimizes your scanner for use. You can launch the Scanner Wizard by clicking on Start > Programs > ScanSoft > OmniPage Pro 11 > Scanner Wizard. If you have OmniPage open, make sure you have your scanner switched on, then click Tools > Options > Scanner. There you will find the Setup button.

If my scanner has both TWAIN and WIA drivers, which should I use with OmniPage Pro 11?

The Microsoft Windows Image Acquisition (WIA) device driver interface is supported on Windows ME and Windows XP systems. If a WIA device driver is available for your scanner and you are using Windows ME or Windows XP, it is recommended that you scan using the WIA interface instead of the TWAIN driver.

Use the Scanner Wizard to select your scanner driver. Follow these steps:

1. Open OmniPage Pro 11.
2. Go to Tools > Options > Scanner.
3. Click the Setup button.
4. Choose Select scanning source.
5. Click Next.
6. The TWAIN or WIA drivers installed on your system will be listed in the window.
7. To change the display to show either the TWAIN or WIA drivers, click the Other drivers button; select the appropriate category of drivers and click OK. If the correct category of drivers is displayed, skip this step.
8. Click once on your scanner's driver to select it.
9. Click Next.
10. Select Yes to test your scanner configuration for use with OmniPage Pro 11.
11. Follow the steps to run the tests on your scanner.
12. Click Finish.

You have now set up your scanner to work with OmniPage Pro 11.

I see the option for Load Image, but not Scan Image.

This error sometimes occurs in early versions of OmniPage if you have reinstalled software drivers. You have to tell OmniPage what scanner driver to use. Make sure the scanner is switched on before you launch OmniPage.

1. Exit out of all open programs.
2. Click Start > Settings > Control Panel.
3. In the Control Panel, select the Scan Manager.
4. Select Add Scanner.
5. Select your scanner from the list and follow the on-screen prompts.
6. If the scanner is TWAIN compliant, select Generic TWAIN Scanner.
7. If the scanner uses ISIS drivers, select Generic ISIS Scanner.

Follow this next procedure only if you have a TWAIN scanner:

1. Close the Scan Manager and then re-open it.
2. Right-click your scanner and select Properties.
3. In the Properties dialog box, select the TWAIN Data Sources tab.
4. Under TWAIN Data Sources, check your current data source to see if it appears to be the correct driver your scanner should be using. If it is not, or if other data sources appear in the available data sources list, try using one of them as your current data source.
5. Select Set as Current and then click Apply to make these changes for setting a new data source.

You can also have the scanner's TWAIN driver software pop up before you scan.

1. Exit all running applications.
2. Click Start > Settings > Control Panel.
3. Select the Scan Manager to display a list of scanners. This list usually contains only one or two scanners.
4. Right-click your scanner and select Properties to display a multi-tabbed Properties dialog box.
5. Click the TWAIN Scanner Settings tab.
6. Set the property Show TWAIN Settings Before Scan to Yes.
7. Close the Scan Manager and the Windows Control Panel.
8. Launch OmniPage. This time, the scanner's TWAIN driver will load and enable you to change its internal settings before scanning.

How can I completely uninstall OmniPage Pro 11?

OmniPage Pro 11 will need to be manually uninstalled, as some files may be left behind. You will find the instructions for the manual uninstall procedure in ScanSoft's OmniPage Pro 11 Knowledge Base.

CHAPTER 14

I get only a quarter or half page once I have scanned my document in OmniPage. Why is this?

When using other programs that access the scanner, for example HP Scanjet or Adobe Photoshop, some scanners remember the settings that were used during that session. One of these settings is the area of the page that was selected, a bit like drawing zones in OmniPage. Also some scanner drivers have their own automatic settings that auto-detect areas of the page that the scanner driver thinks has text or a picture. If you have used an image program or have used the scanner's native interface to scan a photo or selected part of the page, the setting can be remembered when you next use OmniPage. When using OmniPage, the settings for the scanner may not override the selected page area, resulting in displaying only a half or quarter of the page.

There are four ways to fix this:

1. Go back to the scanning program you were using before OmniPage. Scan and select the entire page. This will set the scanner settings back to scan an entire page.

2. In the scanner's native interface, turn off any auto-detect settings such as "auto detect page area" or "auto detect picture."

3. In OmniPage, use the Scanner Setup Wizard, from Tools > Option > Scanner. Click Setup > Test > Configure > Advance. Then select Show native user interface. Then scan a document in OmniPage. The native user interface displays; select the entire page in the scan preview window.

4. For previous versions of OmniPage, go to the Windows Control Panel and open Caere Scan Manager. In the list, choose your scanner and click Scanner Settings. There you will find an option to get available paper sizes from scanner; select this option and experiment. You can download the latest Scan Manager from the ScanSoft Web site.

What should I do if my scanner driver is not listed in the list of scanners?

In the Scanner Setup Wizard, a dialog box will open showing all the drivers in the Windows\Twain and Windows\Twain 32 folders. These folders are where Windows stores the installed scanner drivers. If there is nothing there, it means you haven't installed your TWAIN scanner drivers.

If you are using Windows ME and Windows XP, select the WIA scanner driver for your scanner if it is in the WIA driver list. Older scanners may not be in this list; in that case, use your TWAIN driver.

For Windows 95, 98, and 2000, select your TWAIN driver.

Why does my scanned document come out with white on a black background?

This shouldn't happen if you have run through and completed all of the test scans in the Scanner Setup Wizard.

As we discussed early in the book, computers only know 0's and 1's. The scanner sends pixels to the PC as 0's and 1's. Some scanners use 0 for black and 1 for white, other scanners do the reverse. The Scanner Setup Wizard translates this correctly to black text on a white background.

For previous versions of OmniPage, this translation of black to white is selected through the Scan Manager. Go to the Windows Control Panel and open Caere Scan Manager. In the list, click your scanner, then click Scanner Settings. There you will find options to "invert black and white."

I get a scanner error message when launching OmniPage Pro 11. What's wrong?

The error message will vary depending on the scanner and scanner driver you are using. Generally the error is "Scanner not detected" or " Scanner Error." Follow these steps:

1. Is your scanner switched on? It must be on before you launch OmniPage.

2. Do you have another application open that is using the scanner? Close both OmniPage and the other program and re-launch OmniPage. Only one program at a time can use the scanner.

3. Have you installed the right scanner driver? Try selecting a TWAIN driver. Reboot your computer and try again.

4. Write down the error message, visit http://www.scansoft.com, go to OmniPage, and check the Knowledge Base under Support for information about this error message.

5. Have you installed other scanning programs or uninstalled any other programs? This may have uninstalled some OmniPage files and made changes in the Windows registry. You can try reinstalling OmniPage. Before installing OmniPage Pro 11, disable your anti-virus software and exit out of any other applications that are running on your system.

Why do I get the error message "Error in Format exporting" when exporting as "Send as Mail"?

You will get this error message if you have previously used Export > Send as mail and selected an HTML attachment. Do not use an HTML file as an attachment. The temporary file OmniPage creates when sending an attachment as HTML is not deleted. Until you delete the file and folder, you won't be able to use Send as mail again. See Chapter 10 to resolve this problem.

My ADF is not working; I have to keep pressing "Next."

Have you selected the ADF option in the Scanner Setup Wizard to tell OmniPage your scanner has an ADF? Is the ADF plugged in and working correctly with other programs?

Check that the scanner driver you have installed supports the ADF on your scanner. Use the native user interface to check that the ADF is functioning correctly. If the ADF functions correctly via the native interface and not in OmniPage, use the Scanner Setup Wizard to "Show native interface" and use the native interface to recognize and control the ADF for OmniPage scans. You may have difficulty with old scanners, as the drivers may not be 100 percent compatible with OmniPage 11.

CHAPTER 14

Why are my saved documents so big when they contain images?

If you are scanning color or grayscale documents with lots of pictures, each picture is stored as a 150 dpi BMP image in your Microsoft Word document. BMP is a common and universally accepted format, but it also uses no compression and so is the bulkiest image format. If it's causing a problem, you can try the following to replace the embedded BMP images with smaller JPG images. Here's how:

Scan and save your document as a Word document, then resave the scanned document in HTML format. HTML will create separate JPG image files of all the graphic zones. These JPG files will be much smaller than the BMP images. They will be saved in a sub-folder called filename_dir in the same folder as the one in which you saved the document. Then, in Word, delete the original BMP images and use Insert Picture to insert the JPG images into their place in the document.

I am having problems re-ordering zones. What's wrong?

You can use the re-order zones on pages that do not contain "multi-column text" zones. Re-ordering zones only works with single column text, table, and graphic zones. As soon as you set the properties of a zone to multi-column text zone, all the re-ordering numbers will be lost. This is because OmniPage will break up the "multi-column text" zone into separate "single column text" zones and automatically reorder and renumber all the zones.

I can't select my Microsoft Word Custom dictionary. Why not?

The option to select Microsoft Word custom dictionary is presently not available, though the help file and manuals say it is. In OmniPage versions 9 and 10, this option was available; there is no patch at present. You can import the words from your custom dictionary; see Chapter 13.

Why can't I access extended ASCII characters in my training file?

Previous versions of OmniPage displayed an extended ASCII character set map in the training option. This is not available in OmniPage version 11.

To enter characters not on the keyboard, you can use the Alt key and the decimal number of the character you want. To find the decimal number of the characters, use the Windows Character Map. Click Start > Programs > Accessories > Character Map. Select the character you want and its number is displayed in the lower right-hand corner of the character map window. To enter this character in the training file, hold down the Alt key and type in the three-digit number; when you release the Alt key, the character will be displayed. See Chapter 13 for more on training characters.

When I use "Custom Layout one graphic," why can't I edit my document in the Text Editor?

When using the Options tab Custom Layout, if you select the options one graphic or one table, the entire page is treated as one graphic or one table zone. When using one graphic, the OCR'd result appearing in the Text Editor is a graphic that is the whole page and therefore cannot be edited. Using one table will convert your document to text, but, because it will be converted to a table, it will be difficult to edit. Therefore, it is best to use the auto setting to avoid this, unless of course you have a specific reason for using this option.

Why do I get the error message "the specified page range is invalid" when loading a multi-page image file using "Load File"?

You can get this error loading a multi-page image file when using the Load File Advanced window. When using the Load File function, its dialog box first opens in the Basic view, where you can specify the page range or pages of the image file to load. By clicking on the Advanced button to open the Load Image Advanced view, you can't specify the page range, but you can load a number of files for the OCR session, provided none of them are multi-page image files. If one of them is a multi-page image file, you can get this error message. To process multi-page image files, you will need to use the Load Image dialog box in the Basic view.

Why do my zones overlap?

When using the Perform OCR option Custom Layout with the Flowing Text option set to One column, if your document contains a table, you can get overlapping zones and the table may be broken up into separate zones. Use the auto option instead.

My "Save or Load Settings" doesn't seem to remember my settings. Why not?

Some settings are not saved when using the Save Settings of the Option panel. The AutoOCR, ManualOCR, and OCR Wizard toolboxes are not saved, nor are the Get Page and Export Results options. So when you load your saved settings, these remain as they are currently set. All other settings in the Options panel and the Perform OCR options are restored.

Why do I get a "Scanner Error" message when launching OmniPage Pro 11?

If you have an HP3300C scanner and are using the Windows ME operating system, there is no WIA driver available for the HP3300C scanner. This issue occurred when using HP 3300C scanner with the Precision LT 3.0 Revision 1 software. Please be aware that this can also occur with other scanners.

If the scanner software was installed from the CD that was shipped with the scanner, please go to HP's Web site, http://www.hp.com, to obtain the latest driver; install the driver, then rerun the Scanner Wizard to configure OmniPage Pro 11 for the new driver.

The workaround for this issue would be to scan the document outside of OmniPage Pro 11 in a third-party software such as Imaging or the HP Precision Scan software, and then load the scanned image into OmniPage. To scan a document using Imaging, follow these steps:

1. Open Imaging, which is found in Start > Programs > Accessories.
2. Click File > Scan New to begin the scan.
3. In the scanner user interface, ensure the document has a resolution of 300 dpi; select Black and White, Grayscale, or Color as appropriate.

How do I use the Scanner Wizard once OmniPage is installed?

In OmniPage, click Tools > Options > Scanner > Setup. See Chapter 1 for more on installing and setting up your scanner. You can also run the scanner wizard from Windows by clicking Start > Programs > ScanSoft > Scanner Wizard.

CHAPTER 14

Is OmniPage Pro 11 compatible with Windows XP?

OmniPage Pro 11 is designed to work with your scanner's WIA drivers on Windows XP. Do not install the TWAIN driver onto your Windows XP system if your scanner has both TWAIN and WIA drivers, because the TWAIN driver may overwrite the WIA driver on the system.

Before using your scanner with OmniPage Pro 11 on Windows XP, confirm that your scanner is working properly with its own scanning software and Microsoft Imaging. If you are unable to scan into your scanner's own scanning software or Microsoft Imaging, contact your scanner manufacturer for support.

I get Error 1311 "Source file not found" when trying to install OmniPage Pro 11. What does that mean?

When installing OmniPage Pro 11, the following error message may appear: "Error 1311. Source file not found: C:\Omnipage\Data.Cab. Use windows explorer to verify that file exists and that you can access it."

This can happen with some anti-virus programs that block access to the file "Data.cab." This is one of the many files that are temporarily copied to your hard drive during installation.

Before installing OmniPage Pro 11, disable your anti-virus software and exit out of any other applications that are running on your system. Close all programs except Systray and Explorer.

Will OmniPage Pro 11 work with other SAPI-compliant speech systems installed on my computer?

Speech Application Programming Interface (SAPI) is a standardized interface for text-to-speech applications. OmniPage Pro 11 will detect any other SAPI-compliant text-to-speech programs on a user's system and offer them for use in reading recognized texts aloud. Their voices will be available in the Speech Settings dialog box. Once you have associated a voice with a language, OmniPage Pro 11 will remember this and switch voices according to the recognition language of your document.

"Acquire Text" and "Acquire Text Settings" do not appear in the file menu of registered applications. What should I do?

This is because the application you want to use with Acquire text is not registered in the Direct OCR option in the Options panel. Follow these steps:

1. Open your word processor or other supported application you want to use with Direct OCR.
2. Minimize the application.
3. Open OmniPage Pro 11.
4. Exit out of OmniPage Pro 11.
5. Acquire Text and Acquire Text Settings should now appear in the registered application's file menu.

Or:

1. Open the registered application.
2. Open OmniPage Pro 11.

3. Click Tools > Options > Direct OCR.

4. In the Registered column, click once on the name of the application to select it.

5. Click the Remove button. The name of the application will now be in the Unregistered column.

6. In the Unregistered column, click once on the name of the application to select it.

7. Click the Add button. The name of the application will now be re-added to the Registered column.

8. Click OK to close the Options window.

9. Exit out of OmniPage Pro 11.

10. Acquire Text and Acquire Text Settings should now appear in the registered application's file menu.

When trying to install OmniPage Pro 11, I get an "MSIEXEC" error message. Why?

MSIEXEC is the new Microsoft installer program (MSI). OmniPage makes use of this program during installation; it may be that MSI did not install correctly. If you are running Windows NT, the MSI program may not have administrator privileges. An anti-virus program may be preventing its functioning correctly. This problem can also occur if your computer is infected with the "Win95.cih" virus. Before installing OmniPage Pro 11, make sure all background applications are closed.

How do I access live updates for OmniPage Pro 11?

1. Open OmniPage Pro 11.

2. Go to Help > ScanSoft on the Web > Get Latest Update.

This will bring you to a section of the ScanSoft Web site where you can select different options to install the live updates.

The background of the Windows toolbar is black after installing OmniPage and restarting my computer. Why?

This issue has occurred on computers running Windows 98 First Edition, which does not have Internet Explorer 5.0 installed. Internet Explorer 5.0 or later installs system files that are required for OmniPage Pro 11 to function properly. Install Internet Explorer 5.0 from the installation CD for OmniPage Pro 11. Here's how:

1. Place the OmniPage Pro 11 CD into your CD-ROM drive.

2. When the Autorun feature begins, the OmniPage Pro 11 splash screen will appear. Click the command button for Browse CD.

3. A Windows Explorer window will open, allowing you to browse the contents of the CD.

4. Click the OmniPage\IE5\English sub-folder.

5. Within the English folder, you will find the "ie5setup.exe" file. Click this file to begin the installation process.

As an alternative, go to Microsoft's Web site at http://www.microsoft.com and visit their downloads section to download the latest version of Internet Explorer.

How do I scan legal size documents?

You may have selected "get paper size from scanner" during setup, but your letter-sized scanner will not be able to scan such a document unless you also have an ADF—the ADF moves the paper past the scanner head, so the page could be almost any length. If you do not have an ADF, you will need to reduce the legal-sized document to a letter or A4-sized document using a photocopier.

Can I process and recognize Classical Greek documents using OmniPage Pro 11?

Classical Greek contains additional breath marks, called diacritical marks, on certain characters; these are rendered as special characters. These characters are not contained in the default True Type font sets contained in the standard Windows operating system.

OmniPage Pro 11 is not able to recognize or proofread these special characters. OmniPage Pro 11 supports Modern Greek, which uses a monotonic alphabet. The characters in Modern Greek are found in most default TrueType fonts in the Windows operating system and can be recognized and modified in the Proofreader in OmniPage Pro 11.

As a workaround for processing Classical Greek, follow these steps:

1. In OmniPage Pro 11, click Tools > Options > OCR.
2. In the Fonts in document text box, select Greek.
3. Choose your user dictionary if you have created a custom dictionary for this language. For details on how to create a user dictionary, see "To create a user dictionary" in the OmniPage Pro 11 help menu under "OmniPage Pro Help Topics."
4. Process and recognize the document in OmniPage Pro 11.
5. Edit the document using the Proofreader. To replace suspect characters, use the Character Map utility located in Start > Programs > Accessories > System Tools. The Character Map allows the user to copy and paste characters from different font sets installed on the computer. For best results with the Greek alphabet, use the Arial font. The font can then be changed in the word processing application.
6. Once proofreading is complete, save the document to a word processing application by clicking on Export Results in OmniPage Pro 11.
7. Edit the document in the word processor to render the special Classical Greek characters.

Questions about PaperPort Version 8.0

Can canceling PaperPort installation cause device driver error?

When upgrading to PaperPort Deluxe 8.0 with some Visioneer scanners, canceling the installation before it completes may result in the following error: "PaperPort Device Driver Unable to load DLL" displays and the drivers for your scanner may no longer be available.

To resolve this issue, reinstall the version of PaperPort that came with your scanner, restart your computer, and then reinstall PaperPort Deluxe 8.0. After the installation is complete, restart your computer a second time. You will now be able to use your scanner with PaperPort Deluxe 8.0.

I am unable to scan 8-bit images when using HP Precision Scan.

When you select Precision Scan User Interface from the list of available scanners and select 8-bit color scan, the message "Problem communicating with the TWAIN driver" appears. In this case, select 24-bit to scan your item.

Why are some scanner models not listed in the "Scan" pane?

Some scanner models use proprietary software drivers and thus will not be listed in the Scan pane. For example, if you are using a Visioneer Mx, Ix, Vx, Strobe, Strobe Pro, or Compaq Scanner Keyboard, the model name does not appear in the list of scanners.

To use one of these scanners with PaperPort, simply insert the paper you want to scan into the scanner. The scanner will start automatically, and you will be able to scan your item to the PaperPort desktop.

I am unable to preview scanned fax files with Brother MFL Pro Control Center.

If you are using the Brother MFL Pro Control Center, a GEAR32PD.DLL error may appear when you try to preview faxes you have scanned after installing PaperPort 8.0.

To resolve the issue, you can download an update from the support section of the ScanSoft Web site. Search for GEAR32PD.DLL to locate the update in the PaperPort Support Knowledge Base.

I am unable to import TIFF files that have JPEG compression.

When you try to import a TIFF file that has JPEG compression, PaperPort reports an "Image File Error." To work around this issue, use the source image-editing program to save the image file in a different TIFF format, and then import the TIFF file into PaperPort.

The number of pages in a duplicated image item doesn't match my original item.

When you duplicate a multi-page item as a PaperPort image item (.max file), the number of pages in the duplicate item may be different than the number of pages in the source item. This can occur when some of the formatting in the source item is not retained in the duplicate item. Although the page count may differ, the textual content of the items will be the same.

Overwrite prompt is not displayed when saving a multi-page image item to a single page format.

If you open a multi-page image item (.max file) in the Page View window and save it more than one time to a single page format under the same file name, PaperPort does not ask if you want to overwrite the existing items. Instead, PaperPort will always replace the existing items with your newly saved versions.

Using the "Send To" links: PaperPortOnline with AOL.

To use the new PaperPortOnline feature in conjunction with AOL, log on to your AOL account, minimize the AOL window, and then launch Internet Explorer. You can now use the PaperPortOnline link on the Send To bar.

Existing PaperPortOnline link causes error when upgrading to PaperPort Deluxe 8.0.

If you are upgrading to PaperPort Deluxe 8.0 from an earlier version of PaperPort and have already established PaperPortOnline as a program link, a message reports that the PaperPortOnline link is in use the first time you start PaperPort Deluxe 8.0. To resolve this issue, click OK, and then close and restart PaperPort.

The OmniPage Pro 11 link on the "Send To" bar does not accept PDF files.

If you add OmniPage Pro 11 as a linked program, PaperPort displays the message "Program link does not accept this type of item" when you drag a PDF item to the program icon on the Send To bar. To work around this issue, start your OmniPage Pro 11 program and then load the PDF image item into OmniPage Pro 11.

Some program windows might appear behind the PaperPort window.

When you drag an item to a program icon on the Send To bar, the window for that program may occasionally be displayed behind the PaperPort window. Other types of windows, such as those that display error messages and scanner dialog boxes, might also appear behind the PaperPort window on occasion. To bring any window to the front of other open programs, simply click the program icon in the Windows taskbar at the bottom of your screen display. You can also hold the Alt key and use the Tab key to scroll through icons of open windows and programs on your system. Release the Tab key to open the selected window.

SimpleSearch indexing or "Copy Text" process halts with an error message: "ppocrmg.exe . . . "

If you install TextBridge 9.0 or TextBridge Pro Millennium after you install PaperPort Deluxe 8.0, the SimpleSearch indexing process or the Copy Text feature might halt. The message "ppocrmg.exe has generated an error and will be closed by Windows" may also appear. To resolve this issue, run the TextBridge Update program that is provided in the TBupdate folder on your PaperPort Deluxe 8.0 CD.

When I print browser-viewable e-mail attachments, I get blank pages instead of the attachments.

Browser-viewable (.htm) e-mail attachments print as blank pages if you use the Print command in the browser's File menu or the Print button on the browser's command bar.

To print a browser-viewable (.htm) e-mail attachment, open the attachment in your Web browser and click the Print button located at the bottom of the viewer window. You can also right-click the image and then click Print on the shortcut menu.

On Windows 2000, NT, and XP, certain permissions are necessary to install the browser-viewable plug-in.

On Windows 2000, NT, or XP, recipients of browser-viewable e-mail attachments initially need power user or administrator privileges to download and install the e-mail viewer plug-in from the ScanSoft Web site. When an e-mail recipient does not have the necessary permissions, the image does not appear in the browser window.

To download the plug-in, the recipient will need to log on as a power user or obtain administrator privileges and try again. Otherwise, the e-mail sender should convert the PaperPort item to a .jpg file and send the .jpg file to the recipient as an e-mail attachment.

Note that once the plug-in is installed on a system, all users will be able to view the e-mail attachments. No special permissions are necessary.

On Windows 98 and ME, I have problems using the PaperPort printer with WordPerfect 10.

On a Windows 98 and Windows ME system, the printing process may stop when you print a document from WordPerfect 10 to the PaperPort desktop while PaperPort is closed.

To resolve this issue, simply launch PaperPort before you print a file from WordPerfect 10 to PaperPort. As long as PaperPort is running, you can print from WordPerfect 10 to PaperPort at any time.

I am unable to print high-resolution files to the PaperPort Color print driver.

Depending upon your system configuration, you may be unable to print a high-resolution color file from another program to the PaperPort desktop. If your system does not have sufficient memory, you may receive the message "An error occurred while printing, or printing was canceled" when you select PaperPort Color as the printer. Specify a lower-resolution setting in the PaperPort Color Properties dialog box, or print from the original program.

Questions about OmniForm V5.0

Should I use Scan Manager to install a scanner driver for OmniForm?

Scan Manager is no longer required. OmniForm v5.0 now uses the Scanner Setup Wizard to set up scanners. This is the same Scanner Wizard as in OmniPage Pro 11. To open the Scanner Setup Wizard, in OmniForm's File menu, select Scanner or click Start in the Windows taskbar and choose Programs > ScanSoft OmniForm 5.0 > Scanner Setup Wizard. The Wizard prompts you through the installation.

CHAPTER 14

Some features are not supported when saving as PDF.

Some OmniForm features are not supported when saving a form in PDF format. For example, some calculations will not work, such as those applied to comb fields. Parentheses around numbers will not work to symbolize negative numbers.

I'm having problems with digital signatures using Adobe Acrobat Reader.

You get the following message when you save a form with a digital signature field to PDF format and open the PDF file in Acrobat Reader 5.0, then click the signature field: "The plug-in required by this signature field is unavailable. Information about the missing plug-in might be available on Adobe's Web site." Adobe Acrobat Reader does not have the required plug-in to recognize digital signature fields. The standard free Acrobat Reader does not support digital signatures. You need to purchase Adobe approval or the full Adobe Acrobat program.

If I save a form as HTML and try to print it in Netscape 6, it doesn't come out right.

Netscape 6 cannot print more than one page of a form that has been converted to HTML. Certain form elements are not supported or are handled differently when converted to HTML format.

- ▶ Circle text fields are converted to radio buttons if they are grouped. If they are not grouped, they are converted to check boxes.
- ▶ Comb fields are converted to rectangular-shaped fillable fields.
- ▶ All elements that are aligned will default to top-alignment.
- ▶ When collecting data for forms on the eOmniForm.com site, fillable graphic and signature fields might lose any data entered in them.
- ▶ Autofill fields might not automatically fill other fields.
- ▶ Line elements that are not horizontal or vertical might be dropped.
- ▶ Some calculations, such as Record Count, might not work.
- ▶ The Shrink Text to Fit feature might not work.
- ▶ Prefill fields might be dropped.

I get a kernel32.dll error and OmniForm exits unexpectedly.

When scanning from OmniForm in Windows ME, a known bug in the driver for the CanoScan 650U, CanoScan 670U, and 656U Rev 5.7 (TWAIN) scanners causes OmniForm to exit unexpectedly. ScanSoft is working with Canon to resolve this problem.

I get an ODBC error when exporting data with Entrust signatures.

An ODBC error might occur when exporting OmniForm data digitally signed with an Entrust signature. This is a limitation of the ODBC driver, related to the value of the digital signature, which is exported along with the data.

I get an ODBC error when exporting data to open files.

An ODBC error will occur if you export data from OmniForm to an open file. Close the target file before exporting data to it.

What does the message "Data Must Match Field Type" mean?

This error will occur when data you are exporting to a database is of the wrong type. For example, you can't save alpha text in a time field. OmniForm checks that data matches field type in the following fields only: alpha, number, currency, data, and time. The best way to avoid problems is to have OmniForm create the database and field types at the first export—the data and field types will always match.

You may need to adjust margins when printing forms from Internet Explorer 5.0.

A form opened in Internet Explorer 5.0 might have larger margins than those in the originally designed form. This could cause part of the form to be cut off when printing. To prevent this, use the Page Setup command in Internet Explorer's File menu to adjust page margins as necessary before printing.

Why can't I use Adobe Acrobat to open OmniForm 5.0.PDF file on the installation CD?

The OmniForm 5.0.PDF file in the OmniForm folder on the installation CD is a Microsoft Product Definition File that is required for installation. Although it has a PDF extension, it is not an Adobe portable document format file, and you cannot use Adobe Acrobat to open it.

I get an error when collecting data in eOmniForm.com.

If an error occurs while eOmniForm.com is collecting data and it is unable to collect the data, it might still mark the data as collected. This could prevent collection of additional data due to record limitations in OmniForm. To work around this problem, you must recover the data so that it is again marked as collectible. See OmniForm's help for more information on recovering data.

OLE objects not supported in HTML format.

Graphics inserted into an OmniForm form as OLE objects are not supported when a form is converted to HTML. Instead, insert a graphic by using the Graphic tool in Form Designer. This also applies when publishing forms to eOmniForm.com, because published forms are converted to HTML format.

Uninstalling OmniPage causes error in Scanner Setup Wizard.

If you have OmniPage Pro and OmniForm installed, uninstalling OmniPage will cause an error the next time you start the Scanner Setup Wizard to use with OmniForm. This is because a file necessary for the Scanner Setup Wizard is uninstalled during OmniPage uninstallation. To fix this, insert OmniForm's CD, choose the Repair option, and follow the instructions on the screen; the necessary file will be reinstalled automatically.

Special instruction needed when sending Mailable Filler files to Microsoft Outlook users.

When file attachments are opened directly from the Preview pane of Microsoft Outlook, changes made to the files are not saved. Therefore, if someone double-clicks a Mailable Filler file to open it from the Preview pane of Microsoft Outlook, changes made to the file (such as entered data) will not be retained. If you send a Mailable Filler file as an e-mail attachment, please instruct the recipient to open the actual e-mail message before opening the Mailable Filler file. Or, recipients can save the attachment to their disk before opening it.

CHAPTER 14

Problems exporting data to ODBC databases.

The first time you export data to an ODBC database, an unexpected exit might occur at the end of the export process. This does not result in any data loss; the data will still be successfully exported. This problem might be caused by the ODBC Jet file "odbcjt32.dll" in version 4.00.4403.02 dated 8/8/00. To verify if you have this version, check the properties on your "odbcjt32.dll" file. To avoid this problem, it is recommended that you download and install the latest available version of MDAC, which provides updated ODBC drivers. To do so, go to www.microsoft.com/downloads and search on MDAC.

Go to http://www.scansoft.com/support/ if you are experiencing any installation or error messages. Click support, click the product you need support for, then click Knowledge Base and enter your question.

Index

INDEX

INDEX

We want to hear from you.

We are interested in your ideas and comments. When you provide us the feedback, we'll add you to our monthly announcement list if you wish so you can hear about new books. We won't sell or share your personal information with anyone.

Tell us what you think of this book—what you like and what you don't like or what you would like to see changed.

Let us know what other books you would like to see from Muska & Lipman. You are a valuable resource for us.

Visit our Web site to submit your feedback:

http://www.muskalipman.com/feedback.html

Or send us a letter with your feedback at:
Muska & Lipman Publishing
P.O. Box 8225
Cincinnati, Ohio 45208-8225

Appendix

This appendix contains documents used as exercises in this book. The original image files are available to download from www.omnipagetraining.biz or www.muskalipman.com. You can scan the pages from this appendix or download the image files, print, and scan. Alternatively, download the image files and use the Load image file option to process the pages.

OmniPage Training has been authorized by Scansoft, Inc to use their sample documents in this book. The newspaper articles have been provided with approval by the Fairfax Group in Sydney, Australia. OmniPage Training has provided many different types of documents for the exercises. These documents are for the sole purpose of working through the exercises in the book and must not be used for any other purpose. Copyright on all these documents is owned by the respective owners. Please refer to the Copyright clause in the Introduction.

Some of the example pages for the exercises were installed with OmniPage. If you have upgraded from a previous version of OmniPage, the example files from the previous versions may still be on your hard drive. If you elected to install OmniPage to a different disk drive and folder, please look there for these files. The example files are very good to experiment with. It is much quicker to load the image file than it is to scan it.

OmniPage 11 sample files should be found in the C:\My Documents\My Pictures folder.

Key to Images in This Appendix

Chapter 3: Basic Document Scanning

▶ **test.tif**—Scan using OmniPage. Use Automatic zones or draw a single zone over the entire page and select as Single column text. In the Text Editor view, select Retain Flowing as this retains the text layout. Use True Page to maintain the same layout using frames. Using Retain Font and Paragraph formatting will keep the font and paragraphs together but does not retain the paragraph spacing. No Formatting will save the document as a single font for the entire document. (Note: This file is reused in Chapter 9.)

Chapter 4: Working with Zones

▶ **Skeleton.tif**—Scan using OmniPage. Using AutoOCR will not capture the page correctly. Parts of the graphics will be zoned as text and not recognized correctly, and parts of the graphics not recognized at all. Use ManualOCR and draw the zones as shown in Figure A.2.

▶ **Skeleton zones.tif**—The biology paper showing where the zones must be drawn. Scan using OmniPage. As you can see, you can use OmniPage to recognize and OCR quite complex pages containing graphics and text. Use ManualOCR and draw the zones as shown in this figure. Save using the Text Editor View True Page or Flowing columns. True page is the best, as all the zones will be reproduced in the original positions. Save as a Microsoft Word document.

Chapter 5: Multi-Column Documents

▶ **Tpexmple.tif**—Scan using OmniPage. Use Automatic zones to OCR the entire page or select areas of the page and manually draw a single column text zone around the title and an irregular zone around the three columns of text. Set the zone contents to a multi-column text zone and put a graphic zone around the area of the picture you want to preserve.

Save using the Text Editor View, Retain Flowing Columns. This retains the text layout. Use True Page to maintain the same layout using Frames. Using Retain Font and Paragraph formatting will keep the font and paragraphs together, this but does not retain the paragraph spacing. No Formatting will save the document as a single font for the entire document. (Note: This file is reused in Chapter 9.)

Chapter 6: Direct OCR

▶ **Sample1_single.tif**—This is one of the sample files installed with OmniPage. It is a single page tif file. If you print this image file and then scan it, you may not get a very good result. This is because the file on your PC is very compressed, and the way the printer interprets the image file will not give a very good "original" to scan.

Scan (load file) using OmniPage. Use Automatic zones to OCR the entire page. Or to select areas of the page, manually draw a single column Text zone around the Title, an irregular zone around the three columns of text and set the zone contents to a Multi-column text zone. Draw a graphic zone around the area of the picture you want to preserve, and a Table zone around the Table.

Chapter 7: Tables and Spreadsheets

▶ **phone.tif**—Scan using OmniPage. Use Automatic zones to OCR the entire page. Or, to select areas of the page manually, draw a Table zone around the Table. Use the manual zone to exclude the unwanted shading. If you regularly scan this type of document layout, then save the table zone as a template file to use in the future. Make the size of the table zone in the template large enough to accommodate the largest size the table could be. Save as a Word or Excel spread sheet file. When saving tables to Excel you will find you may get better format and layout using the Text Editor View No Formatting.

Chapter 8: Logos, Signatures, Line Art, and Color Photos

▶ **Logo.tif**—Scan using OmniPage. Scan using B&W for line Art and text logos, Gray and color if the logo contains a colored graphic or colored text you want to retain. Use manual OCR. Draw a Graphic Zone over the entire

Logo. If you use AutoOCR, you may need to manually rezone the logo and reprocess the page. To maintain the integrity and format of logos, capture the entire logo, graphics, and text as a single graphic. Manually draw a single graphic zone around the logo. Sometimes you may need to draw an irregular zone to capture the entire logo.

▶ **Signature.tif**—Scan using OmniPage. Use Scan Black & White for best results. Capture signatures in the same way as logos. Draw a single graphic zone around the signature. Sometimes you may need to draw an irregular zone to capture the entire signature.

▶ **Lineart.tif**—Scan using OmniPage. Use Scan Black & White for best results. Use Manual OCR. Line art that contains text must be captured using a graphic zone for the entire drawing. If not, OmniPage will zone the text and graphic separately. Capture line art drawings in the same way as logos. Draw a single graphic zone around the drawing. Sometimes you may need to draw an irregular zone to capture the entire drawing.

▶ **Letter.tif**—Scan with OmniPage or PaperPort. As this is a letter from someone else, you should not change any of the text. If you do want to OCR the text, use OmniPage. You will need to draw a single column zone around the text in order to OCR it. If you wanted to scan a letter and keep the logo and signature in their original places, OCR the text, then draw a graphic zone around the logo and one around the signature. A graphic zone will prevent OmniPage from interpreting graphics as text. To store the letter as an image, use PaperPort. If you are using OmniPage, draw a graphic zone over the entire page. Scan B&W. Use ManualOCR, and draw an irregular graphic zone around the logos and a regular graphic zone around the signature. Draw a single column text zone around the entire text in the letter.

Perform the OCR process. In the Text Editor view select Retain Flowing columns or True Page. Save as a Microsoft Word document.

Chapter 9: Multiple-Page and Long Documents

▶ **Spexmple.tif**—Scan using OmniPage. Scan as B&W. Use AutoOCR and Automatic OCR Process.

▶ **Mpexmple.tif**—Scan using OmniPage. Scan as B&W. Use AutoOCR and Automatic OCR Process.

▶ **Test.tif**—Use file from Chapter 3.

▶ **Tpexmple.tif**—Use file from Chapter 5.

▶ **Xmas100.tif**— Download from http://www.omnipagetraining.biz or http://www.muskalipman.com.

Chapter 12: Form Scanning with OmniForm

▶ **Form2.tif**— While you could use OmniPage for this job, it's better suited to OmniForm. If you scan using OmniPage, the results may be variable. The saved document will not be easy to fill in using Microsoft Word as the "dotted lines" for the fields are already "filled in" with dots.

To process using OmniPage, scan in Black & White. Use AutoOCR to process the page, with the Perform OCR option set to Automatic. Choose True Page format in the Text Editor view. In the Options settings > Text Editor > Option Word Wrap, select No Wrap. This stops the text flowing on to the next line. In the "Save As" options, click the Advanced save button. Select Hard Carriage return after every line. Save the document as a Microsoft Word document and launch the application. Once the document is open in Microsoft Word, select the entire document (Ctl+A) and shrink the font as required to fit the lines of text to one line.

This does work using OmniPage but requires performing more steps and the result is a printable form. OmniForm will produce a superior result and a form that can be filled in on the PC.

Further Examples and Exercises

More OmniPage exercises for your scanning enjoyment are available from www.omnipagetraining.biz or www.muskalipman.com. You'll learn how to scan handwritten text, recipes, legal forms, and much more!

Chapter 3: Basic Document Scanning

Figure A.1
Test.tif

BUSINESS

Caere designs, develops, manufactures and markets information recognition software and systems products. The Company's products provide a low cost, accurate means of converting text, numeric and bar code data into computer usable form. For many applications, the Company's products are an attractive alternative to manual data entry, which is slow, tedious and error prone. Caere currently offers two families of information recognition products. OmniPage, which was first shipped in September 1988, is a page recognition software product with versions for the Apple Macintosh II and SE/30, the IBM PC AT and compatibles (with a coprocessor card) and 80386-based computers. The Company also markets a line of OCR and bar code data entry products. Caere introduced its OCR products in 1977 and its bar code products in 1983. As a pioneer in the OCR market, the Company believes that information recognition markets, whether OCR, bar code or page recognition, are technology driven, cost sensitive and often slow to develop. Building upon its extensive experience in OCR, the Company's strategy is to identify and pursue markets in which manual entry of information can be cost effectively automated.

Desktop Recognition Products

The earliest information recognition systems required proprietary hardware and were expensive. Lower cost recognition systems were subsequently introduced, but these systems were only capable of recognizing a few type styles and sizes and were unable to recognize typeset pages or pages organized in columnar format. As a result, these lower cost systems met with limited market acceptance.

OmniPage is a software product that uses widely available, powerful personal computers and low cost scanners to bring capabilities to the user's desktop previously available only on expensive, dedicated recognition systems. A user can scan a page of text or numeric data and then use OmniPage software to capture, edit, save and load the scanned image into popular word processing, spreadsheet and database programs running on industry standard personal computers. The desktop recognition market encompasses a wide range of document processing applications, including general office, desktop publishing, legal, educational and governmental.

OmniPage is currently available in three versions: a software-only version that runs on Apple Macintosh II and SE/30 computers; a version for the IBM PC AT and compatibles that requires a coprocessor card to supply additional computing power and memory; and a software-only version for computers utilizing the Intel 80386 microprocessor. Both of the PC versions run under Microsoft Windows. The Macintosh version was first shipped in September 1988, the AT version in December 1988 and the 386 version in July 1989.

The three versions of OmniPage are virtually identical in features and functions. OmniPage recognizes text which has been scanned from a printed or typed page and captures the text in a computer usable form. The speed with which a page is recognized is dependent upon the type and speed of processor, the quality of the scanned image and the graphical elements, headers and variety of fonts included on the scanned page. On a 386-based 20 megahertz personal computer, the page you are now reading takes approximately one minute to be scanned and converted by OmniPage into a text file. OmniPage is capable of recognizing letters and numbers in many different layouts and presentations including landscape, single and multiple columns and financial (spreadsheet) forms.

OmniPage is "omnifont"—it recognizes virtually all nonstylized fonts in sizes ranging from 8 to 72 points without training or programming. In addition, OmniPage accelerates when reading a consistent font, achieving speeds in excess of 100 characters per second (about 25 seconds per typical typed page). During page recognition, OmniPage displays sample characters from the scanned document in a character window, allowing the user to monitor and improve the recognition process, primarily by adjusting the scanner contrast settings. Once scanned and recognized, text may be edited within the OmniPage transitional editor prior to transferring it to an application file.

Appendix

Chapter 4: Working with Zones

Figure A.2
Skeleton.tif

SKELETAL SYSTEM
VERTEBRAE & VERTEBRAL COLUMN*

PLATE 1

CN 6
1. Color the individual cervical vertebra and the 7 cervical vertebrae in both posterior and lateral views.
2. Do the same for the thoracic and lumbar vertebrae as well as the sacrum and coccyx. Avoid the intervertebral foramina (–¦–) seen in the thoracic and lumbar regions of the column, lateral view. Also avoid the 8 foramina in the sacrum, posterior view of the column.
3. Color in the intervertebral discs.
4. Do not color the skull.

7 CERVICALₐ
This flexible group of *cervical* vertebrae supports the skull and neck. Holding the head erect develops and maintains its curvature. The 1st and 2nd cervical vertebrae are unique as is the 7th with its prominent spine. The foramina in the transverse processes of C1–C6 transmit the vertebral arteries to the base of the brain. The series of vertebral foramina form a canal for the spinal cord.

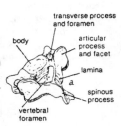

12 THORACICᵦ
This rather rigid group of *thoracic* vertebrae and the 24 ribs with which they articulate support the thorax. Its prominent curvature is developed in fetal life. Thoracic vertebrae are characterized by long slender spines, heart-shaped bodies, and facets for rib articulation.

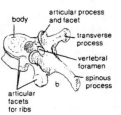

5 LUMBAR𝒸
These stubby, quadrilateral *lumbar* vertebrae, the most massive of the column, carry a large share of the body weight, balancing the torso on the sacrum. The lumbar curvature results from walking and standing erect. This vertebral group is quite mobile; when lifting from the floor by flexing this group, great pressure is often put on their discs, which may induce their rupture. This may injure the spinal nerves which pass from the spinal cord through the intervertebral foramina.

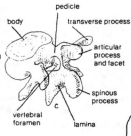

SACRUM𝒹
Five *sacral* vertebrae fuse to form this single bone. It transmits the body weight to the hip joints via its articulation with the pelvic girdle.

COCCYX𝑒
Consisting of 2 to 4 fused coccygeal vertebrae, the functionally insignificant *coccyx* represents the vestigial tail of our forebears.

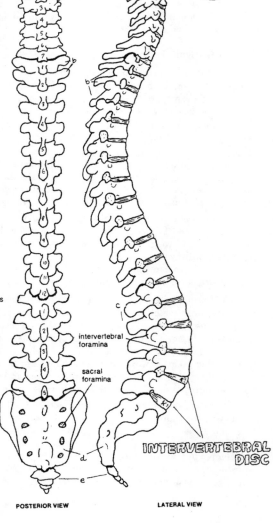

POSTERIOR VIEW   LATERAL VIEW

INTERVERTEBRAL DISC

http://www.muskalipman.com

Figure A.3
Skeleton zones.tif

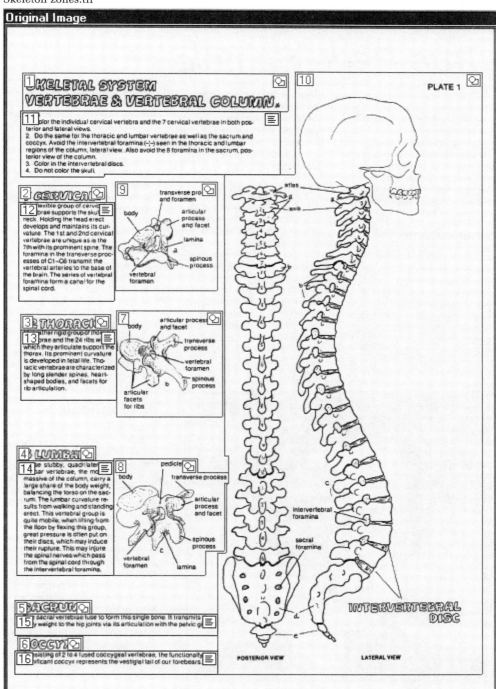

Chapter 5: Multi-Column Documents

Figure A.4
Tpexmple.tif

True Page Sample

OmniPage Professional allows you to recognize, edit, and save documents in their original, full page formats when you use True Page recognition. With True Page, you can even edit any images on the page by simply clicking on the image. This opens a complete set of editing tools in our Image Assistant editing package. Image Assistant features are highlighted below.

Image Editing for Every Business

Image Assistant has automatic, intelligent tools that anyone in your office can use. And, for the professional graphic artist, it has the most complete set of professional features available in image editing software. Whether your business consists of you and your computer or you and a cast of thousands,

Image Assistant is your image editing tool. Image Assistant is a 24 bit color image editor that lets just about anyone, even beginners, produce professional color output: from a color slide to a four color separation.

Assist Mode

You may not be a graphic artist; but you know how your image should look. In Assist Mode, you choose just the right effect for your image by looking at sample thumbnails onscreen. For example, if you're setting contrast, you'll see 15 samples of how your image will look with 15 different contrast settings. You just click on the sample that looks right to you, and your image is transformed. And, multiple levels of Undo and Redo let you experiment to your heart's content.

Imaging for Pros

Image Assistant's true power and versatility are clear to the professional graphic artist. You can edit in bilevel, grayscale, RGB, or CYMK and access complete PANTONE color support. Image Assistant has all the tools and features you expect from a high end image processing product.

Automatic Scanning Controls

Image Assistant completely automates the task of capturing images. For example, it can separate a scanned photo from unwanted text, crop it and rotate it. It determines whether you're working with a line art, grayscale, or color image and opens it in the appropriate environment. You also have complete manual control for all settings if you need it.

Editing Tools

Image Assistant provides all the features you need to edit color, grayscale and black and white images. It can even convert images to a different type; for example, you can convert grayscale images into line art and vice versa. Grayscale images are made of various shades and tones. Consequently, the editing tools in Image Assistant let you paint and edit in shades and tones of grays. You can smudge grays together, paint with any gray from within an image, and even create custom brushes from different patterns and textures in the image. Electronic tools such as the pencil, eraser, paintbrush and airbrush are also available.

Chapter 6: Direct OCR

Figure A.5
Sample1_single.tif

Tropical Vacations

Volume 5. October

Surf Angels

Ladies, have you ever dreamed of an endless summer of surf and fun? Splash Adventures now offers "women only" surfing camps in Los Cabos, Mexico. Miles of sparkling private beaches are the perfect learning ground for would-be Lady Kahunas. Prices start from $1,000 per week for an all-inclusive package. Call Splash Adventures for more information.

Paradise Rediscovered

Nestled along a half-mile stretch of The Big Island's sunniest coastline, the Royal Hilo Resorts Hualalai is being heralded as a return to Hawaii's Golden Age. With its stunning natural beauty and understated elegance, the casual observer might at first mistake this 243-room resort as a naturally occurring oasis that had arisen from its black-lava surroundings. Yet, once on the property, the warm, personal service and attention to detail gently reminds you that this is indeed a Royal Hilo Resort.

Now through April 18th, book four nights at the Royal Hilo Resorts Hualalai and receive a fifth night free.

ROOM RATES	High season	Low season	Super saver
Partial ocean view	$149	$110	$89
Ocean view	$225	$168	$112
Ocean view	$300	$220	$198

Caribbean Underwater Treasure

World renowned for its spectacular diving, Negril has always been a favorite destination for divers. For many, the crystal clear water of the Caribbean sea offers an escape into the beautiful underwater world that lies below. In an attempt to match the allure of the sea, Grand Palms Negril is now offering special diving packages to their guests.

For years, travel critics have lauded the Grand Palms Negril as the "Best Caribbean/Atlantic Resort." Now the readers of Monte Claire Diver magazine have made it official. In its annual poll, readers cited the resort's gourmet cuisine, luxurious accommodations, and super inclusive policy as reasons why the Grand Palms Negril earned the top spot on this very exclusive list.

For a limited time, you can experience the Grand Palms Negril and save up to $555 per couple on an all-inclusive stay of seven nights or more.

Travel Tips

1. When making airline reservations, remember to ask for special discounts if you have younger children.

2. Make photocopies of your passport, airline tickets, and credit cards. This will help you get replacements if you lose any of these items.

3. Keep receipts of all your purchases when you shop. Custom officials may ask for proof of purchase.

4. Carry different forms of currency such as cash, traveler's checks and credit cards.

5. Keep extra batteries and film in your camera bag. It's handy for any traveler.

Chapter 7: Tables and Spreadsheets

Figure A.6
Phone.tif

10 Aug	01:05 pm	Mobile	015435482	Peak	0:21	0.25
12 Aug	10:02 am	Mobile	018259253	Peak	0:37	0.25
17 Aug	12:15 pm	Mobile	018415485	Peak	0:35	0.25
17 Aug	01:27 pm	Mobile	018865586	Peak	2:35	1.00
17 Aug	02:53 pm	Mobile	018415485	Peak	0:27	0.25
22 Aug	09:14 am	Mobile	015230053	Peak	0:51	0.50
22 Aug	11:31 am	Mobile	018265761	Peak	1:24	0.75
22 Aug	02:56 pm	Mobile	018415485	Peak	0:32	0.25
26 Aug	09:07 am	Mobile	018617249	Peak	0:44	0.50
26 Aug	01:34 pm	Mobile	018415866	Peak	0:42	0.50
29 Aug	10:11 am	Mobile	018969363	Peak	0:29	0.25
30 Aug	12:30 pm	Mobile	015431007	Peak	2:34	1.00
30 Aug	12:54 pm	Mobile	018044682	Peak	11:03	4.50
30 Aug	04:14 pm	Mobile	018153040	Peak	0:26	0.25
31 Aug	12:21 pm	Mobile	018256063	Peak	0:19	0.25
31 Aug	12:45 pm	Mobile	018256063	Peak	0:32	0.25
31 Aug	02:27 pm	Mobile	018617249	Peak	0:31	0.25
31 Aug	03:02 pm	Mobile	018617249	Peak	1:27	0.75
05 Sep	02:12 pm	Mobile	018969363	Peak	0:48	0.50
05 Sep	02:59 pm	Mobile	018212472	Peak	0:30	0.25
05 Sep	03:17 pm	Mobile	018212472	Peak	4:04	1.75
05 Sep	04:34 pm	Mobile	018617249	Peak	0:43	0.50
Telephone Service						
10 Aug	12:08 pm	Mobile	015435482	Peak	1:00	0.50
23 Aug	10:23 am	Mobile	018617249	Peak	0:20	0.25
31 Aug	04:49 pm	Mobile	018293791	Peak	4:38	2.00
01 Sep	10:22 am	Mobile	018617249	Peak	1:35	0.75
05 Sep	03:06 pm	Mobile	018617249	Peak	0:23	0.25
Telephone Service						
24 Aug	11:46 am	Mobile	018278366	Peak	0:44	0.50

Continued page **5**

Chapter 8: Logos, Signatures, Line Art, and Color Photos

Figure A.7
Logo.tif

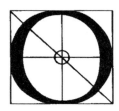

Omnipage Training

Figure A.8
Signature.tif

Figure A.9
Lineart.tif

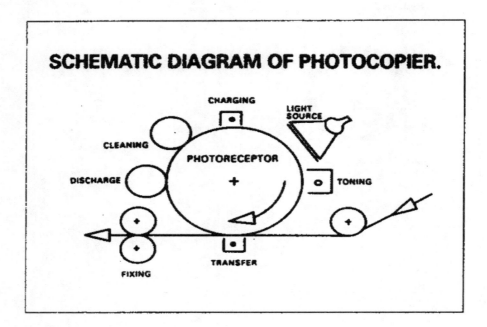

Figure A.10
Letter.tif

Copyright Laws do not permit reproduction of this client's Logo, Letterhead, Address, Signature or Name. This is where the logo and letterhead would be displayed.

T E C H N O L O G Y   ●   S I M P · L E

4 June 1998

Chief of Division:

OmniPage Training
Fax: 9888 7400

Dear Sir

I attended an OmniPage Pro 8 Training course last week at Parramatta and just wanted to let you know how informative it was. I have been using Omnipage for a few years now, mostly making it do what I wanted, but now I realise I was doing things a very long way around indeed.

To be able to scan tables and spreadsheets (a big part of my job) and have them arrive in Word or Excel correctly is just wonderful, something I had never got totally right before. Knowing how to now handle graphics and text together, and those odd shaped pieces you need from time to time put the finishing touches on very informative day.

I particularly liked before the course started the trainer asked everyone in the room what they used Omnipage for and what they would like to do and made a very long list, but by the end of the day every item on the list was crossed off.

Great trainer, great program. great day.

Many thanks indeed

Signature went here

Chapter 9: Multiple-Page and Long Documents

Figure A.11
Spexmple.tif

Single Column Page Sample

Dear OmniPage Customer,

Thank you for purchasing OmniPage. Our OmniPage products have been specifically designed to meet your needs as you enter and add value to information on your desktop.

As an OmniPage user, you join a large group of users in over 35 countries who have looked to Caere to set new standards for accurate and affordable OCR since 1988.

In our latest versions of OmniPage we are proud to incorporate new technologies in addition to our patented core OCR technology. Our corporate mission is to continue to make it easier and more efficient for you to enter, retrieve, and work with documents on your desktop.

In a recent survey of OmniPage customers conducted by an independent research company, these factors were identified as most important when purchasing an OCR product.

Accuracy	96 %
Reliability	92
Ease of use	89
Speed	87
Scanner support	82
Ease of learning	82
Text editing capabilities	75
Price	69
Sophistication of features	66
Image handling capabilities	65
Number of features	64
Direct application input	57
Multi-language recognition	21

Figure A.12
Mpexmple.tif

Multiple Column Page Sample

The introduction of the personal computer has caused dramatic changes in the way businesses and individuals access, retrieve, share, store, analyze, and present information.

Today, more than 60 percent of the work force spends its time creating, processing, or distributing information, compared to just 17 percent in 1950. Yet in spite of the widespread use of computers, the promise of a paperless office is far from a reality. More than 90 percent of the information generated today resides on paper. In fact, more than 150 billion pages of information are generated each year.

An estimated 10 percent of the information used by an organization is reused in some way, and research shows that percentage is increasing. Employees in large and small businesses, educational organizations, and government offices all deal with information that is reused, reformatted, or revised.

To manage their paper flow, workers need easy-to-use, inexpensive, yet sophisticated information recognition devices that quickly transfer printed material into computers.

Caere met that challenge with its OmniPage and Typist text-recognition products, which were hailed as information recognition breakthroughs for the personal computer market. Caere continues to improve its product line.

The Solution: Information Recognition and Management

Caere Corporation is a pioneer and leader in the information recognition market, developing tools for information recognition and information management that increase employee productivity. The company has combined its extensive experience in optical character recognition (OCR), with powerful new personal computer technologies.

Caere's products recognize 11 western European languages and have received numerous international industry awards. OmniPage is a leading desktop page recognition software. Caere's newest products are PageKeeper, OmniScan, and Image Assistant. Each of Caere's new products depends on one or more of the new technologies to come out of Caere's research and development efforts in the last year. They include Caere's new SuperCompression technology which offers efficient storage of text and images.

Caere Corporation was founded in 1976 by Dr. Robert Noyce, the inventor of the integrated circuit and the founder of Intel Corporation. Noyce believed that keyless data entry was the most efficient and productive method of entering data into computers. That belief defined the company's mission: to develop economical tools that accurately render data in computer-compatible form.

Appendix

Chapter 12: Form Scanning with OmniForm

Figure A.13
Form2.tif

INFORMATION PAGE – PLEASE COMPLETE ALL INFORMATION

COMPANY NAME .... ACN NO .... YEARS EST ....

ADDRESS .... STATE .... POST CODE ....

FULL INDIVIDUAL/DIRECTOR/PARTNER NAME .... DATE OF BIRTH ...../...../.......

ADDRESS .... STATE .... POST CODE ....

HOME OWNER/RENTER .... REAL ESTATE VALUE $ .... MORTGAGE (WITH WHOM?) $ ....

FULL INDIVIDUAL/DIRECTOR/PARTNER NAME .... DATE OF BIRTH ...../...../.......

ADDRESS .... STATE .... POST CODE ....

HOME OWNER/RENTER .... REAL ESTATE VALUE $ .... MORTGAGE (WITH WHOM?) $ ....

BANK & BRANCH .... NATURE OF BUSINESS ....

ACCOUNTANTS NAME .... CONTACT .... PH NO ....

TRADE REFERENCE (1) .... CONTACT .... PH NO ....

TRADE REFERENCE (2) .... CONTACT .... PH NO ....

SALESPERSON .... COMPANY .... PH NO ....

EQUIPMENT DESC .... COST PRICE $ ....

TERM (MONTHS) .... MONTHLY PAYMENT (INCL. STAMP DUTY & FID) $ .... RESIDUAL $ ....

PRIVACY ACT AUTHORISATION

AUTHORISATION BY APPLICANT:

I/WE AGREE TO YOU OBTAINING A REPORT ABOUT MY/OUR CONSUMER OR COMMERCIAL CREDIT WORTHINESS FROM A CREDIT REPORTING BUSINESS RESPECTIVELY, FOR THE PURPOSE OF ASSESSING THIS LOAN APPLICATION OR COLLECTING ANY OVERDUE PAYMENTS; IN SO DOING , I/WE ACKNOWLEDGE THAT INFORMATION FROM THIS APPLICATION OR CONCERNING THE LENDERS CURRENT CREDIT PROVIDER STATUS MAY BE DISCLOSED. I/WE ALSO AGREE THAT YOU MAY GIVE TO AND RECEIVE FROM ANOTHER CREDIT PROVIDER A REPORT ABOUT MY/OUR CONSUMER OR COMMERCIAL CREDIT WORTHINESS FOR THE PURPOSE OF ASSESSING A LOAN APPLICATION MADE BY ME/US TO ANOTHER CREDIT PROVIDER OR COLLECTING ANY PAYMENT THAT IS OVERDUE TO A CREDIT PROVIDER.

SIGNED ....

GUARANTORS AUTHORITY:

I/WE AGREE TO YOU OBTAINING A REPORT ABOUT ME/US FROM A CREDIT REPORTING AGENCY FOR THE PURPOSE OF ASSESSING THIS GUARANTEE OR FOR RELYING UPON IT AT ANY TIME; IN SO DOING, I/WE ACKNOWLEDGE THAT INFORMATION FROM THIS AUTHORISATION OR CONCERNING THE LENDERS CURRENT CREDIT PROVIDER STATUS MAY BE DISCLOSED. I/WE ALSO AGREE THAT YOU MAY GIVE TO AND RECEIVE FROM ANOTHER CREDIT PROVIDER A REPORT ABOUT MY/OUR CONSUMER OR COMMERCIAL CREDIT WORTHINESS FOR THE PURPOSE OF: ASSESSING A LOAN APPLICATION MADE BY ME/US TO ANOTHER CREDIT PROVIDER; OR COLLECTING ANY PAYMENT THAT IS OVERDUE TO A CREDIT PROVIDER BY ME/US OR THE PERSON HEREBY GUARANTEED.

SIGNED ....